ACSM's
Health/Fitness Facility
Standards and Guidelines

SECOND EDITION

American College of Sports Medicine

James A. Peterson, PhD, FACSM
Monterey, CA

Stephen J. Tharrett, MS
Club Corporation of America
Dallas, TX

Editors

Human Kinetics

Library of Congress Cataloging-in-Publication Data

American College of Sports Medicine.
  ACSM's health/fitness facility standards and guidelines / American College of Sports Medicine; James A. Perterson, Stephen J. Tharrett, editors. -- 2nd ed.
       p.   cm.
   Includes bibliographical references (p.   ) and index.
   ISBN 0-87322-957-6
   1. Physical fitness centers -- Standards -- United States.
  2. American College of Sports Medicine.   I. Peterson, James A., 1943- . II. Tharrett, Stephen J., 1953- . III. Title.
GV429.A45   1997
613.7'1--dc21

97-10276
CIP

ISBN: 0-87322-957-6

Copyright © 1992, 1997 by American College of Sports Medicine

Permission notices for material reprinted in this book from other sources can be found on page v.

Photos on pages 3,7,9,15,21,25,28,38,44,46,51,52,57,61,62,67,72,76,89,96, and 102 are courtesy of the International Health, Racquet & Sportclub Association. Photo on page 87 is © Mike Sinclair, Howard & Helmer architects p.a.

Acquisitions Editor: Scott Wikgren; **Developmental Editor:** Holly Gilly; **Assistant Editors:** Chad Johnson, Sarah Wiseman, and Coree Schutter; **Editorial Assistant:** Amy Carnes; **Copyeditor:** Karen Bojda; **Proofreader:** Sue Fetters; **Indexer:** Theresa Schaefer; **Graphic Designer:** Judy Henderson; **Graphic Artist:** Tom Roberts; **Photo Editor:** Boyd LaFoon; **Cover Designer:** Jack Davis; **Illustrator:** Gretchen Walters; **Printer:** Braun-Brumfield

Human Kinetics books are available at special discounts for bulk purchase. Special editions or book excerpts can also be created to specification. For details, contact the Special Sales Manager at Human Kinetics.

Printed in the United States of America   10 9 8 7 6 5 4 3 2

Human Kinetics
Web site: http://www.humankinetics.com/

United States: Human Kinetics, P.O. Box 5076, Champaign, IL 61825-5076
1-800-747-4457
e-mail: humank@hkusa.com

Canada: Human Kinetics, Box 24040, Windsor, ON N8Y 4Y9
1-800-465-7301 (in Canada only)
e-mail: humank@hkcanada.com

Europe: Human Kinetics, P.O. Box IW14, Leeds LS16 6TR, United Kingdom
(44) 1132 781708
e-mail: humank@hkeurope.com

Australia: Human Kinetics, 57A Price Avenue, Lower Mitcham, South Australia 5062
(088) 277 1555
e-mail: humank@hkaustralia.com

New Zealand: Human Kinetics, P.O. Box 105-231, Auckland 1
(09) 523 3462
e-mail: humank@hknewz.com

Contents

Credits   v

Editors and Contributors   vi

Notice   vii

Preface   ix

Acknowledgments   xi

PART I   STANDARDS FOR HEALTH/FITNESS FACILITIES   1

Chapter 1 Standards for Health/Fitness Facilities   3

Chapter 2 An Overview and Discussion of the Standards   5

PART II   GENERAL CONSIDERATION GUIDELINES   11

Chapter 3 Guidelines for Enhancing Physical Plant Safety   13

Chapter 4 Guidelines for Signage   19

Chapter 5 Guidelines for Organizational Structure and Staffing   23

Chapter 6 Guidelines for User Screening   27

Chapter 7 Guidelines for Emergency/Safety Procedures   29

PART III   PROGRAM ACTIVITY AREA GUIDELINES   35

Chapter 8 Guidelines for the Fitness-Testing, Health Promotion, and Wellness Area   37

Chapter 9 Guidelines for the Exercise Classroom   43

Chapter 10 Guidelines for the Fitness Floor   49

Chapter 11 Guidelines for a Multipurpose Recreation Area (Gymnasium)   55

Chapter 12 Guidelines for Sports Court Areas   59

Chapter 13 Guidelines for Pool Areas   67

Chapter 14 Guidelines for Outdoor Recreational Areas   75

Chapter 15 Guidelines for Running Track Areas   81

PART IV   NONACTIVITY AREA GUIDELINES   85

Chapter 16 Guidelines for External Grounds   87

Chapter 17 Guidelines for the Control Desk Area   89

Chapter 18 Guidelines for the Laundry Room Area   91

Chapter 19 Guidelines for the Locker Room Area   95

PART V   SPECIALTY AREA GUIDELINES   99

Chapter 20 Guidelines for a Youth Supervision Area   101

Chapter 21 Guidelines for Spa Areas   105

Appendix A   Supplements   109

Appendix B   Forms   151

Appendix C   The Americans With Disabilities Act (ADA) As It Applies to
             Health/Fitness Facilities   185

Appendix D   Climbing-Wall Areas   193

Appendix E   Bibliography   197

Appendix F   Trade and Professional Associations for Fitness, Health,
             and Related Recreational Concerns   201

Appendix G   About the American College of Sports Medicine   203

ACSM Certifications for Health/Fitness Professionals   205

Index   207

Credits

Supplements

Supplement 1: From C.G. Ramsey and H.R. Sleeper [J.R. Hoke, Jr., of the American Institute of Architects, Ed.], 1988, *Architectural graphic standards*, 8th ed. (New York: Wiley), 116. Copyright © 1988 by John Wiley & Sons. Reprinted by permission of John Wiley & Sons, Inc.

Supplement 2 and Forms 15 and 20: From Club Corporation of America, 1995, *Standards of design and construction of an athletic facility* (Dallas: Club Corporation of America). Reprinted with permission of Club Corporation of America.

Supplements 3 and 4: Reprinted, by permission, from Heart Healthy Fitness Center, 1990, *Operations manual* (Dallas: Heart Healthy Fitness Center).

Part of Supplement 8 (sound level pressure chart and table): From C.G. Ramsey and H.R. Sleeper [J.R. Hoke, Jr., of the American Institute of Architects, Ed.], 1988, *Architectural graphic standards*, 8th ed. (New York: Wiley), 43. Copyright © 1988 by John Wiley & Sons. Reprinted by permission of John Wiley & Sons, Inc.

Supplement 23: Reprinted, by permission, Copyright © 1989, D.E. Arnold and *Athletic Business* magazine.

Supplement 24: From R.T. Packard and S.A. Kliment, 1989, *Architectural graphic standards* [student edition abridged from the American Institute of Architects' 7th ed.] (New York: Wiley), 33. Copyright © 1989 by John Wiley & Sons. Reprinted by permission of John Wiley & Sons, Inc.

Supplement 25: From R.T. Packard and S.A. Kliment, 1989, *Architectural graphic standards* [student edition abridged from the American Institute of Architects' 7th ed.] (New York: Wiley), 34. Copyright © 1989 by John Wiley & Sons. Reprinted by permission of John Wiley & Sons, Inc.

Supplement 31: From C.G. Ramsey and H.R. Sleeper [J.R. Hoke, Jr., of the American Institute of Architects, Ed.], 1988, *Architectural graphic standards*, 8th ed. (New York: Wiley), 121. Copyright © 1988 by John Wiley & Sons. Reprinted by permission of John Wiley & Sons, Inc.

Supplement 32: From R.T. Packard and S.A. Kliment, 1989, *Architectural graphic standards* [student edition abridged from the American Institute of Architects' 7th ed.] (New York: Wiley), 29. Copyright © 1989 by John Wiley & Sons. Reprinted by permission of John Wiley & Sons, Inc.

Forms

Form 1: Reprinted with permission from the Canadian Society for Exercise Physiology, Inc., Copyright © 1994.

Forms 2, 3, 4: Reprinted, by permission, from Fitcorp, 1990, *Fitcorp program manual* (Boston: Fitcorp).

Forms 5, 8, and 18: Reprinted, by permission, from B.E. Koeberle, 1990, *Legal aspects of personal fitness training* (Canton, OH: Professional Reports Corporation).

Form 6: Reprinted, by permission, from D. Herbert, 1989, "Avoiding allegations of misrepresentation/fraud in program documents," *The Exercise Standards and Malpractice Reporter* 3(2): 30-31.

Forms 7, 9, 10, and 14: Reprinted, by permission, from D. Herbert, 1994, *Legal aspects of sports medicine* 2nd ed. (Canton, OH: Professional Reports Corporation).

Form 11: Reprinted, by permission, from Herbert and Herbert, 1983, *Legal aspects of preventative, rehabilitative, and recreational exercise programs*, 3rd ed. (Canton, OH: Professional Reports Corporation).

Form 17: Reprinted, by permission, from Fitcorp, 1990, *Fitcorp program manual* (Boston: Fitcorp), 7.

Form 19: Reprinted, by permission, from Fitcorp, 1990, *Fitcorp program manual* (Boston: Fitcorp), 12.

Form 25: Reprinted with permission from the Canadian Society for Exercise Physiology, Inc., Copyright © 1995.

Editors and Contributors to Second Edition

Editors

James A. Peterson, PhD, FACSM
Monterey, CA

Stephen J. Tharrett, MS
Club Corporation of America
Dallas, TX

Contributing Authors

William C. Day, PhD, FACSM
Concord Athletic Club
San Antonio, TX

David Herbert, JD
The Belpar Law Center
Canton, OH

Carl Foster, PhD, FACSM
Sinai Samaritan Medical Center
Milwaukee, WI

Gary Klencheski, MEd
Fitcorp
Boston, MA

Jennifer Harding
Eastside Athletic Club
Milwaukie, OR

Frank Napolitano, JD
Highpoint Athletic Club
Chalfont, PA

Editors and Contributors to First Edition

Editors

Carl Foster, PhD, FACSM
Sinai Samaritan Medical Center
Milwaukee, WI

Neil Sol, PhD, FACSM
The Houstonian
Houston, TX

Contributing Authors

David Herbert, JD
The Belpar Law Center
Canton, OH

James A. Peterson, PhD, FACSM
Consultant
Monterey, CA

Gary Klencheski, MEd
Fitcorp
Boston, MA

Stephen J. Tharrett, MS
Club Corporation of America
Dallas, TX

Additional Contributors

David Camaione, PhD, FACSM
University of Connecticut
Storrs, CT

John McCarthy
IHRSA
Boston, MA

Lawrence Golding, PhD, FACSM
University of Nevada-Las Vegas
Las Vegas, NV

Lyle Micheli, MD, FACSM
Children's Hospital Medical Center
Boston, MA

David Hillery
Cross Conditioning Systems
Boulder, CO

L. Joy Prouty
The Fitness Connection
West Palm Beach, FL

Thomas Kelly, MS
Milwaukee County Medical Complex
Milwaukee, WI

Michael Sharratt, PhD, FACSM
University of Waterloo
Waterloo, ON, Canada

Robert C. Larsen
Institute for Quality Health
University of Virginia
Charlottesville, VA

Jack Young, MD, FACSM
Doctors' Hospital
Coral Gables, FL

Notice

This document has been developed to represent a nationally derived consensus statement concerning the standards set forth in chapter 1 of this document. In addition, it provides guidelines, which appear in chapters 3 to 21, that are applicable to the design and operation of health and fitness facilities. The guidelines should not be deemed to be all-inclusive in their treatment of various areas of concern, nor should they be considered to be exclusive of other methods or modalities of service rendition. The ultimate responsibility for development and application of services and procedures lies with the facility providing services. Moreover, individual circumstances may necessitate deviation from what is stated herein. In the application of this statement, facility personnel must exercise professionally derived judgment as to what is appropriate for individuals or groups under particular circumstances.

By the development and publication of this document, the American College of Sports Medicine, its officers, its trustees, its agents, its employees, the editors, the authors, the drafting committee, or any of their successors or assignees do not assume any duty owed to third parties by those utilizing this publication. The duty owed to such parties remains with those providing services. Responsibility for service provision is a matter of personal and professional judgment using many resources, of which this document is but one.

Any activity, including those carried out within a health and fitness facility, carries with it some risk of harm, no matter how prudently and carefully services may be provided. Health/fitness facilities are not insurers against all risks of untoward events; rather their mission should be directed at providing facilities and services in accordance with the applicable standards. The standard of care that is owed by facilities is ever changing and emerging. As a consequence, facilities must stay abreast of relevant professional developments in this regard.

By reason of authorship and publication of this document, neither the editors, the authors, nor the publisher are or shall be deemed to be engaged in the practice of medicine or any allied health field, the practice of delivering fitness-training services, or the practice of law or risk management. In performing such services, facilities and professionals must engage the services of appropriately licensed individuals.

The words *safe* and *safety* are frequently used throughout this publication. Readers should recognize that the use of these terms is relative and that no activity is completely safe.

Preface

Members of the medical and exercise science communities are generally well aware that the need and value of exercising on a regular basis has never been greater (reference: 1996 U.S. Surgeon General's Report on Physical Activity and Health). The benefits of engaging in a sound physical activity program on an individual's level of health and sense of well-being are both numerous and well documented. In order to achieve these benefits in a safe and time-efficient manner, however, it is critical that an individual adhere to a few well-defined training principles and exercise guidelines while exercising. Accordingly, millions of individuals have chosen to join organizations that can help facilitate their desire to be physically active (YMCAs, JCCs, health/fitness clubs, corporate fitness centers, etc.).

In response to guidance given by the ACSM president at that time, Dr. Lyle Micheli, ACSM initiated the process of assembling a team of academic, medical, and health/fitness industry experts to develop and write a manual on standards and guidelines for delivering quality physical activity programs and services to consumers. In 1992, the end product of the collective efforts of that team was published as a text on standards and guidelines for designing and operating a health/fitness facility. The comprehensive nature of that work was reflected by the fact that it contained 353 separate standards, plus an additional 397 guidelines.

In the approximately five years since *ACSM's Health/Fitness Facility Standards and Guidelines* was published, a number of steps were undertaken to evaluate the need for and the format of a second edition of that book. The primary action in this regard was the appointment of an ad hoc committee of leaders from the medical, exercise science, and health/fitness facility communities to discuss and study the matter. The committee subsequently issued a consensus report that concluded that a second edition of the book was needed to resolve various industry, professional, and consumer-oriented concerns. The committee felt that a second edition of the book would enable the information in the text to be updated while allowing essential features of the publication to be reorganized into what was designed to be a more balanced format. Compared with the first edition, the revised work would place greater emphasis on taking into account the views and input of industry trade organizations and of a wide variety of fitness associations. In this regard, the primary focus was to develop a document that would be more reflective of a true consensus of the health/fitness industry.

In response to the findings of the ad hoc committee, ACSM appointed a committee to develop a second edition of *ACSM's Health/Fitness Facility Standards and Guidelines*. This text is the result of the efforts of that committee. In an attempt to earn broader support in the health/fitness industry, this edition of the book features a number of major changes from the first edition.

First and foremost, the myriad standards and guidelines presented in the first edition have been consolidated into six standards and approximately 500 guidelines. Responding to a charge given by the ACSM committee that reviewed the first edition, the editorial committee for the second edition reduced the original list of 353 standards that must apply to all health/fitness facilities to six standards. As opposed to the original open ended tabulation of standards, the six standards identified in the second edition represent the standard of care that must be demonstrated by all health/fitness facilities toward their users.

In contrast to the substantial reduction in the number of standards that are presented in the second edition, the quantity of guidelines included in this text increased by over 20 percent. Designed to serve as possible tools for health/fitness facility owners and managerial staff to improve their operations, these guidelines set forth design considerations and operating procedures that, if employed by a facility, would enhance the quality of service that a facility provides to its users. *These guidelines are not intended to be standards of practice or to give rise to duties of care.*

Finally, the second edition features an augmented appendix section. Several additional supplements and forms have been included in appendices A and B, respectively. Furthermore, two chapters that were included in the first edition of this book have been modified and included as appendices in the second edition (appendix C, "The Americans With Disabilities Act As It Applies to Health/Fitness Facilities," and appendix D, "Climbing-Wall Areas"). The primary purpose of the appendices is to provide readers with primary resources and forms that can assist them with implementing many of the standards and guidelines in this book.

It is important to keep in mind that this book is intended to provide standards and guidelines for facility staffing, programming, safety, design, and equipment. It is not intended to present general exercise standards and guidelines. The fundamental principles of sound exercise are relatively well documented and readily available in the literature.

In a fashion similar to the first edition of this book, this text has been organized into the following components:

Part I: Standards for Health/Fitness Facilities. This section presents a list of the standards for health/fitness facilities and an overview and discussion of those standards.

Part II: General Consideration Guidelines. This section sets forth guidelines concerning the physical plant safety, signage, organizational structure and staffing, user screening, and emergency/safety procedures.

Part III: Program Activity Area Guidelines. This section chronicles the guidelines that govern pro-

gramming, staffing, and safety, as well as those that deal with facilities and equipment in the following areas of a facility: fitness-testing, health promotion, and wellness areas; exercise classroom; fitness floor; gymnasium; sports court areas; pool areas; outdoor recreational areas; and running track areas.

Part IV: Nonactivity Area Guidelines. This section lists the guidelines that govern programming, staffing, safety, and facilities and equipment in the following physical plant areas of a facility: external grounds, control desk, laundry, and locker rooms.

Part V: Specialty Area Guidelines. This section articulates the guidelines that govern programming, staffing, safety, and facilities and equipment for the following areas of a facility: youth supervision areas and spa areas.

One of the primary goals of the American College of Sports Medicine is to ensure that every individual is given the opportunity to achieve the innumerable benefits of being physically active on a regular basis. To the extent that health/fitness facilities implement the standards and recognize the importance of incorporating the guidelines into their operating procedures and design considerations, the ability of these organizations to provide quality care within an appropriate environment will be greatly enhanced.

Acknowledgments

ACSM and the editors of this edition of this book wish to acknowledge and thank the two teams of nationally recognized experts who collaborated in writing the two separate editions of this text. A particular sense of appreciation is extended to Neil Sol and Carl Foster, the editors of the first edition of *ACSM's Health/Fitness Facility Standards and Guidelines*, for their efforts in ensuring that the initial project was successfully completed.

ACSM and the editors would also like to express special gratitude to the corporate sponsors for funding and supporting this project: Club Corporation of America for its efforts with the second edition of this text and StairMaster Sports/Medical Products, L.P.; *Fitness Management*; and Nordic Track for their assistance with the first edition.

In addition, the editors would also like to recognize the IHRSA Board of Directors, as well as ACSM's Executive Committee, for their input into this document.

Special thanks are also extended to the more than 60 professional organizations who reviewed the draft manuscript for content. (Refer to supplement 35 for a complete list of the organizations that were invited to participate in the review process.) Their feedback and comments have been included in the final text. The editors would also like to give special recognition to Dr. JoAnn Eickoff-Shemer, whose doctoral dissertation, titled "Opinions of ACSM Professional Members Regarding Selected ACSM Health/Fitness Facility Standards and Guidelines," provided a valuable resource for the efforts to develop this edition of this book.

Finally, the editors would like to thank Roseanne Kiesz for her untiring word processing efforts with the second edition and Kay Gorman for her adept administrative assistance with various aspects of the developmental process for the second edition.

PART

I

STANDARDS FOR HEALTH/FITNESS FACILITIES

This section of the book provides a list of standards for health/fitness facilities and presents an overview of those standards. A standard is a practice that gives rise to duties of care and is expected of all health/fitness facilities. These standards represent base performance criteria that each facility must meet in order to satisfy its obligation to provide users with a relatively safe environment in which every physical activity or program is conducted in an appropriate manner.

This section includes two chapters. In chapter 1, the six standards to which all health/fitness facilities must adhere are identified. A discussion of the rationale of each standard is presented in chapter 2.

1 Standards for Health/Fitness Facilities

ACSM has identified six fundamental standards to which all health and fitness facilities (hereinafter called a "facility") must adhere. Collectively, these standards ensure that every physical activity or program offered by a facility is held in what is considered to be a relatively safe environment and is conducted in an appropriate manner.

Standards of Care for Health and Fitness Facilities

1. A facility must be able to respond in a timely manner to any reasonably foreseeable emergency event that threatens the health and safety of facility users. Toward this end, a facility must have an appropriate emergency plan that can be executed by qualified personnel in a timely manner.

2. A facility must offer each adult member* a preactivity screening that is appropriate to the physical activities to be performed by the member.

3. Each person who has supervisory responsibility for a physical activity program or area at a facility must have demonstrable professional competence in that physical activity program or area.

4. A facility must post appropriate signage alerting users[†] to the risks involved in their use of those areas of a facility that present potential increased risk(s).

5. A facility that offers youth services or programs must provide appropriate supervision.

6. A facility must conform to all relevant laws, regulations, and published standards.

With regard to addressing the issue of to which organizations or groups the standards should apply, it is important to note that ACSM has not attempted to define precisely what types of physical activities and programs collectively constitute a "facility." It is the position of ACSM that any business or entity that provides an opportunity for individuals to engage in activities that may reasonably be expected to involve placing stress on one or more of the various physiological systems (cardiovascular, muscular, thermoregulatory, etc.) of a user's body must adhere to the six standards.

* A member is an individual who has entered into an agreement with a fitness facility that allows her access to the facility for a fee. The definition of adult may vary from state to state but at the least would describe an individual who is capable of making an educated decision about his readiness for physical activity based on the results of a preactivity screening.

† Users are individuals of any age who have access to a facility, either on an individual or a group basis. Users may or may not be under a fee-based agreement to use the facility.

2 An Overview and Discussion of the Standards

In order to better understand ACSM's rationale for the recommended standards, this chapter presents an overview of each of the six standards and provides a discussion of some of the reasoning behind each standard. ACSM recognizes that given the diverse array of entities to which the standards should apply, each health/fitness facility must be accorded some degree of flexibility in fulfilling its responsibility for user care. It is also important to note that the information presented in this chapter is not intended to modify or augment the standards set forth in chapter 1 or to create any additional duty of care.

Standard #1

> A facility must be able to respond in a timely manner to any reasonably foreseeable emergency event that threatens the health and safety of facility users. Toward this end, a facility must have an appropriate emergency plan that can be executed by qualified personnel in a timely manner.

The objective of this standard is straightforward: Every health/fitness facility must be able to respond in an appropriate manner to reasonably foreseeable emergencies that threaten the safety of its users. Accordingly, a facility must meet three key criteria: First, a facility must have an appropriate emergency response plan; second, a facility must have qualified personnel to execute its emergency response plan; and finally, a facility must be able to execute its emergency response plan in a timely manner. One of the primary steps involved in meeting this standard is understanding what is involved in each of the three criteria.

What is an appropriate emergency plan, and how might such a plan differ from one health/fitness facility to another? An appropriate emergency plan is in writing and is posted within the facility.

Which staff members are qualified to execute an emergency plan depends on the type of emergency event. In the case of a cardiopulmonary event, it would be personnel trained and certified in basic CPR (cardiopulmonary resuscitation) or BLS (basic life support) and first aid. In the case of other medical emergencies, it would likely be personnel who have first-aid training. A facility must also take steps to ensure that its entire staff fully understands its emergency plan and each person's role in implementing it. The overriding concern is to have enough appropriately trained personnel on duty at any given time to respond to any reasonably foreseeable emergency in a timely manner.

What is a proper time frame when dealing with an emergency? Obviously, "timeliness" is a relative term that has to be applied to each situation. The important point to remember is that the more rapidly a facility can respond to an emergency, the more likely it is to protect the safety of the user.

Standard #2

> A facility must offer each adult member a preactivity screening that is appropriate to the physical activities to be performed by the member.

This standard has a twofold objective. First, every facility must provide a preactivity screening device to its adult members that will allow them to determine whether they have medical conditions or risk factors that would require particular actions to be undertaken (e.g., physician approval, fitness testing, program modification) before they would be permitted to engage in physical activity. Second, every facility must provide a preactivity screening device to its adult members that is appropriate for the activity being undertaken by each user. In order to better understand this standard, two questions must be addressed: What are the medical conditions and risk factors that would require special consideration before a member should be allowed to participate in physical activity? What is an appropriate preactivity screening device?

While risk factors will vary somewhat from one medical condition to another, a facility has a greater responsibility to probe for some potential risk factors than for others. For example, because of the inherent potential for having a life-threatening impact, a facility must provide preactivity screening for primary coronary risk factors. According to the American Heart Association, the primary risk factors for coronary problems are high blood pressure, high cholesterol, smoking, and a sedentary lifestyle. In addition to coronary risk factors, a facility should also consider preactivity screening for any other serious medical conditions, such as diabetes, arthritis, and orthopedic restrictions.

After a facility develops a general idea of what risk factors and medical conditions it needs to screen, the next step is to select a preactivity screening device. Such screening devices range from the relatively simple Physical Activity Readiness Questionnaire (PAR-Q) to more extensive health history questionnaires and computerized health-risk appraisal schemes. Examples of the PAR-Q and an extensive health history questionnaire are presented in appendix B (Forms 1, 2, and 3).

Just as preactivity screening devices tend to vary from instrument to instrument in their level of detail, the approach to administering such devices also ranges from device to device and facility to facility. For example, some facilities may choose to post the screening device (e.g., the PAR-Q) in a conspicuous place so that adult members can read it prior to participating in physical activity, while other facilities may have a staff member administer the device. In most instances, the decision regarding how to give the screening device is basically a subjective one for a facility, although in a few cases, the nature of the device requires more staff involvement.

Ultimately, however, the choice of a preactivity screening device may depend on several factors, including the types of individuals expected to use the facility, the kinds of activities offered by a facility, and the philosophy of the facility regarding how extensive the level of information provided by preactivity screening should be. Whatever combination of factors influences a facility's subsequent decision of what screening device to use, one tenet should apply to all facilities: Each facility must in some systematic way inform its adult members of any potential risks for participating in physical activity. It must also provide adult members with the opportunity to engage in physical activity after they have been made aware of those risks if the members either receive clearance from their physicians or agree to assume personal responsibility for their decisions to participate.

Accordingly, each facility should have the prerogative to require an individual to execute an assumption of risk or prospective release or waiver of claims document. Such a document is appropriate should the responses of an individual to a preactivity screening device indicate that an increased risk of untoward events exists if the individual engages in physical activity and if that person subsequently fails to obtain clearance from a physician for participating in physical activity. Furthermore, a facility should have the option of denying an individual the opportunity of participating in its program offerings if the individual fails to either secure medical clearance or sign the applicable form. It is important to note that the Americans With Disabilities Act (ADA) may preclude a facility from denying any individual access to the facility. As a result, facilities should obtain appropriate legal advice before deciding whether to deny access to individuals who fail to secure medical clearance or sign the applicable form.

Standard #3

> Each person who has supervisory responsibility for a physical activity program or area at a facility must have demonstrable professional competence in that physical activity program or area.

The objective of this standard is to ensure that health/fitness facilities provide credible and professional supervision of all physical activity areas and programs. The successful implementation of this standard requires that the operator of a health/fitness facility has a thorough understanding of what constitutes supervisory responsibility for a physical activity program and what is meant by demonstrable professional competence.

What is supervisory responsibility for a physical activity program or area? In general, supervisory responsibility for a physical activity program refers to having accountability for one or more of the following elements of a program conducted in a health/fitness facility: program content, program staffing, and the programming space. An example of a physical activity program supervisor is a fitness director who is responsible for the fitness floor, the fitness programs, and the instructors of the fitness programs. Another example is an aerobics coordinator who is responsible for the aerobics room, the aerobics programs, and the aerobics instructors (group exercise leaders).

What is demonstrable professional competence? In general, it refers to having some combination of education and professional experience that would be recognized by both the industry and the public at large as representing a relatively high level of competence and credibility. For example, in fields outside the health/fitness industry, two instances of individuals with demonstrable professional competence in their chosen profession are United States Professional Tennis Association Level 1 Professionals and Professional Golf Association Class A Professionals. Within the health/fitness industry, three examples of what would be considered demonstrable professional competence for individuals who are assigned to supervisory roles within a health/fitness facility include the following:

Physical activity program area	Indication of professional competence
Fitness director	Four-year college education in a health/fitness-related field or substantially equivalent work experience; certification from a nationally recognized association/organization in the health/fitness industry*; CPR certification; one year of work experience in the fitness field.
Aerobics coordinator	A two-year college education in a health/fitness-related field or substantially equivalent work experience; certification from a nationally recognized association/organization in the health/fitness industry; CPR certification.
Aquatics director	Certification in advanced lifesaving; certification in water safety instruction; one year of work experience in aquatics; pool operation training; CPR certification.

*A certification from a nationally recognized association in the health/fitness industry is one in which the actual certification is based on job performance–related criteria that has been validated by documented research.

While the aforementioned list of examples is not exclusive, it does provide a representative overview of three of the more common positions involving supervisory responsibility for physical activity programs or areas and the professional competence that could be expected for each position. It should be noted that in some areas of the country, the requirements for demonstrable professional competence for some professional positions may be governed by local or state rules and regulations.

Standard #4:   A facility must post appropriate signage alerting users to the risks involved in their use of those areas of a facility that present potential increased risk(s).

Each health/fitness facility has an inherent responsibility to provide appropriate signage that alerts individuals to the potential risks involved in using the facility—in particular, those areas of a facility that expose users to an increased level of potential risk. Examples of facility areas that would be expected to have signage alerting users to potential risks are those areas where users are exposed to temperatures in excess of core body temperature or where the possibility of drowning exists. Specific examples of areas in a facility in which appropriate signage must be posted include the following:

• *Saunas, steam rooms, and whirlpools.*   Due to the high heat and/or humidity levels and suction of drains, a facility must provide signage providing warnings and information notices indicating the risks inherent in the use of these areas, particularly for those with special considerations or medical conditions (e.g., people with hypertension or cardiac problems, pregnant women, children under 12 years of age).

• *Swimming pools.*   Due to the inherent risk of drowning (whether the pool area is supervised or unsupervised), a facility must provide signage that clearly indicates the dangers associated with using the pool and the steps that an individual can take to reduce that risk. It should be noted that the requirements of state and/or local laws may mandate the presence of qualified lifeguards at such sites.

Although the two aforementioned examples are not meant to be an exhaustive list, they are intended to point out that every facility has at least a few areas that need signage indicating the potential risks inherent in using such areas. While this standard is not intended to imply that health/fitness facilities should aimlessly post signage in all areas of their facilities, it does state that a facility must post signage in those areas of the facility that carry a high potential of risk to users and alert users to that risk. Examples of appropriate signage are presented in supplement 2, appendix A.

Standard #5:

> A facility that offers youth services or programs must provide appropriate supervision.

This standard clearly states that any facility that offers youth programs or services must ensure that those programs and services are adequately supervised at all times. It should be noted that each facility may define "youth" somewhat differently. Examples of youth programs and services that are offered in health/fitness facilities include babysitting, organized youth activities, unstructured activity times for youth summer camps, open recreation periods for youths, and so on. In other words, every time a facility offers services or programs to youths or opens areas of the facility to involve youths, the facility must ensure that the youths are provided appropriate supervision.

In most instances, appropriate supervision would be considered either a staff person or volunteer over the age of 16 who has demonstrable competence in the supervision of youth. In some areas of the country, demonstrable competence in this area of responsibility may involve specific training and/or formal licensure. Many states also require that staff personnel given the responsibility for supervising youths must be screened for prior criminal behavior. Such a screening helps to ensure that youths are not placed at undue risk while being supervised.

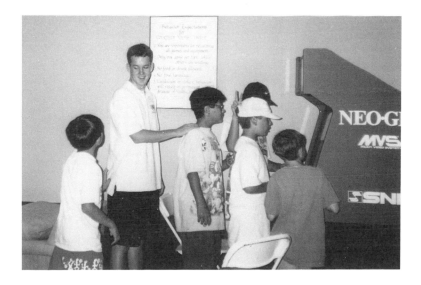

The term "appropriate supervision" also raises quantitative issues regarding what constitutes an appropriate ratio of supervisors to youths. While nationally derived (and validated) ratios of supervisors-to-youths do not exist, many states have specified what constitutes a suitable proportion of supervisors-to-youths for various age categories. Each facility has the responsibility of determining whether any local or state regulation or statute in its area governs the proportional level of supervision it must provide.

Standard #6:

> **A facility must conform to all relevant laws, regulations, and published standards.**

As should be expected, health/fitness facilities must conform to all relevant laws and regulations that apply to the jurisdiction in which they are located. Examples of relevant laws and regulations that would apply to health/fitness facilities include the following:

- United States federal laws such as the ADA and the laws and regulations of the Occupational Safety and Health Administration (OSHA).
- Local government laws and regulations, such as those developed and enforced by a local Department of Public Health.
- Building codes, zoning ordinances, and planning and zoning regulations.

PART

II

GENERAL CONSIDERATION GUIDELINES

This section of the book presents general consideration guidelines that are designed to enhance the safety and the effectiveness of service delivery in a health/fitness facility. Unlike the standards that were chronicled in part I, guidelines are intended as tools for health/fitness owners and operators that, if adopted, will help advance design considerations and operating procedures that will improve the quality of service that a facility provides to its users. It is important to note that these guidelines are not standards and do not give rise to duties of care.

For discussion purposes, these general consideration guidelines are grouped into five basic categories: physical plant safety, signage, organizational structure and staffing, user screening, and emergency/safety procedures. The guidelines that apply to each category are discussed in a separate chapter.

Chapter 3 presents guidelines for enhancing physical plant safety. These guidelines focus on helping operators enhance the safety level of their properties and facilities.

Chapter 4 provides guidelines for signage. Proper signage can assist facility operators in a number of ways, including warning users of any potential increased risks in a particular area or program in the facility, showing users where clear pathways (access and egress) exist in a facility, and serving as an effective means of communication to users concerning specific programs, policies, and procedures.

Chapter 5 discusses guidelines that concern organizational structure and staffing. Given the fact that one of the primary factors affecting the success of a particular organization is the people within the organization, the better people know their jobs and how their jobs relate to other aspects of the organization, the better they will perform their duties and provide quality service to the user. The guidelines presented in this chapter are designed to assist a facility in recruiting, selecting, and training staff.

Chapter 6 enumerates guidelines involving user screening. In order to make a physical activity or a program effective, relatively enjoyable, and reasonably safe, a facility should screen users before they participate in the offerings of the facility. The guidelines listed in this chapter are designed to show how a facility can safely and effectively identify the individual health needs and conditions that may limit user participation.

Chapter 7 offers guidelines on emergency/safety procedures. Being adequately prepared to handle emergencies is one of the primary hallmarks of a quality facility. The guidelines presented in this chapter are designed to help a facility develop a sound system for effectively dealing with emergency events in a manner that protects users and staff alike.

3 Guidelines for Enhancing Physical Plant Safety

Physical plant safety is an important issue for all health/fitness facilities. Physical plant refers to the grounds, facilities, and equipment that are part of a health/fitness facility. Accordingly, owners, developers, and managers of health/fitness facilities should consider user safety with regard to the equipment, internal spaces, external spaces, and surrounding areas that are adjacent to the facility. This chapter presents guidelines that address the following physical plant issues:

- External areas (grounds)
- Floor surfaces
- Internal illumination
- Signage
- Electrical safety
- Sharp objects
- High-temperature and high-humidity areas
- Equipment
- Air circulation
- Telephones
- Water fountains

It should also be noted that although it is not listed as a separate guideline, facilities are encouraged to conduct regular inspections of their physical plant as part of an overall risk-management program to enhance the level of safety involving their physical plant.

External Areas (Grounds)

3.G1 A facility should provide properly designed, produced, and erected signage indicating entries, exits, speed bumps, hazardous locations, vehicle speed limits, pedestrian walkways or crosswalks, traffic direction, and location of facilities.

3.G2 An appropriate level of external illumination should be provided, in accordance with governmental and architectural requirements. It is extremely important that all areas of a facility have sufficient levels of lighting. Refer to supplement 1 in appendix A for outdoor lighting guidelines.

3.G3 All walking surfaces should be periodically inspected and cleared of hazards that could cause an individual to slip, trip, or fall; users should be warned of uncorrected conditions that are not readily observable. Walking surfaces that are not level or that have cracks, elevations, or bumps should be promptly repaired. Until repaired, these problems should be brought to the attention of users via signage. Also, areas that have inadequate drainage should be repaired to prevent pooling of water, unnatural accumulation of snow and ice, and resultant increased hazards. Finally, in geographic areas that receive snow and ice, facilities should have removal systems to handle such potential hazards, as well as signage denoting the increased risk due to possible snow and ice accumulation.

3.G4   Building structures and other large objects on the grounds (such as trees) should be periodically inspected and maintained to ensure that falling debris or objects do not pose hazards. It is extremely important that facilities trim hedges, trees, and other plants that might create hazards because of their proximity to walkways and parking lots. Facility operators should also regularly inspect the building structures and correct dangerous conditions (or provide signage that warns of them until they are corrected) to ensure that protruding or loose objects do not expose the facility's users to undue risk.

Floor Surfaces

3.G5   A facility should take precautions to ensure that the proper floor surfaces are provided for each activity to avoid the possibility of acute injuries that can result from slip-and-fall situations. (*Acute*: Injuries that are sudden in onset, or conditions that occur quickly, are typically characterized by sharp or intense pain or symptoms that last a short time.)

3.G6   Floor surfaces should be designed and constructed to safely accommodate the activities intended for that area. Floor surfaces should also be periodically and reasonably maintained. All surfaces should periodically be checked for cracks, broken tiles, exposed seams, loose impediments, exposed power cords, and warping that could increase the likelihood of user injury. Any defects should be corrected within a reasonable time, and until corrected, appropriate signage should provide a warning to users. If a defect creates unreasonably dangerous conditions, the area should not be used until corrected or repaired. Floors and surfaces should also be cleaned and disinfected on a regular basis to prevent an undue risk of foreign substances being transmitted to users as they use the facility. In addition, floor surfaces should be kept free of oil, wax, liquid, and dust, which can cause slippery conditions. If a surface is known to be slippery, the facility should provide the appropriate warnings to the facility's users and should eliminate such a condition.

3.G7   A facility should provide slip-resistant surfaces (e.g., slip-resistant tile, special rubber matting) in all wet areas.

Internal Illumination

3.G8

A level of internal illumination should be provided in accordance with governmental and architectural requirements. Refer to supplement 10 in appendix A for general illumination guidelines.

Signage

3.G9

A facility should provide relevant, communicative, and properly posted signage for certain areas of the facility. *Relevant* refers to signage that is appropriate for its intended purpose, place of posting, and audience. *Communicative* refers to signage that is able to convey the precise message or signal that is intended. *Properly* refers to signage that is posted in such a way and in such a place as to be appropriate for its intended purpose and audience. A list of the types of signage that are frequently used in health/fitness facilities is provided in supplement 2 in appendix A.

Electrical Safety

3.G10 In areas in which users are exposed to electrically operated equipment, a facility should provide grounded electrical outlets. In areas in which users might come in contact with moisture in conjunction with electrically powered equipment (e.g., locker rooms, rest rooms, food and beverage areas, and pool), facilities should provide ground-fault circuit interrupters that will automatically shut down power in the event of a short due to water or insulation breakdown.

Sharp Objects

3.G11 A facility should make sure that no sharp objects protrude into areas that are frequented by users (i.e., activity areas, nonactivity areas, and specialty areas).

High-Temperature and High-Humidity Areas

3.G12 In areas in which users are exposed to a high level of thermal stress (e.g., sauna, steam room, whirlpool), a facility should have control mechanisms that will automatically shut off the equipment in predetermined (i.e., potentially dangerous) situations. A facility should also have an ongoing monitoring system that ensures that the temperature in each area is properly controlled. Finally, facilities should avoid placing steel or other heat-conducting materials in areas of high temperature or humidity (e.g., no metal handles on the doors to the sauna or the steam room).

Equipment

3.G13 All equipment should be inspected prior to installation to ensure that no major or observable defects are evident. Furthermore, all equipment should be installed and located in a facility in accordance with the manufacturers' and/or sellers' instructions. Once installed, all equipment should again be thoroughly inspected before it is used.

3.G14 A facility should provide appropriate signage and user instructions for all equipment. This signage should include the following for each piece of equipment:

- A full description of the equipment's mechanical function (each manufacturer should be asked to provide this information)
- Instructions on how to use the equipment
- Posted warnings for any relevant risks that may be associated with use of the equipment

3.G15 A facility should provide initial and ongoing user instruction for all equipment, as well as initial and ongoing user supervision.

3.G16   An ongoing inspection and preventive maintenance program should be conducted for all equipment (refer to supplements 3 and 4 in appendix A).

3.G17   A system should be developed to promptly remove from use equipment that is known to be defective and potentially dangerous. Equipment that is known to be defective and/or potentially dangerous because it is in a state of disrepair or because it is otherwise hazardous must be removed from utilization by facility members and guests.

Air Circulation

3.G18   Negative air pressure (a situation in which external air is drawn into a room) should be established in all facility areas by designing and installing an air-handling system that ensures the existence of negative air pressure.

3.G19   Air filters for the HVAC systems should be changed on a regular basis.

Telephones

3.G20   A working telephone or another mode of emergency calling system, such as a public address system, should be available within or adjacent to all physical activity areas.

Water Fountains

3.G21   A system for dispensing water (e.g., water fountain, cooler) should be available within or adjacent to all physical activity areas.

4 Guidelines for Signage

Communication is one of the most potentially complex and demanding issues that operators of health/fitness facilities have to address on a daily basis. Successful communication requires that the desired message be both conveyed correctly and received correctly. Inadequate efforts to communicate, on the other hand, can result in distorted messages. One of the best methods for overcoming barriers to clear communication is effective signage. In a health/fitness facility, proper signage can help ensure satisfactory communication by providing both the user and the operator with universally clear messages. Because of its ability to have a positive impact on the capacity of a facility to meet the needs and interests of the facility's users, the importance of signage should not be underestimated. Depending on the situation, signage can provide direction, warning, instruction, motivation, and enjoyment to both staff and users. This chapter provides guidelines on key signage issues. By incorporating the recommended guidelines into the design and operation of heath/fitness facilities, operators enhance the likelihood that individuals will have safe, productive, and satisfying experiences while using the facility. This chapter presents guidelines that address the following signage issues:

- Purpose of the signage
- Explicit signage
- Appearance
- Readability
- Placement

Purpose of the Signage

4.G1

The purpose of each sign and the message that is to be conveyed by a particular sign should be determined. For example, some signs identify places and things or give directions. Others are intended to protect public health and safety. Within health/fitness facilities, signs are frequently used to enumerate facility area or program policies. A facility operator should also determine what audience each sign is intended to reach and what signs will best serve each specific audience. Facility operators should keep in mind that a sign may serve one purpose with one audience and an entirely different purpose with another audience. In addition, signs may also serve more than one purpose with the same audience.

Explicit Signage

4.G2   A facility should include entryway and exit signage. All entrances to and exits from the facility to hallways or external grounds should be identified by the appropriate signage.

4.G3   A facility should include operational policies and rules signage. Those areas of the facility such as the pool, whirlpool, sauna, steam room, free-weight area, exercise classroom, cardiovascular area, resistance-training area, racquet sports courts, and gymnasium should have signage posted that communicates the general policies and rules that govern that area. (Refer to supplement 2 in appendix A for examples of signage used in a health/fitness facility.)

4.G4   A facility should provide message boards or bulletin boards for the communication or dissemination of facility and user information. These boards should be located in appropriate areas, such as the lounge, locker rooms, fitness areas, aerobics studio, and physical activity areas.

4.G5   A facility should have signage that identifies its staff and their relevant credentials.

Appearance

4.G6   The appearance of each sign should carefully be considered. Signs should be professional in appearance. For example, signs should be harmonious with the colors and materials of the adjacent wall finishes and furnishings in particular and with the entire facility in general. On the other hand, signs should be color coded in such a way that they readily stand out and catch the intended audience's attention.

4.G7   Signs should be of colors consistent with expectations within the culture. For example, in Western culture red connotes blood or fire and, by extension, danger. Therefore, the color red should be used in emergency or danger-related warning signs (e.g., signs designating the location of the fire extinguisher). Furthermore, in Western culture signs that involve some element of caution should be yellow, and so forth.

4.G8   The factors that affect an individual's perception of colors should be considered when a sign is being designed. The three primary factors are the lighting conditions under which the colors are seen, the sources of light for the sign, and the colors that surround the sign.

Readability

4.G9   The language to be used on a sign and the message to be conveyed by the sign should be carefully considered. Accordingly, sign designers should consider what words, symbols, pictures, and colors best convey the intended message. Technical terms (if any) should be avoided. Layperson's language and standard nomenclature should be used for all signage. Depending on the location, a facility may need to consider bilingual issues with regard to signage (i.e., a sign may need to be made in another language in addition to English).

4.G10 Whenever appropriate, words should be replaced by symbols or photographs. For example, a wheelchair symbol has more communication value than does the word *wheelchair.* A photograph is a very useful tool because it provides a literal representation of an idea.

4.G11 All symbols and words used on a sign should be carefully reviewed to ensure that no culturally based ambiguity or disparagement exists.

4.G12 Every sign should be as legible as possible. Sign legibility is enhanced by the careful selection of letter style, size, spacing, design, color contrast, and placement. The signage for a particular facility should maintain consistency in typeface style, design factors, placement, and, If possible, color within each category of signs in order for signage to achieve greater overall visual authority and effectiveness. It should be noted, however, that although color consistency is important, it should not take precedence over the purpose of the sign if another specific color will communicate the intended message more clearly.

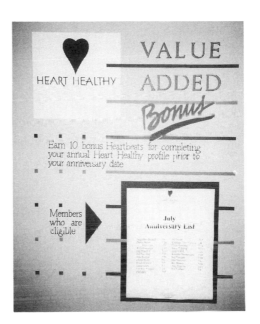

4.G13 The typefaces used on signs should be simple and uncluttered. The size of the letters used on a sign should be based on three factors: the type of illumination the sign will have, the distance from which the sign will be read, and the number of signs within a particular area or location.

4.G14 The number of alphabetic or numeric characters per line, the number of words per sign, and the percentage of the sign occupied by lettering should be carefully considered when designing a sign. As a general rule, the following parameters for designing a sign are recommended: The length of a line should not exceed 26 characters, including spaces; a single sign should include 16 words or less; and no more than 50 percent of any sign face should be occupied by text, including words and numbers.

4.G15   Emphasis within a given sign can be achieved in several ways. For example, larger letters can be used, all capital letters can be used, or the word to be emphasized can have a different typeface or style.

Placement

4.G16   The location of each sign and the visibility afforded by that location should be carefully considered. As a general rule, signs on a wall within a facility should be affixed five to seven feet above the floor. To help create a cohesive appearance within a facility, signs should be mounted at a uniform height throughout, with due consideration given to the visibility or placement needs of the specific individuals using a particular area of the facility (e.g., children, the disabled).

4.G17   Signs should have a substantial amount of open space surrounding them. For example, as a general rule, no more than 50 percent of the wall space in an information area (zone) should be occupied by signage.

5 Guidelines for Organizational Structure and Staffing

One of the major keys to any successful organization is the people within the organization. All factors considered, the better that people know their jobs and how their jobs relate to other aspects of the organization, the better they perform and the better the service they provide to the user. Qualified and knowledgeable staff can go a long way toward providing users with relatively safe and satisfying physical activity. The first issue that should be addressed with staff members is their ability to carry out their job responsibilities. In a health/fitness facility, those responsibilities include two very important areas: user safety and user satisfaction. It is important that users receive the appropriate attention, instruction, and motivation so they can achieve their personal physical activity goals without harm. Although on-the-job training can go a long way toward helping staff members to be prepared to aid users to achieve their objectives, it generally cannot totally replace experience and formal academic preparation.

What determines or demonstrates that an individual is qualified to provide appropriate and effective physical activity programming for a facility user? Under most circumstances, it should include some combination of formal academic preparation, professional certification, and professional experience. As a general rule, front-line personnel will demonstrate either formal training or professional certification; front-line supervisory personnel should have both formal academic training and professional certification; and senior-level supervisors should have advanced academic preparation in addition to advanced levels of certification. For a staff position with highly technical requirements, such as an exercise physiologist, the combination of academic preparation (e.g., a master's degree in exercise science) with an advanced professional certification (e.g., ACSM's Health/Fitness Director) is recommended. This chapter addresses guidelines for selecting qualified staff for most areas of a health/fitness facility, including the following:

- Individual responsible for the daily operations of a facility (e.g., owner, manager)
- Individual responsible for overall direction of a major component of the physical activity program (e.g., fitness director, athletic director)
- Fitness/physical activity instructors/leaders
- Support staff
- Medical liaison personnel
- Coordinator/specialist
- Continuing education

It should be noted that the level of staffing for a facility is often influenced by a variety of factors, including its size, budget, and the number of members. As a result, it is a common practice for one staff person often to assume multiple job functions. In other instances, certain positions in a health/fitness facility may require certification. The certification process for personnel in those positions may be administered by a governing body or an organization that oversees a given physical activity area. Also, in many situations, a position may require licensure or registration as a prerequisite qualification. The key is to verify the qualifications of those staff members through evidence of licensure, registration, or the appropriate certification. In addition to ensuring proper staff qualifications, a facility manager should structure the staff so that it works efficiently and appropriately. Sample organizational and staffing structures, respectively, are illustrated in supplements 6 and 7 of appendix A.

Director of Daily Operations

5.G1 A facility should have a manager/executive director who is responsible for the daily operations and strategic planning for the facility.

Director of Physical Activity Programs

5.G2 A facility should have an individual who is responsible for the programming, staff, and operation of the physical activity areas of the facility. This individual should have an undergraduate degree in a health/fitness-related field or have substantially equivalent work experience and should be knowledgeable in the areas of exercise science, programming, and operations. This individual should also have a current professional certification from a nationally recognized organization in the health/fitness industry, have earned a current CPR certification, have completed first-aid training, and have evidence of work experience in the health/fitness industry.

Fitness/Physical Activity Instructors/Leaders

5.G3 A facility should have instructors/leaders who are responsible for providing instruction, guidance, and motivation to the facility's users. These instructors/leaders should be hired to work in areas that require direct interaction with a facility's users. Individuals assigned to these positions should have a minimum of two years of college-level courses in a health/fitness-related field or equivalent work experience, have earned a current CPR certification, have completed first-aid training, and should have current professional certification from a nationally recognized organization in the health/fitness industry.

Support Staff

5.G4 A facility should provide appropriately trained support staff for each area of the facility based on user needs and governmental regulations (e.g., housecleaning staff, gymnasium staff, control desk attendants, and child-care attendants). Efforts to provide such support staff should be based on user needs, user safety, and the requirements of federal, state, and local laws. For example, it is recommended that support staff have a current CPR certification. In addition, certain specialty areas and programs should be supervised and instructed by professionals who have specific training in their given specialty area, for example:

- Lifeguard (certification)
- Nutrition (college degree and certification)
- Weight management (college degree and/or certification)
- Physical therapy (licensure from state)

Medical Liaison Personnel

5.G5

A facility should have a medical liaison who assists in reviewing and witnessing emergency plans, witnessing and critiquing drills, and reviewing and critiquing incident reports. This medical liaison should be a licensed physician or an Advanced Cardiac Life Support (ACLS)–trained registered nurse (RN) or an emergency medical technician (EMT). This individual does not have to be a member of the facility's staff. As appropriate, a facility can employ an outside contractor or consultant as a medical liaison.

Coordinators/Specialists

5.G6

A facility with a pool or other aquatic amenities should have an individual who is responsible for its maintenance. This individual should have formal training from an appropriate pool operators' teaching/licensing organization/agency and have a current CPR certification.

5.G7

A facility should have a sufficient number of CPR-certified individuals or BLS-certified and first aid–trained individuals on duty at any given time to be able to respond to a cardiorespiratory emergency within the facility within four minutes as outlined in the guidelines formulated by the American Heart Association.

5.G8   A facility should have a sufficient number of first aid–trained individuals on duty at any given time to be able to respond to an emergency within an appropriate time period.

5.G9   A facility that provides valet parking should provide a properly trained attendant who has a valid, current drivers license to handle parking responsibilities.

5.G10   A facility that provides salon or spa services (e.g., massage, manicures, pedicures) should provide properly trained staff who also have appropriate licensure and/or certification.

Continuing Education

5.G11   A facility should provide continuing education opportunities to all instructors/leaders and directors, so that these employees can keep abreast of changes in the industry and the body of knowledge relating to health, wellness, and physical activity.

5.G12   A facility should also verify on a regular basis the licenses, certifications, and so on of all staff members to make sure that these measures of professional competence are currently valid.

6 Guidelines for User Screening

Considerable evidence supports the fact that physically active individuals are less likely to suffer from a wide array of medical conditions, including coronary heart disease. On the other hand, when participating in physical activity, the risk of cardiovascular incident or death is greater than when not participating in physical activity. Because of the increased risk of cardiovascular incident during physical activity, staff members prescribing programmed physical activity for facility users should ensure that users are screened for conditions that might indicate the heightened possibility of cardiovascular incident or death. This recommendation is also applicable in instances where facility users participate without staff guidance. Research indicates that individuals with coronary risk factors or other medically significant risk factors, as identified through a preactivity screening process, run a greater chance of a cardiovascular incident during physical activity than do individuals with no risk factors. As a result, it is prudent that individuals be screened for coronary and other medical risk factors with a preactivity screening protocol before engaging in any physical activity program. In addition, users should undergo fitness evaluations prior to engaging in a physical activity program. One of the benefits of such an evaluation is that it affords the staff an opportunity to better educate and motivate users to adopt healthier lifestyles. Fitness evaluations also allow staff members to identify adverse signs and symptoms that might otherwise compromise user well-being and that should be promptly evaluated and assessed by qualified medical personnel.

This chapter addresses the recommended guidelines that should govern the screening of users prior to their participation in a physical activity program. These guidelines are designed to protect users from troublesome medical events or death while engaging in physical activity and to enhance the ability of the facility to meet an appropriate standard of care. Among the issues related to user screening that are addressed in this chapter are the following:

- Preactivity screening
- Informed consent
- User screening

Preactivity Screening

6.G1

A screening procedure given to an individual before that person engages in a physical activity program should incorporate either a general screening device (e.g., PAR-Q and You) or a specific screening device (e.g., the Health History Questionnaire). Refer to Forms 1 through 3 in appendix B for samples of preactivity screening devices.

6.G2   When an individual who has completed a preactivity screening instrument, fitness test, or health promotion evaluation is identified as having a condition or risk factor that could be adversely aggravated by physical activity, that person should be advised in writing or verbally to see a physician before engaging in physical activity. For a clarification of coronary risk factors, facility staff members should refer to the fifth edition of *ACSM's Guidelines for Exercise Testing and Prescription* and the American Heart Association's *Exercise Standards: A Statement for Health Professionals.* Examples of the forms that can be used to obtain physician approval for individuals with identified coronary risk factors are illustrated by Forms 4 and 5 in appendix B.

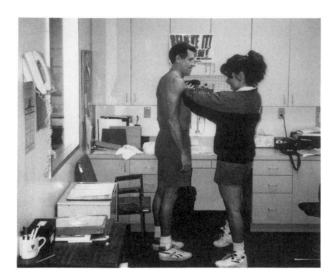

Informed Consent

6.G3   As part of its efforts to prescreen users, to conduct fitness evaluation protocols, and to prescribe physical activity, health/fitness facilities should encourage all users to complete an informed consent form. An informed consent form is generally designed to advise all users of the benefits and risks of participation, testing, and physical activity and to advise users that their participation is voluntary in nature. Samples of informed consent sheets are provided in Forms 7 through 10 in appendix B.

User Screening

6.G4   Individuals who decide not to participate in preactivity screening prior to engaging in programmed physical activity should be required to complete and sign an assumption of risk or a prospective release or waiver of claims form (or other form legally recognized as such within the jurisdiction of the facility), by the terms of which the individual assumes all risks of participation. Examples of prospective release, assumption of risk, and waiver of claims forms are provided in Forms 6, 11, and 13 in appendix B.

7 Guidelines for Emergency/Safety Procedures

Although giving careful consideration to all procedures and actions relating to such areas as physical plant safety, signage, staffing, and preactivity screening can reduce the likelihood of users' experiencing injuries or health-related problems, such attention cannot totally eliminate the risks attendant on physical activity. As a result, all health/fitness facilities must be prepared to handle situations that arise unexpectedly. A major component of the efforts to be prepared must be a comprehensive emergency plan. An emergency plan should provide guidelines for the staff to react to untoward incidents and to perform their duties in a way that will minimize the consequences of any incident. A prudent emergency plan addresses more than procedures; it also addresses staff skills, supplies and equipment, support personnel, practice, training of staff, and even risk management. Often it is the emergency plan that ensures that minor incidents don't become major incidents and that major incidents don't lead to a fatality. In all instances, the emergency plan that a health/fitness facility has adopted should ensure that all events are handled in as safe, efficient, and effective a manner as possible.

This chapter provides guidelines for developing and implementing emergency plans and procedures for a health/fitness facility. Among the issues related to emergency/safety procedures that are addressed in this chapter are the following:

- Emergency plan
- Minor incidents
- Major incidents
- Incidents involving blood
- Communications system
- First-aid kit
- Documentation
- Drills
- Chemical storage
- Risk management

Emergency Plan

7.G1   The emergency plan should include provisions for physical access to all areas of the facility, as well as a plan for the handling and disposition of bystanders.

7.G2   The emergency plan should include provisions for documenting all events to provide a basis for the orderly evaluation of a situation after it occurs and the subsequent follow-up actions that may be taken. A sample of such documentation is provided by Form 20 in appendix B.

7.G3   An emergency plan should include provisions for securing and using specific protocols and emergency supplies. Accordingly, a written emergency plan should be developed that lists specific steps that the staff should perform to satisfy the basic goals enumerated in guidelines 7.G1 and 7.G2. Refer to Form 26 in appendix B for an example of an emergency plan.

7.G4   The emergency plan should include contact and interaction with a predetermined community emergency resource.

Minor Incidents

7.G5   A facility should ensure that minor incidents (e.g., abrasions, contusions, and strains) are promptly evaluated and then managed within the facility or triaged to a community medical resource. An incident report should be completed on all incidents and kept on file at the facility.

7.G6   The supervising staff member should assess the condition of any individual who is injured. Based on the results of the evaluation, the supervising staff member should decide to respond in-house or to send the individual to a community medical resource. When necessary, the supervising staff member should then arrange for transport to a community medical resource.

7.G7   Other staff members (as assigned on the spot or detailed in the emergency plan) should be responsible for crowd control and for requesting additional assistance, if needed.

7.G8   The incident should be documented in writing by the individual assigned the responsibility and followed up with appropriate actions.

Major Incidents

7.G9   A facility should ensure that major incidents (those that are life or limb threatening or that may lead to disabilities) are appropriately addressed initially by the staff and then referred to a predetermined community emergency resource. All factors considered, staff members tend to function most effectively if they are assigned the following duties: first responder, team leader, communications staffer, and crowd control staffer.

7.G10   The individual designated as the first responder is the person who witnesses the event or is the first staffer to reach the victim. That person should promptly render immediate care, consistent with the protocols of CPR or rules of first aid. In this text, CPR is defined as the American Heart Association's Basic Cardiac Life Support (one-person adult CPR and the Heimlich maneuver).

7.G11   The team leader is the highest-level staffer on duty. After arriving on the scene, that individual should direct the general flow of care.

7.G12 The individual designated as the communications staffer should contact the appropriate community medical service by dialing 911 or other emergency medical system (EMS) contact and should provide the service with the following information: victim description, exact location of the facility, and specific point of entry into the facility. This person should then obtain an estimated time of arrival (ETA), communicate this ETA to the team leader, gather any pertinent victim records, proceed to the specific point of entry, and direct the EMS to the scene.

7.G13 The individual assigned the responsibility of serving as the crowd control staffer should clear the area of other users and of any equipment that may be in the way to ensure EMS access to the victim and ease of evacuation.

7.G14 The incident should be documented by the individual assigned the responsibility (usually the team leader) and followed up with appropriate actions.

Incidents Involving Blood

It should be noted that all incidents in a health/fitness facility involving blood are regulated by OSHA's Blood-Borne Pathogen Rule. As such, the handling of blood falls under Standard #6. The information and guidelines presented in this section are designed to help clarify certain issues pertaining to the handling of blood.

7.G15 A facility must take precautions as established by the Centers for Disease Control (CDC) and as highlighted in OSHA's Blood-Borne Pathogen Rule for the management of incidents involving blood or other body fluids likely to contain blood. For example, all staff members must wear protective barriers, such as latex gloves, when touching any surface, body, or other area soiled with blood or body fluids. In addition, all staff members must wash their hands with soap and water immediately after being exposed to blood or body fluids. Areas exposed to such substances must be cleaned with a solution of water and household bleach in accordance with CDC guidelines.

7.G16 All persons must take extreme care to avoid puncture wounds by contaminated sharp objects, such as lancets for obtaining finger-stick blood samples, and should clean any holders associated with such devices, as specified by the CDC.

7.G17 Mouthpieces or resuscitation bags must be available in a facility for emergency situations requiring mouth-to-mouth resuscitation.

7.G18 Soiled linens and medical equipment must be disposed of with the appropriate disposal equipment as required by law (for a more detailed explanation of how to properly dispose of such materials, refer to the Medical Waste Tracking Act of 1988, Section 3745.01, 42 U.S.C., Section 67992-67992K).

7.G19 All situations and incidents involving the handling of blood must be documented by the appropriate staff member and followed up with appropriate actions.

Communications System

7.G20 A facility should have established a systematic line of communication with community medical resources that is designed to facilitate communication when emergencies occur. This communications system should include appropriate signage and displays.

For example, emergency contact numbers should be displayed at all phones within the facility. These numbers should include those for EMS, police, and fire departments, according to local availability.

7.G21   An outline of the full emergency plan should be displayed at a central staff location.

7.G22   A telephone or another emergency calling system should be available within or adjacent to all physical activity areas.

First-Aid Kit

7.G23   A facility should have a first-aid kit available within the facility for use in the treatment of medical incidents. The kit should be stocked in accordance with the recommended supplies detailed in supplement 34 in appendix A. Supplies in the kit should all be checked at least once a month. Possible areas in a facility where a first-aid kit might be located are the fitness floor, the youth activity area, the control desk, the aerobics studio, and so on.

7.G24   The kit should be easily transportable and located in a well-marked and easily accessible area. In large facilities, it may be necessary to have several first-aid kits.

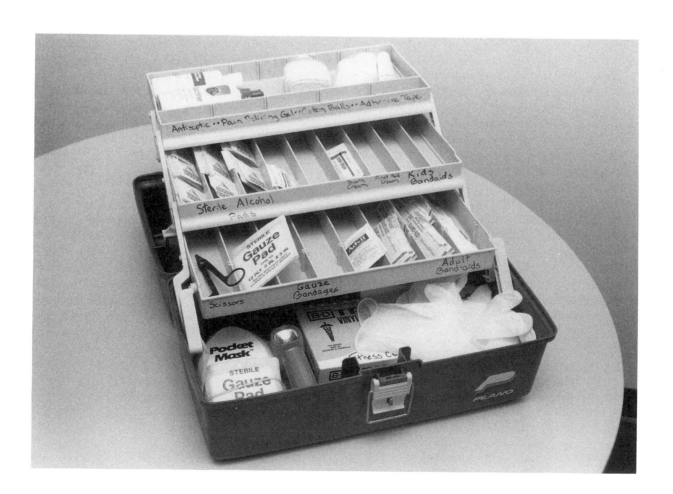

Documentation

7.G25

A facility should ensure that its emergency plan and all activities resulting from rehearsing and implementing its emergency plan are documented and retained for a period of time consistent with the statute of limitations of that locale or as advised by the facility's own legal counsel. At a minimum, such documentation should include the following:

- A copy of the emergency plan for the facility
- Written reports of all minor or major incidents (refer to Form 20 in appendix B for an example of an incident report)
- Written reports of incidents involving staff or user exposure to blood or other body fluids
- Evidence of current and relevant staff certification (e.g., CPR and first-aid certification)
- Reports of engaging in emergency drill practice, which contain the information indicated in 7.G28, including documentation of any problems that are uncovered during drills and need to be rectified
- Documentation that the first-aid kits have been restocked if utilized; a written record that the kits have been evaluated for completeness on an annual basis and have been restocked as necessary for dated items

Drills

7.G26

A facility should periodically practice its emergency plan. Such practice should help ensure that the facility's staff is fully prepared to handle emergencies, that new staffers are familiar with the emergency plan, that the plan is readily workable and responsive to facility needs, and that the emergency plan will be periodically re-evaluated and revised as needed. Emergency plan practice drills should address numerous typical health/fitness facility scenarios to cover a broad range of potential emergencies and contingencies that may occur within the facility.

7.G27

Emergency plan practice drills should be performed at least two times per year. At a minimum, one scheduled and one unannounced full rehearsal drill should be performed. Staff members should participate in emergency plan drills as an integral part of their job responsibilities.

7.G28

All emergency plan practice drills should have an after-action report that documents the date, time, nature of drill, staff participants, action taken, and recommendations for future similar drills.

Chemical Storage

7.G29

All chemicals used for cleaning should be clearly marked with an ingredient label (material data sheet) supplied by the manufacturer.

7.G30   A facility should have adequate storage for all cleaning, pool, and spa chemicals. This area should be locked and have appropriate ventilation and signage.

7.G31   A facility should provide easy access to the material data sheets for all chemicals.

Risk Management

7.G32   A facility should establish a safety committee consisting of employees who are responsible for overseeing the safety and emergency policies for the facility.

7.G33   A facility should conduct regular risk-management audits to assist in the maintenance of all emergency and safety procedures.

PART

PROGRAM ACTIVITY AREA GUIDELINES

This section of the book presents guidelines for selected program activity areas within a health/fitness facility. Collectively, the guidelines in this section are designed to help a facility attain and sustain a high quality level of service in developing and providing individual and group physical activity programs. It is important to note that these guidelines are not meant to be standards or to give rise to duties of care.

For discussion and organizational purposes, the guidelines for each particular type of program activity area that is examined in this section are separated into the following components: programming, staffing, safety, and facilities and equipment. Chapters 8 through 15 provide guidelines for eight different program activity areas within a facility: the fitness-testing, health promotion, and wellness area (chapter 8); the exercise classroom (chapter 9); the fitness floor (chapter 10); the multipurpose recreation area, for example, the gymnasium (chapter 11); sports court areas (chapter 12); pool areas (chapter 13); outdoor recreational areas (chapter 14); and running tracks (chapter 15).

8 Guidelines for the Fitness-Testing, Health Promotion, and Wellness Area

The fitness-testing, health promotion, and wellness area can be one of the most significant areas in a health/fitness facility for identifying and addressing the needs and interests of users. The potential benefits of activities conducted in this area are substantial. For example, information collected in this area may allow physical activity programming to be tailored to specific individual needs and capabilities and should enhance the ability of the staff of the facility to develop a personalized exercise prescription for each user. In order for either goal to be achieved, qualified staff members are essential.

Because of the level of expertise that is intrinsically expected from personnel who staff this area, the need for professionalism is particularly acute. Accordingly, some facilities employ off-site medical consultants to staff this area. In other situations, staffing decisions may be less subjective in nature. For example, some aspects of staffing in this area may be subject to regulation by governmental agencies if licensed or registered health professionals are involved. In those instances where government regulations do not apply, the most prudent approach that a facility can adopt to ensure that it has well-qualified staff in this area is to require that all employees in this area possess an appropriate combination of formal education, experience, and professional certification.

Fortunately, the evaluative procedures and other programs typically offered in this area of a facility are ordinarily very safe. Even clinical exercise testing on clinical populations carries a myocardial infarction risk ratio of 3.6 per 10,000 and a death risk ratio of 0.5 per 10,000. In addition, for submaximal fitness testing, a review of approximately 130,000 tests performed in work-site health promotion programs shows even lower risk levels than for those of clinical exercise testing. Nevertheless, the fact that users sometimes undertake heavier-than-usual levels of exertion in this area confirms the need for appropriate screening procedures and a well-conceived emergency protocol. Furthermore, because some activities in this area may involve the collection of body fluids, the necessity for appropriate care in the collection, handling, and disposal of these substances is critical. This chapter presents guidelines that address issues related to the fitness-testing, health promotion, and wellness area of a health/fitness facility.

Programming

8.G1   A facility should offer health promotion/wellness programs to its users. Because health promotion/wellness information has become an important part of the efforts to educate consumers, a commitment to make such programs available is important to the health/fitness facility intent on serving the needs of its users. Of particular importance for the activities conducted in this area are the fitness-testing programs that are in many instances a critical element of the safe prescription of physical activity. Examples of other assessment and intervention program offerings in this area that help identify, educate, and favorably change the lifestyle patterns of users include smoking cessation, AIDS awareness, stress management, nutrition education, and so on.

8.G2   A facility should provide fitness testing for its users. A fitness-testing protocol should incorporate measurements of body composition, cardiorespiratory fitness, flexibility, and muscular fitness. All protocols should be conducted in accordance with professionally derived standards and guidelines as adapted to particular programs (refer to *ACSM's Guidelines for Exercise Testing and Prescription,* fifth edition). A written record of all such measurements should be made and retained, using a form such as Form 15 in appendix B.

8.G3   The cardiovascular assessment portion of the fitness evaluation should be submaximal in nature and should not require physician supervision for users who have passed preactivity screenings and who are apparently healthy. (Refer to *ACSM's Guidelines for Exercise Testing and Prescription*, fifth edition, for additional information.) Cardiovascular information should be recorded using a form such as Form 15 or 17 in appendix B.

8.G4

If maximal cardiovascular assessments are incorporated into a fitness evaluation procedure, the assessment may be performed without a physician or Advanced Cardiac Life Support (ACLS)–trained personnel when the individual (if a male under 40 years of age or a female under 50 years of age) has been screened for and cleared of medical risks either by a preactivity screening form or by a physician.

8.G5

Maximal cardiovascular assessments using a 12-lead electrocardiogram (ECG) should be incorporated into a fitness evaluation procedure only if the procedure is supervised by a physician and if the facility has the appropriate emergency equipment available.

8.G6

Wherever the law allows, a facility has the option of providing a comprehensive offering of assessment procedures including the following:

- Blood pressure screening
- Blood screens for cholesterol, high-density lipoprotein (HDL), and low-density lipoprotein (LDL)
- Blood screens for glucose and triglycerides

Such procedures are usually governed by local or state laws and typically require professionally licensed or certified individuals to administer them (e.g., an RN, a medical technician, a physician). The results of these procedures should be provided to users, who should be encouraged to review the results with their physicians.

8.G7

A facility should provide, when feasible, a comprehensive offering of health promotion/wellness intervention programs, including these:

- CPR classes
- Eating management and nutrition
- Smoking cessation
- Stress management
- Back care
- Blood pressure screening
- Cholesterol screening

Because this list is not inclusive, it should be supplemented by programs that are relevant and of interest to users and the community.

Staffing

8.G8

A facility should ensure that all fitness tests are administered by individuals who, at a minimum, have the following credentials:

- A college degree in health/fitness or a related exercise science field
- Current professional certification from a nationally recognized organization in the health/fitness industry
- Current CPR certification

8.G9

If blood screens, maximal graded exercise tests, or similar medically oriented tests are offered, they should be supervised by a physician or another qualified health care professional authorized by law to administer such programs.

Safety

8.G10   A facility should have an operations manual that outlines the policies and procedures for programming, safety, and staff for the fitness-testing, health promotion, and wellness area.

Facilities and Equipment

8.G11   Provided that a facility has staff members who are legally authorized to use such items, a facility should incorporate the following equipment into its fitness-testing area if maximal graded exercise tests are performed:

- Crash cart
- ECG defibrillator
- Spine board

8.G12   Appropriate temperature, humidity, and air circulation levels should be maintained for the fitness-testing, health promotion, and wellness area. The following levels are recommended:

Temperature:	68 to 72 degrees Fahrenheit
Humidity:	60 percent or less
Air circulation:	8 to 12 exchanges per hour

Air exchanges should have an appropriate mix of outside and inside air. This mix is usually 10 percent outside air and 90 percent inside air, though a ratio of 40 to 60, outside to inside, is preferred. The specific ratio of outside air to inside air (recirculated air) is most often governed by local engineering codes. These codes should be followed when any air-handling system is installed. Additional information on what constitutes appropriate temperature levels is presented in supplement 9 in appendix A.

8.G13   The fitness-testing, health promotion, and wellness area should have an appropriate level of light. The illumination level should be at least 50 foot-candles at the floor surface. Additional information on what constitutes appropriate illumination levels is presented in supplement 10 in appendix A.

8.G14   A facility should allocate the following space for its health promotion, fitness-testing, and wellness area:

Fitness testing:	100 to 180 square feet
Counseling room:	90 to 120 square feet
Seminar room:	20 square feet per participant

8.G15   A facility should provide antistatic carpet with antifungal and antibacterial treatment for all health promotion, fitness-testing, and wellness spaces.

8.G16   A facility should ensure that every fitness-testing space either has a sink or has access to a sink.

8.G17   A facility should ensure that its fitness-testing area has the following equipment: a bicycle ergometer, a treadmill or a fixed step device (e.g., a bench) of a desired height, skinfold calipers or other body composition measurement device, sit-and-reach bench or goniometer, tensiometer or other device for measuring muscular strength and endurance, perceived exertion chart, clock, metronome, sphygmomanometer (blood pressure cuff), stethoscope, tape measure, scale, and first-aid kit.

8.G18   A facility should ensure that its other health promotion spaces have the following equipment: computer, overhead projector, video system, slide projector, conference table, and chairs.

8.G19   A facility should ensure that its fitness-testing, health promotion, and wellness area has a system that provides for and protects the complete confidentiality of all user records and meetings. User records should be released only with an individual's authorization. An example of a form for such purposes is Form 18 in appendix B.

9 Guidelines for the Exercise Classroom

The exercise classroom is the area in a facility where selected physical activity classes (e.g., step aerobics, yoga, martial arts) are conducted. An exercise classroom is an essential component of a health/fitness facility. Some exercise classrooms, such as an aerobics studio, are used strictly for a specific activity, while other exercise rooms may serve as a location where several activities are held. As a result, guidelines for this area should take into consideration the sometimes diverse uses of such areas.

It is essential that all users are aware of the types of group exercise classes a facility offers and when they are offered. Accordingly, a facility should develop a written schedule of class offerings to enable users to better plan their personal physical activity programs.

Group exercise classes are sometimes the only form of physical activity in which many facility users engage. As a result, it is imperative that programming efforts for group classes adhere to the basic principles of exercise activity that are professionally derived, formulated, and referenced (refer to the fifth edition of *ACSM's Guidelines for Exercise Testing and Prescription*). In addition to sound programming, facilities should consider how staffing, safety, design, and equipment factors affect an exercise classroom. Toward that end, this chapter presents guidelines that address exercise classrooms in health/fitness facilities.

Programming

9.G1 A facility should provide an individualized exercise program for users who have completed a preactivity screening and are cleared to participate in physical activity. This program should adhere to the exercise variables and principles outlined in the *ACSM's Guidelines for Exercise Testing and Prescription*, fifth edition. Individuals who fail to take a preactivity screening or who fail such a screening and, as a result, do not receive clearance should be required to sign an assumption of risk or a prospective release or waiver of claims form before being allowed access to the facility. (Note: Such individuals should not be provided with an exercise program.)

9.G2 A facility should ensure that individualized programming recommendations for physical activity are reviewed by the fitness staff on a regular basis and modified if necessary. Any changes in the recommended activity regimen should then be reviewed with the user. An example of a form that could be used for such reviews is Form 16 in appendix B.

9.G3 A written schedule of group exercise programs that are to be conducted in the classroom should be made available to facility users. These schedules should be available at least one week in advance and should include information on class location, time, and description.

9.G4   A set of written policies should be made available to users that outlines the rules and regulations governing participation in and use of the exercise classroom.

9.G5   Group exercise participants should be informed of the risks, limitations, and benefits of any group physical activity programs scheduled.

9.G6   All group physical activity programs taught in the exercise classroom should incorporate a warm-up phase, conditioning phase, and cool-down phase, in accordance with professionally derived, formulated, and referenced guidelines for exercise prescription and programming (refer to the fifth edition of the *ACSM's Guidelines for Exercise Testing and Prescription*).

9.G7   All group physical activity programs should closely adhere to the following fundamental principles of exercise: overload, progressive resistance, specificity, maintenance, detraining, individuality, and reversibility. (Refer to the fifth edition of *ACSM's Guidelines for Exercise Testing and Prescription* for further information concerning these principles.)

9.G8   Group physical activity programming should enable those individuals with unique physical, physiological, or other limitations to safely participate in the scheduled activities.

9.G9   Attendance should be recorded for all group physical activity functions conducted in the exercise classroom.

9.G10   A facility should make an effort to incorporate a variety of types of group physical activity classes into its program offerings, including low-impact, combination, circuit training, stretch, progressive resistance, step, dance, and martial arts activities.

Staffing

9.G11   A professionally trained instructor should be available in the classroom immediately before, during, and immediately after the group physical activity class to ensure that all users are safely prepared, instructed, monitored, and cared for if needed.

Safety

9.G12   Instructors/leaders should remove users from the classroom who are endangering the safety of either themselves or other users.

9.G13   A facility should provide a clock and a target heart rate or perceived exertion chart in the exercise classroom and should instruct users in self-monitoring techniques so they can safely monitor their own levels of exertion.

9.G14   The user-to-instructor/leader ratio, while usually dependent on the specific nature of the class being taught and the capabilities of each particular instructor, should not exceed 50 to 1. As a result, users can be assured of receiving an appropriate level of personal attention and instruction. In those classes in which more than 50 users participate, a second instructor should be provided.

9.G15   Food or drink should not be allowed into the exercise classroom during class, with the exception of water in a closed container

9.G16   Users should warm up before entering an exercise classroom after class has begun.

9.G17   Users should wear the appropriate footwear (i.e., sports shoes) for a class when participating in physical activity.

9.G18   Instructors/leaders should inform users of any physical movements that may expose them to an undue risk of injury while they are engaged in a particular physical activity.

9.G19   Instructors/leaders should encourage all users to participate in a program of cool-down exercises prior to leaving the exercise classroom. If for some reason individuals have to leave the exercise classroom prior to performing a planned routine of cool-down exercises, they should be encouraged to conduct an alternate cool-down program prior to leaving the facility.

Facilities and Equipment

9.G20   Exercise classrooms should be designed to provide at least 40 to 50 square feet of space per expected user. The exact space requirements are dictated by the program activity conducted in the exercise classroom.

9.G21   Whenever possible, the exercise classroom should have a minimum ceiling height of 10 feet.

9.G22   The exercise classroom should have mirrors on at least two of its four walls. These mirrors should extend from six inches above the floor to the ceiling.

9.G23
The exercise classroom should have a wood or comparable floor surface in conjunction with a subfloor system that eliminates dead spots and provides for adequate absorption of the impact created by users. Numerous options for achieving such a level of deflection exist, including spring systems, floating floors, resilient rubber padding, and wood furring strips. Additional information on designing and constructing floors for exercise classrooms is provided in supplement 11 in appendix A.

9.G24
A facility should insulate the walls of the exercise classroom to avoid having an excessive level of sound heard outside of the classroom. One of the most effective forms of insulation is a double layer of plasterboard or a sound board and a single layer of plasterboard, along with at least four inches of fiberglass insulation.

9.G25
A facility should provide an adequate sound system for the exercise classroom, including a wireless microphone for the instructor/leader.

9.G26
A facility should provide equipment that will enhance participation in the group physical activity class. Among the types of equipment that are often included are the following:

- Exercise mats
- Weights
- Tubes and bands
- Benches or steps
- Slides
- Resist-a-balls
- Body bars (weighted bars)

9.G27
Appropriate temperature, humidity, and air circulation levels should be maintained in the exercise classroom. The following levels are recommended:

Temperature: 66 to 70 degrees Fahrenheit
Humidity: 60 percent or less
Air circulation: 8 to 12 exchanges per hour

Air exchanges should have the appropriate mix of outside and inside air. This mix is usually 10 percent outside air and 90 percent inside air, though a mix of 40 to 60, outside to inside, is preferred. The specific ratio of outside air to inside air (recirculated air) is most often governed by local engineering codes. These codes should be followed when any air-handling system is installed. Additional information regarding what constitutes appropriate temperature levels is provided in supplement 9 in appendix A.

9.G28   The exercise classroom should have an appropriate level of light. The illumination level should be 50 foot-candles at the floor surface. Additional information regarding what constitutes appropriate illumination levels is provided in supplement 10 in appendix A.

9.G29   Sound levels in the exercise classroom should be kept no higher than 70 to 80 decibels and should not exceed 90 decibels.

10 Guidelines for the Fitness Floor

The fitness floor is the area that most often addresses the physical activity needs of users in a health/fitness facility. In most instances, this area houses the cardiovascular, resistance, and free-weight training equipment offered by a facility. Because of the variety of program options available on the fitness floor, this area represents the nucleus of the facility for many users.

Accordingly, a facility should take every step to ensure that all of the activities conducted on the fitness floor are worthwhile to participants. One of the major keys toward achieving that objective is to keep in mind that individuals are most likely to realize the benefits of physical activity when they engage in a physical activity program that incorporates the appropriate dose of frequency, intensity, and duration of exercise. The appropriate quantity and quality of exercise should be determined from an individual's health profile, needs, and, ideally, responses during evaluation procedures. In other words, a user's physical activity program should be based on sound principles of exercise training (e.g., the precepts presented in the fifth edition of *ACSM's Guidelines for Exercise Testing and Prescription*).

Another primary key for ensuring that users maximize the benefits of their physical activity regimen involves activity instructors' or leaders' showing each individual exactly how the various parts of the exercise program should be performed. In addition to leading users through each of the components of their activity endeavors, instructors should monitor individuals as they perform their individualized programs to ensure that users receive the maximal level of benefits from their efforts with minimal exposure to injury. Finally, instructors should periodically adjust each user's individual physical activity program to ensure that, to the extent possible, personal goals are achieved. Toward that end, a facility should offer a wide variety of activities (e.g., personal training, circuit training) on the fitness floor to further enhance the users' opportunities to meet their needs and interests.

This chapter presents guidelines that address the safe and effective operation of the fitness floor.

Programming

10.G1

Before users begin participating in any activity on the exercise floor, a facility should provide them with a physical walk-through of the facilities and hands-on instruction on how to use each piece of equipment involved in their programs.

10.G2

A facility should provide supervision of all fitness areas during operating hours to provide a safe and motivating environment for physical activity. Supervision refers to a staff member being present on the floor and actively involved in monitoring the activities that are occurring to ensure that they are being performed safely and properly.

10.G3 A facility should prescribe an individualized exercise program only for users who have received preactivity screenings and are cleared to participate in physical activity. After they have completed the appropriate waiver or assumption of risk form, individuals who either fail to take a preactivity screening or fail the screening and who do not receive subsequent medical clearance should be provided with a conservative program of light-to-moderate physical activity in accordance with CDC/ACSM guidelines.

10.G4 A facility should have procedures that ensure that individualized exercise programs are reviewed by the fitness staff on a regular basis and modified if necessary. Any changes in an individualized exercise program should be reviewed with the user involved. A sample of a form that could be used for such review procedures is Form 24 in appendix B.

10.G5 A facility should provide at least one instructor/leader for every 50 or fewer users who are engaged in a physical activity program on the fitness floor.

10.G6 A facility should make an effort to offer exercise programs that include the following components and factors:

- Warm-up, conditioning, and cool-down stages
- Cardiovascular, muscular strengthening, and flexibility exercises
- Adherence to the appropriate doses of duration, frequency, and intensity of exercise
- Accommodation for the special needs of each user, including individuals who have physiological limitations or are otherwise challenged physically or emotionally

10.G7 A facility should provide users with a wide variety of program offerings on the fitness floor, including the following activities:

- Personal training (one-on-one instruction and coaching)
- Group exercise orientations
- Circuit-training classes
- Competitive fitness events or fitness-type challenges
- Fitness incentive programs that reward users for participating in individualized fitness or group physical activity programs

10.G8 As an integral part of their responsibilities as floor supervisors, all fitness floor staff members should continually educate and motivate users.

10.G9 A facility should provide written descriptions of the fitness programs and services available to users and should make this information readily available to all users.

Staffing

10.G10 A facility should assign staff members who have demonstrable professional competence to work the fitness floor. Refer to chapter 5 under guideline 5.G3 for an example of such professional competence.

Safety

10.G11 A facility should provide a clock and a target heart rate or perceived exertion chart for the fitness floor and should ensure that users are instructed in self-monitoring techniques so they can safely monitor their own levels of exertion.

10.G12 A facility should provide signage that clarifies for the user the warning signs and symptoms related to exercise (nausea, dizziness, a pain in the chest, etc.).

Facilities and Equipment

10.G13 A facility should provide adequate space on the fitness floor for an appropriate amount of cardiovascular-conditioning equipment, resistance-training equipment, and stretching equipment and/or activities.

10.G14 The design and layout of a facility should provide at least 20 to 40 square feet for each piece of exercise equipment. The exact amount of space to be occupied is determined by the size of each particular piece of equipment and the recommendations of the manufacturer.

10.G15 A facility should allow for 20 to 25 square feet of space for each person expected to be using the fitness floor at any one time. (This is not in addition to the space allocation for equipment in 10.G14.)

10.G16   A facility should provide the following types of floor coverings for the fitness floor area:

Cardiovascular area:	Antistatic carpet treated with antifungal and antibacterial agents
Resistance-training area:	Same as for cardiovascular area, or rubber-based resilient floor
Stretching area:	Nonabsorbent mats or antistatic carpet treated with antifungal and antibacterial agents

10.G17   A facility should consider providing a variety of types of equipment for the cardiovascular area, including treadmills, mechanical stair-climbing machines, bicycle ergometers, computerized cycles, rowing ergometers, upper-body ergometers, and total-body-conditioning machines.

10.G18   A facility should consider providing at least one circuit of progressive resistance-training equipment for the fitness floor (other than free weights) that includes either a machine or a workout station for each of the following muscle groups: gluteus, quadriceps, hamstrings, calves, chest, upper back, lower back, shoulders, triceps, biceps, and abdomen.

10.G19   A facility should arrange the circuit for resistance training in a fashion that allows users to train the largest muscle groups first and then proceed to the smaller muscle groups. All compound movement machines* should be placed in the circuit before isolated movement machines involving the same muscle(s).

*A compound movement while strength training is an exercise that elicits the involvement of multiple muscles and multiple joints (e.g., a squat, a bench press).

10.G20 A facility should consider providing a variety of types of free-weight equipment, including a supine bench press with safety pins, incline bench with safety pins, Smith-type machine, supine bench, adjustable incline bench, cable crossover system, pull-up or pull-down system, abdominal system, dumbbells, and Olympic-style bar and plates.

10.G21 The fitness floor should have a sound system that provides equal sound distribution to all areas.

10.G22 Sound levels should be kept at no more than 90 decibels.

10.G23 Appropriate temperature, humidity, and air circulation levels should be maintained in the fitness floor area. The following levels are recommended:

Temperature:	68 to 72 degrees Fahrenheit
Humidity:	60 percent or less
Air circulation:	8 to 12 exchanges per hour

Air exchanges should have the appropriate mix of outside and inside air. This mix is usually 10 percent outside air and 90 percent inside air, though a mix of 40 to 60, outside to inside, is preferred. The specific ratio of outside air to inside air (recirculated air) is usually governed by local engineering codes. These codes should be followed when any air-handling system is installed. Additional information on what constitutes appropriate temperature levels is provided in supplement 9 in appendix A.

10.G24 The fitness floor should have an appropriate level of light. The level of illumination should be at least 50 foot-candles at the floor surface. Additional information on what constitutes appropriate illumination levels is presented in supplement 10 in appendix A.

10.G25 The fitness floor should provide users with access to entertainment-related media (e.g., televisions, magazines, and newspapers) while they are exercising.

11 Guidelines for a Multipurpose Recreation Area (Gymnasium)

A gymnasium is a large, multipurpose room within a health/fitness facility in which various indoor activities (usually games) are conducted (e.g., basketball, badminton, roller hockey, and volleyball). Accordingly, a gymnasium offers a multiopportunity setting in which activities can be scheduled to serve a wide array of distinct audiences and meet a multitude of specific organizational goals. In order to ensure that a gymnasium is utilized in an appropriate manner, programming efforts should take many factors into consideration. One such factor is the importance and relative time share of scheduled play (e.g., leagues) versus "pick-up" (i.e., unstructured) activities. This usage ratio may affect the scheduling of other activities at the facility, the need for personnel with officiating credentials, and the overall tone set for the facility. This chapter presents guidelines that address the safe and effective use of a gymnasium area.

Programming

11.G1   A facility should provide a regularly scheduled program of both structured and unstructured activities in the gymnasium area that are appropriate for the needs, interests, and personal goals of the facility's users. Examples of such activities include the following:

Structured:
- Sports camps (e.g., youth basketball and volleyball) and leagues (e.g., basketball, volleyball, badminton, soccer, softball, pickleball)
- Tournaments (e.g., basketball, volleyball, badminton, soccer)
- Special events (e.g., dances, carnivals)

Unstructured:
- Open play (e.g., basketball, volleyball, badminton)

11.G2   A facility should post monthly an activity schedule for its gymnasium that lists all activities scheduled for that month.

Staffing

11.G3   The gymnasium area should be supervised on a regular basis by qualified staff members who are aware of and sensitive to the unique characteristics and needs of the facility's users.

11.G4   When organized competition is conducted within a gymnasium, individuals serving as officials should be certified or licensed by an appropriate governing body. At the very least, those serving as officials must have a thorough knowledge of the rules and regulations that apply to the specific activity. Organized competition includes those situations that require payment for entry and that award some level of recognition or prize for winning the competition.

Safety

11.G5   All participants should be encouraged to comply with eye-guard and footwear requirements.

11.G6   All activities should be conducted in accordance with rules and guidelines that prohibit flagrantly unsafe actions by the participants.

11.G7   The wall area immediately behind each backboard area should be padded.

11.G8   All backboards in the gymnasium should have breakaway rims.

Facilities and Equipment

Size

11.G9   The gymnasium should be large enough to include (at the minimum) space for one full-size basketball court (50 feet by 84 feet is recommended) with at least 6 to 10 feet of unobstructed area around the court. Note that all measurements are from the inside lines. Exact dimensions for activity courts in a gymnasium are provided in supplements 12 through 14, appendix A. For those facilities that are unable to provide such space but wish to offer basketball as an activity, other options need to be explored. For example, a converted racquetball court (20 by 40 feet) may suffice.

11.G10   The height from the floor to the ceiling beams should be a minimum of 23 feet (Note: A clearance height of 30 feet is strongly recommended) so that in normal use of any of the court areas in the gymnasium, any sports equipment used in the activity (e.g., balls, badminton birds) will not strike the lowest ceiling beam.

11.G11   If spectator seating is to be provided, three square feet of space per spectator should be allocated. Portable, folding bleachers that can be easily moved offer a desirable option for providing seating.

11.G12   The ceilings in the gymnasium should be constructed of materials that help reduce noise levels.

11.G13   The walls in the gymnasium should be constructed of concrete or cinder blocks.

11.G14 The walls in the gymnasium should have a wainscot from the floor up to a height of eight feet. From that point to the ceiling, the walls should be painted with a light-colored paint. The wall area immediately behind each backboard area should be padded for safety.

11.G15 The floors in the gymnasium should have a concrete base covered by a sleeper system and a hardwood surface. Maple tongue-and-groove and pressure-treated beech are two of the more common types of wood used for the surface of gymnasium floors. Additional information on gymnasium floors is provided in supplement 11 in appendix A.

Floor Markings

11.G16 The gymnasium floor should be marked for the activities that are planned for the gymnasium. Where appropriate, a facility should consider having the following (overlapping) markings on its gymnasium floor:

- One full-size basketball court (50 feet by 84 feet is recommended). Supplement 12 presents the dimensions and the markings for a full-size basketball court and the recommended dimensions of a backboard and the off-court encroachment allowances for backboards.
- One full-size volleyball court. Supplement 13 presents the dimensions and the markings of a full-size volleyball court.
- One full-size badminton court. Supplement 14 presents the dimensions and the markings of a full-size badminton court.
- Side-by-side basketball courts, if space permits and user interest dictates.

Equipment

11.G17 The gymnasium should be adequately equipped and furnished to meet the material requirements for all activities scheduled to be conducted in the area (e.g., basketball, volleyball, badminton).

11.G18 At least one clock with a second hand that is visible to all users to help facilitate self-monitoring during exercise should be located in the gymnasium.

Environment

11.G19 Appropriate temperature, humidity, and air circulation levels should be maintained in the gymnasium. The following levels are recommended:

Temperature:	68 to 72 degrees Fahrenheit
Humidity:	60 percent or less
Air circulation:	8 to 12 exchanges per hour

Air exchanges should have the appropriate mix of outside and inside air. This mix is usually 10 percent outside air and 90 percent inside air, though a mix of 40 to 60, outside to inside, is preferred. The specific ratio of outside air to inside air (recirculated air) is most often governed by local engineering codes. These codes should be followed when any air-handling system is installed. Additional information on what constitutes appropriate temperature levels is presented in supplement 9 in appendix A.

11.G20 The gymnasium should have an appropriate source and level of light. Mercury vapor, metal halide, or fluorescent lights are recommended. The illumination level should be at least 50 foot-candles at the surface of the floor. Additional information on what constitutes appropriate illumination levels is presented in supplement 10 in appendix A.

11.G21 Sound levels in the gymnasium should be kept at no more than 90 decibels.

Accessibility

11.G22 The gymnasium should be adjacent to storage rooms that can house the equipment and supplies used in the activities conducted in the gymnasium.

12 Guidelines for Sports Court Areas

Sports courts are physical activity areas designed for specific types of sport activities (e.g., tennis, racquetball, squash, handball, badminton, paddle tennis, platform tennis) that are played on courts. A facility can have sports courts that are indoors, outdoors, or both. Depending on the interests and needs of the users and the organizational goals of the facility, sports court activities can be scheduled to serve a wide array of distinct audiences and meet a multitude of specific goals (e.g., competition, exercise, social opportunities).

To ensure that a facility's sports court areas are utilized in an appropriate manner, personnel who program activities for the sports courts should consider not only the interests, needs, and goals of both the facility and its users, but also the many factors that may be affected by programming decisions. For example, decisions regarding how activities in the sports court areas are structured and implemented should be considered relative to the proportion of time allotted to formal competition, recreational league play, and open play. Such decisions can be perceived by one group of a facility's users as positive and by another group as negative. By the same token, such decisions could facilitate one particular outcome for users (e.g., enhancing the opportunities for social interaction), while concurrently inhibiting another outcome (e.g., developing individual levels of physical fitness). This chapter presents guidelines that address ensuring that sports court areas are operated safely and effectively.

Programming

12.G1 A facility should provide a regularly scheduled program of both structured and unstructured activities in the sports court areas that are appropriate for the needs, interests, and goals of the facility's users. Programming options for a structured court sport activity include organizing the activity by skill or experience level (all participants in a particular event are grouped by comparable skill or experience), by sex (men only, women only, or mixed), and by the number of on-the-court participants (singles, doubles, or cutthroat).

12.G2 A monthly (or weekly) schedule of activities to be conducted in a particular type of sports court should be posted outside the area in a conspicuous, appropriate location.

Staffing

12.G3   The sports court areas should be monitored on a regular basis by qualified health/fitness professionals with demonstrable professional competence to ensure that all activities are being conducted in a fashion that enhances user safety and enjoyment.

Safety

12.G4   All participants should comply with eye-guard and footwear requirements.

12.G5   All activities should be conducted in accordance with rules and guidelines that prohibit flagrantly unsafe actions by the participants.

12.G6   All doors and windows on enclosed sports courts should be made of shatterproof glass.

12.G7   If the tennis and platform tennis court areas include a court designated primarily for teaching, that court should be separated from adjacent courts by a divider net.

Facilities and Equipment

The guidelines in this section are divided into five subsections: general guidelines, enclosed courts, open courts, indoor courts, and outdoor courts. Information about open indoor courts, for example, can be found in both the subsection on indoor courts and on open courts.

General Guidelines

12.G8   All sports court areas should be of regulation size. The national governing organization for each court sport recommends the following dimensions:

Racquetball/handball	20 feet wide by 40 feet long by 20 feet high
Squash (singles/North American)	18 feet 6 inches wide by 32 feet long by 16 feet high
Squash (singles/international)	21 feet wide by 32 feet long by 16 feet high
Squash (doubles)	25 feet wide by 45 feet long by 16 feet high
Tennis	36 feet wide by 78 feet long
Platform tennis	20 feet wide by 44 feet long
Paddle tennis	20 feet wide by 50 feet long
Paddle	32 feet 6 inches wide by 65 feet long

Diagrams of the dimensions and the markings for some of these courts are presented in supplements 15 through 19 in appendix A.

12.G9   The surface of tennis and paddle tennis courts should consist of a hard base (asphalt or concrete) covered by a poured coating. The type of coating depends on which type of base—concrete or asphalt—is installed. A number of different brands of

coatings are on the market; all generally offer a rubberized, latex-type covering that purports to ensure an all-weather surface, true ball response, cushioned give to minimize leg fatigue, ease of maintenance, and long-term durability. Clay is another surface that is used on some outdoor tennis courts, particularly on courts located in southern climates. Har-Tru, a synthetic clay surface, is a popular alternative to clay.

12.G10   The surface of a platform tennis court should be a raised, level platform that is constructed of treated wood or an aluminum superstructure with an undercarriage set on concrete piers.

12.G11   Storage rooms for equipment and supplies used in sports court areas should be located adjacent to the courts.

12.G12   For both enclosed and indoor open courts, at least one clock should be hung in the area just outside the courts to facilitate exertional self-monitoring (via heart rate) during activity.

12.G13   The ball marks on the walls of enclosed courts should be removed on a regular basis.

12.G14   The glass walls of enclosed courts should be cleaned on a regular basis.

12.G15   All windows to enclosed courts should be cleaned on a regular basis.

12.G16   The lenses of light fixtures in open courts should be wiped with a damp cloth on a regular basis.

12.G17   The light fixture louvers in open courts should be dipped in a cleaning solution, then dipped in clear water, and allowed to dry without wiping at least quarterly.

12.G18   When the lamps in the open sports courts are approaching the end of their estimated lifetimes, they should all be replaced at the same time.

Enclosed Courts

12.G19 When more than one enclosed sports court of a specific type is to be constructed, the new courts should be placed in two rows adjacent to each other and arranged in such a manner that the back walls of the two rows of courts are separated by a corridor approximately 10 feet wide and 8 feet high.

12.G20 For enclosed courts that do not have glass viewing walls, a facility should consider having an open-balcony corridor (at least 12 feet above ground level). Such a corridor is constructed immediately above the floor level of the courts and is designed to serve either as an area for an instructor to observe play in the courts or as a spectator area.

12.G21 Enclosed squash and racquetball courts should have cushioned hardwood floors.

12.G22 The ceilings of enclosed courts should be made of either plaster or laminated composition panels.

12.G23 The walls of enclosed courts should be constructed of hard plaster, concrete, shatterproof glass, laminated composition panels, or a nonsplintering, durable wood. In general, hardwood, such as maple, is recommended. Plaster walls are the most expensive to maintain, whereas the initial cost of glass walls may be prohibitive.

12.G24 The front walls of enclosed courts should be constructed of hard maple laid on diagonal wood sheathing or laminated composition panels.

12.G25 The studding on the front walls of enclosed courts should be placed close enough to prevent dead spots. Studs should not be placed farther than 16 inches apart.

12.G26 If feasible, at least one enclosed sports court (of each type) should have a glass back wall that permits spectator viewing.

12.G27   A small, shatterproof window should be installed flush with the interior surface of the door into each enclosed court and should be located at a height of approximately five feet.

12.G28   The entrance doors to enclosed courts should open toward the corridor and have flush pulls and hinges.

12.G29   Enclosed court areas should be adequately equipped and furnished to meet the material requirements for all activities that may be conducted in a particular area. Examples of items with which a facility should consider equipping and furnishing an enclosed court area include the following:

- Racquets and racquetballs
- Handballs and handball gloves
- Squash racquets and squash balls
- Eye guards
- Movable metal "telltales" (a metal baseboard over which a squash ball must be hit) for placement in racquetball and handball courts so that they can be used for squash (if the health/fitness facility does not have squash courts)

12.G30   Appropriate temperature, humidity, and air circulation levels should be maintained in both enclosed and indoor courts. The following levels are recommended:

Temperature:	60 to 68 degrees Fahrenheit (for squash courts, 60 to 65 degrees Fahrenheit)
Humidity:	60 percent or less
Air circulation:	8 to 12 exchanges per hour for enclosed courts

Air exchanges should have the appropriate mix of outside and inside air. This mix is usually 10 percent outside air and 90 percent inside air, though a mix of 40 to 60, outside to inside, is preferred. The specific ratio of outside air to inside air (recirculated air) is usually governed by local engineering codes. These codes should be followed when any air-handling system is installed. Additional information on what constitutes appropriate temperature levels is presented in supplement 9 in appendix A.

12.G31   The ventilation ducts on all enclosed courts should be flush with the ceiling surface.

12.G32   All enclosed sports courts should have appropriate sources and levels of light. Mercury vapor or warm white fluorescent lights are recommended. The illumination level should be at least 50 foot-candles at the surface of the floor or, in the case of tennis courts, at the height of the net. Additional information on what constitutes appropriate illumination levels for tennis courts is presented in supplements 20, 21, and 22 in appendix A.

12.G33   A single light switch to control all lights in each enclosed court should be placed on the corridor side near the entrance door.

12.G34   The corridors and galleries adjacent to enclosed sports courts should be illuminated with indirect light.

12.G35   All courts should have a clock either in or visible from the court.

Open Courts

12.G36

As a general rule, a health/fitness facility should have one open indoor sports court per 50 to 100 estimated users and one open outdoor sports court per 25 to 50 estimated users .

12.G37

Open courts should have sufficient border space surrounding them. The recommended space for tennis courts is 12 feet on the sides and 21 feet on each end. The recommended clearance area for a platform tennis court is five feet on each side and eight feet at each end. Paddle tennis courts require a 10-foot minimum space on each side and a 15-foot minimum space on each end. Tennis, platform tennis, and paddle tennis courts should be allotted a ground space of approximately 7,200, 1,800, and 3,200 square feet per court, respectively.

12.G38

Open courts should be placed side by side if the facility has less than six open courts. If a facility has six or more open courts, half of the courts may be placed end to end with the other half.

12.G39

Spectator traffic lanes between open courts should be clearly marked.

12.G40

Open court areas should be adequately equipped and furnished to meet the material requirements for all activities that may be conducted in a particular area. These materials include the following:

- Two net posts and one net per court
- Racquets
- Tennis balls, platform tennis balls, and paddle tennis balls
- Extra nets
- Manually operated water squeegee (for outdoor court use)
- Ball retriever for teaching courts
- Ball machines (optional)

12.G41

Appropriate temperature, humidity, and air circulation levels should be maintained in open indoor courts. The following levels are recommended:

Temperature:	60 to 68 degrees Fahrenheit
Humidity:	60 percent or less
Air circulation:	Six to eight exchanges per hour

Additional information on temperature-related factors is presented in supplement 9 in appendix A.

12.G42

All open courts should have appropriate sources and levels of light. The illumination level should be at least 50 foot-candles at the level of the net. Additional information on illumination-related factors is presented in supplements 20, 21, and 22 in appendix A.

Indoor Courts

12.G43

On indoor open sports courts, backdrop curtains should be approximately 12 feet high at the back wall. Above these levels and on the sides of the courts, the walls should be painted a very light, uniform color with a matte finish.

12.G44

The height of the ceiling of an indoor open sports court should be at least 30 feet.

12.G45

Ceilings of a facility with indoor open courts should have a matte finish and be light in color. No contrasting colors should be used.

12.G46 All indoor open sports courts should have appropriate sources and levels of light. The level of illumination should be at least 50 foot-candles (measured 36 inches above the court surface with a light-sensitized cell facing upward). Supplement 20 in appendix A presents a matrix of the foot-candle (illumination) requirements for different levels of competitive indoor tennis play. (Note: These levels also apply to both platform tennis and paddle tennis.)

12.G47 Lighting for the entire playing area in an indoor sports court should be uniformly distributed.

12.G48 Background colors on indoor sports courts should be light in order to improve light reflection.

12.G49 Concentrated sources of high-intensity light in a small area should be avoided.

12.G50 Lenses and louvers should be used to reduce glare. Diffusing lenses should be sufficiently far from the source of light, or the louvers should be sufficiently close together. Louvers should completely cut off direct light at approximately 45 degrees when the individual is looking parallel to the length of the court and at right angles to the length of the court.

12.G51 Direct, indirect, or combination lighting systems should be used to provide indoor lighting. At least 30 percent of all light sources should be directed upward to reduce the contrast between lighting above and below the light fixtures.

12.G52 The required number of lighting fixtures should be determined by the level of lighting desired and the height of the ceiling. A wide variety of light-fixture types can be used, provided they are of sufficient quantity, minimize the contrast between the ceiling above the court and the light source, and uniformly distribute a low intensity of surface brightness. High-intensity lights, if used, should be mounted no closer than six feet from the ceiling or structural members. If fluorescent lights are used, they should be placed 16 to 22 feet over or outside the alleys, parallel to both the length of the court and the court surface.

12.G53 Visible light sources should not be placed directly over the playing area.

12.G54 Lamps should be protected from balls (including balls that may strike from above or below the lamps). Louvers (if used) should be strongly resistant to damage (e.g., bending) from a direct hit. Lenses (if used) should be either protected from a direct hit or should be shatterproof.

Outdoor Courts

12.G55 Outdoor open courts should be oriented so that the long axis lies north-south.

12.G56 Outdoor courts should have a proper drainage system. The drainage system for both tennis and paddle tennis courts may be end to end, side to side, or corner to corner diagonally, at a minimum slope of one inch in 10 feet. The drainage system for platform tennis should be provided by a quarter-inch pipe between the six-inch deck planks or channels.

12.G57 A 10-foot-high chain link fence should be constructed on all sides of outdoor tennis and paddle tennis court areas.

12.G58 Platform tennis courts should have tension fencing that is 12 feet high and made of 16-gauge, hexagonal, galvanized, one-inch flat-wire mesh fabric.

12.G59   Light colors, such as tan, are recommended as background colors for all outdoor sports courts to improve light reflectivity and to provide a more pleasant playing environment.

12.G60   Depending on the geographic location, outdoor platform tennis courts should have heating units with fans located under the platforms.

12.G61   All outdoor open sports courts should have appropriate sources and levels of light. Outdoor court lighting is provided by three primary sources: high-intensity discharge source (e.g., mercury vapor, metal halide, and high-pressure sodium); incandescent bulbs (e.g., quartz or tungsten halogen); and fluorescent bulbs. Each source has its own unique qualities and requires a specific luminal design. Supplement 21 in appendix A presents an overview of the general advantages and disadvantages of each lighting source.

12.G62   The level of illumination should be sufficient for the playing conditions. Supplement 22 in appendix A presents a matrix of the illumination requirements for different levels of competitive outdoor tennis play. (Note: These levels also apply to both platform tennis and paddle tennis.)

12.G63   Light levels should be distributed as uniformly as possible within both the primary playing area and the adjacent court area.

12.G64   Light sources should be placed on the outside of the court area so that the beams of light are directed across the courts.

12.G65   Light poles should be located either between the net posts or immediately outside adjacent fences (no closer, however, than 10 feet from the sidelines). All freestanding light poles should be heavily padded.

12.G66   Light sources should be mounted at heights that are appropriate to the unique characteristics of that source, which will ensure proper uniformity of light distribution, low glare, reduction of light spill onto surrounding areas, and ease of maintenance.

12.G67   All outdoor lighting should use underground wiring.

13 Guidelines for Pool Areas

A facility may have indoor, outdoor, or both types of pools. Within a health/fitness facility, a swimming pool serves as an aquatics area with a variety of potential uses. Accordingly, swimming pool activities can be scheduled to serve a wide array of distinct audiences and meet many specific organizational objectives and goals. To ensure that the pool area of a facility is used in an appropriate manner, staff members should keep in mind that swimming pools represent one of the greatest potential hazard areas within a health/fitness facility. In addition to the serious (and obvious) risk of drowning, pool users can be exposed to the risks of infection and effects of hazardous chemicals. (Note: In most states, the design, construction, operation, and supervision of a pool is strictly governed by state and local laws.) This chapter presents guidelines that address relevant issues (particularly safety) for pool areas.

Programming

13.G1 A facility should provide a regularly scheduled program of both organized and free-time activities in the pool areas that is appropriate for the needs, interests, and goals of the facility's users. Examples of activities for the pool area include the following:

Organized:	Swim lessons (individual and group), master swim program, aquatic exercise classes, scuba classes, youth swimming program, water basketball, water volleyball, water polo, and swim teams
Free-time:	Lap swimming, recreational swimming, and family swim times

13.G2 The maximum number of individuals using the pool area (including the deck area) should be limited to one person per 20 square feet of pool and deck area combined. Local laws will govern the specific number.

13.G3 A schedule of activities to be held in the pool areas should be posted outside the facility in a conspicuous, appropriate area or should be available at the control desk.

Staffing

13.G4 A facility should ensure that the pool areas are adequately supervised. A minimum of one lifeguard per 75 pool users is the recommended level of supervision at all times that the pool area is open. During those times that lifeguards are scheduled for duty, they should not perform other duties. In locations where state and/or local laws do not require lifeguards to be present and the facility chooses not to have a lifeguard on duty, the pool should be monitored on a regular basis by a staff person capable of initiating emergency response procedures. All lifeguards should be certified by an appropriate agency.

Safety

Safety Equipment

13.G5 Appropriate lifesaving equipment (e.g., rescue tube, shepherd's crook, spine board, ring buoys) should be readily accessible. The exact number and specifications for such items are usually dictated by local codes.

(The rescue tube should be with the lifeguard (if a lifeguard is on duty); otherwise it should be readily accessible to staff members in the event of an emergency.)

Security

13.G6 Pool areas should be securely locked when they are not open for use.

13.G7 Pool areas should have emergency lighting.

Safety Checklist

13.G8 All staff members involved with the pool areas should be made aware of the safety factors relevant to such areas. Supplement 23 in appendix A provides a checklist of the recommended safety considerations for aquatic areas.

Signage

13.G9 Pool users should be warned through signage of inappropriate actions in the pool area (e.g., "no diving," "no running on deck," "lifeguard not on duty—swim at your own risk").

13.G10 The depth of the water should be plainly marked at or above the water surface on the edge of the deck or the walk next to the pool. In addition, each pool should have appropriate depth and lane markings. Supplements 24 and 25 in appendix A present the recommended dimensions and markings for 25-yard and 50-meter pools, respectively. Furthermore, the depth of the water should be marked at maximum and minimum points on both sides and ends of the pool and at the immediate depth breakpoints between the deep and shallow ends, spaced at not more than 25-foot intervals. All depth marks must be in numerals at least four inches in height and of a color that contrasts with the background.

Lightning

13.G11 When a lightning strike is possible, an outdoor pool should be evacuated.

Cleaning

13.G12 The pool filter should be backwashed according to the procedures and schedule recommended by the manufacturer.

13.G13 Pool filters, chlorinators, and heaters should be checked on a regular basis for routine maintenance and wear.

13.G14 All drains and skimmers should be cleaned as often as needed. As a general rule, drains and skimmers are normally cleaned daily in outdoor pools and as needed in indoor pools. At a minimum, they should be cleaned at least quarterly.

13.G15 The lane lines should be cleaned and scrubbed as often as needed or as required by local codes.

13.G16 The pool should be drained and cleaned as often as needed, preferably at least once a year.

Facilities and Equipment

13.G17 The pool should include an area with an appropriate minimum and maximum water depth to accommodate the types of programs the facility will offer and the unique needs and interests of the expected users.

13.G18 A pool in which diving is permitted should have sufficient area and depth of water for safe diving. A facility should take steps to prohibit diving in areas where pool depth is insufficient to accommodate such activity. Supplement 26 in appendix A lists the recommended basic springboard and platform dimensions for safe diving.

13.G19 Every pool should have a system for accommodating the overflow of water from the pool. A number of options for pool gutters exist: fully recessed, semirecessed, roll-out, rim flow, deck level, surface skimmer, or semirecessed prefabricated steel. The choice of which system to use can be based on many factors, including cost and the planned uses of the pool. Supplement 27 in appendix A lists the basic advantages and disadvantages of the most commonly used overflow systems.

13.G20 The wiring for the pool areas must conform to National Electric Code guidelines for installing electric wiring or equipment in or adjacent to swimming pools, for metal accessories in or within five feet of the pool, and for the auxiliary pool equipment, such as pumps, filters, and similar equipment.

13.G21   All water circulation and filtration equipment and piping for a pool should be sized for the desired turnover rate.

13.G22   The design parameters of a pool should be based on a number of considerations, including the following: the intended programs that will be conducted in the pool, the location of the pool on the site, the traffic pattern for both pedestrians and user vehicles, the shape and dimension of the pool, the location of the diving boards, the floor plan of the bathhouse or locker room, the location of equipment (both safety and other types), and the location of any adjacent fences. Supplement 28 in appendix A presents a list of agencies that offer construction standards for aquatic facilities and of associations that serve the field of aquatics.

13.G23   An outdoor pool should be located where it is not a nuisance to surrounding businesses and residents.

13.G24   An outdoor pool should be located where it will get the maximum amount of sun during the swimming season.

13.G25   Pool areas should be readily accessible to men's and women's locker rooms or bathhouses.

13.G26   The foundation of a pool should be constructed of one of three types of inert and durable materials (poured, reinforced concrete; pneumatically applied concrete product; or stainless steel) designed to withstand all anticipated loading when the pool is full and when it is empty.

13.G27   The surface walls and floor finish for a pool should be constructed of an inert, impervious material and should be reasonably durable. Among the more popular materials used for finishing a pool surface are pneumatically applied plaster, fiberglass, and tile. In some instances, aluminum or stainless steel inserts are then installed. Depending on the surface, epoxy, chlorinated rubber, and water-based paints are then also applied.

13.G28   Pool wall and floor finishes should be moderately smooth and white or light colored.

13.G29   All materials used in an indoor pool should be moisture- and chemical-resistant.

13.G30   Any metal doors, trims, or railings in a pool area should be stainless steel.

13.G31   A minimum ceiling height of 15 feet should be provided for a one-meter diving board. (Note: In some locales, this guideline is subject to state and local codes.)

13.G32   The ceiling on an indoor pool area should be constructed using acoustic, moisture-resistant materials.

13.G33   Acoustic units should be installed in the pool area on or over deck areas.

13.G34   Each pool should have at least one elevated lifeguard chair per 2,000 square feet of pool surface area.

13.G35   If a pool has more than one lifeguard chair, the chairs should be located on opposite sides of the pool.

13.G36   A lifeline should be provided at or near the break in the grade between the shallow and deep ends of a pool. The lifeline should be marked with colored floats spaced five feet or less apart. In addition, the lifeline should be securely anchored with corrosion-resistant terminals that are recessed so that they do not constitute a hazard.

13.G37 At least two entry areas should be provided for any pool. An entry area is considered either steps, a lift, or a ladder. A minimum of one entry area per 75 feet of perimeter area is the recommended guideline for large pools.

13.G38 A facility should have at least one clock, visible to all users, that is hung in the area adjacent to each pool to facilitate exertional self-monitoring during activity.

13.G39 Outdoor pool areas should be surrounded (contained) by a wall or fence at least six feet high. (Note: In many locales, this factor is governed by local codes.) In addition to a wall or fence, pools should be separated from adjacent areas by appropriate signage.

13.G40 Spectator space (if provided) should be located slightly above deck level. Spectator space should be separated from the pool deck.

13.G41 A pool should have a continuous walkway around it with a minimum width of five feet of unobstructed clearance between the curb at the pool edge, if such a curb is used, and any other physical structure such as a wall, a window, or deck chairs. In addition, a pool area should have a walkway that is a minimum of three feet wide on the sides and to the rear of any piece of diving equipment. All walkways in the pool area should have a slip-resistant texture.

13.G42 All walkways and decks should have a minimum slope of one-quarter inch per foot to drains or to points at which the water will at all times flow unobstructed to disposal.

13.G43 Adequate storage room should be provided for aquatics instructional equipment and other pool items, such as starter blocks, buoys, and kickboards.

13.G44 The pool areas should be adequately equipped and furnished to meet the safety and material requirements for all aquatics activities scheduled to be conducted in the facility. Among the items of equipment that should be present in the pool area are the following:

- Lifeguard chairs
- Lifeguard whistles
- At least one water fountain
- Water-testing equipment
- Manual pool-cleaning equipment (brushes and hoses)
- Spine board
- Water treatment systems
- Recirculation systems
- Pumps
- Filters/filtration system
- Ring buoys (minimum of two)
- Shepherd's crook
- First-aid kit
- Life jackets (minimum of two)
- Lifeline (25 feet)
- Rescue tube
- Blankets

13.G45 Based on its programming needs, a facility should provide the following types of equipment in its pool areas:

- Kickboards
- Deck umbrellas
- Competitive starting platforms
- Buoyancy belts/devices
- Deck furniture
- Swimming aids (ear plugs, goggles, bathing caps, and nose clips)

13.G46 As a general rule, the water temperature in the pool should range between 78 and 86 degrees Fahrenheit, but this will depend on the types of activities performed in the pool.

13.G47   The room temperature in the pool area should be, at minimum, 80 degrees Fahrenheit and should be at least 2 degrees Fahrenheit higher than the water temperature. (Note: This guideline helps to ensure that the room air will not draw the warmth from the water.) When spectators are present for an indoor swimming event or meet, the room temperature can be lowered slightly.

13.G48   Neither the water nor the room temperature in a pool area should vary more than two degrees Fahrenheit per day.

13.G49   Humidity within the pool area should be kept as close as possible to 60 percent or less, consistent with the somewhat contrary goal of keeping air circulation at minimal levels.

13.G50   Air velocity in the pool area should be kept relatively low (four to six air exchanges per hour) to avoid chilling wet skin.

13.G51   The pool water should be pumped, filtered, chemically treated, heated, and circulated continuously at a minimum turnover rate of every eight hours—every six hours if the pool is in extensive use.

13.G52   Water pumps for the pool area should be located below the water line.

13.G53   The filter system for a pool should be either granular-media pressure filters (sand and gravel or Anthrasilt) or diatomaceous filters (pressure or vacuum).

13.G54   Each pool should have adequate surge tank capacity. The recommended minimum capacity is one-half gallon of water for every square foot of pool surface.

13.G55   A facility should ensure that every pool in the facility receives the appropriate chemical treatment, which includes the following:

- Chlorine or bromine is recommended for water purification.
- The system of supplying chlorine to the water should provide one pound of chlorine per eight hours for each 10,000 gallons of water. (Note: User activity will dictate actual chlorine requirements.)
- The chlorine level should be maintained at a range of 1.0 to 3.0 parts per million.
- Bromine levels should be kept in the range of 1.0 to 2.5 parts per million.
- The pH level should be maintained at a range of 7.4 to 7.6; alkalinity should range from 80 to 120 parts per million.
- Calcium levels should be maintained at a range of 200 to 300 parts per million.

13.G56   The pool areas should have appropriate sources and levels of light. Mercury vapor, metal halide, or fluorescent lights are recommended. The illumination level should be at least 60 foot-candles at the surface level of the water. Additional information on illumination-related factors is presented in supplement 10 in appendix A.

13.G57   The light fixtures in the pool area should be shatterproof. Special light bulbs with an outer coating to contain the glass in the event of breakage should be used.

13.G58   When underwater lighting is provided in the pool, it should be at least one watt per square foot of the pool area.

13.G59   The pool area should have an emergency lighting system.

14 Guidelines for Outdoor Recreational Areas

Among the most popular types of outdoor recreational areas are playgrounds, ball fields, and volleyball courts. The size and number of outdoor activity areas and the purposes for which they are used often vary from one health/fitness facility to another.

The presence of outdoor recreational areas expands the facility's options for audience focus and programming. Activities can be scheduled in outdoor recreational areas to serve a wide array of distinct audiences and meet many specific organizational objectives and goals. For example, facility users with young children can often take advantage of the inherent benefits offered by a playground area. In addition, a playground area can be used for programming that would be enhanced by the availability of child-care services. Furthermore, sports activities and competitive leagues for all ages can be conducted if a facility has outdoor sports areas (e.g., ball fields, volleyball courts). This chapter presents guidelines that address the design and safe operation of outdoor recreational areas.

Programming

14.G1 A facility should provide a regularly scheduled program of both structured and unstructured activities in the outdoor recreational areas that are appropriate for the needs, interests, and goals of the facility's users. Examples of such activities include the following:

Structured:	Leagues (e.g., softball, soccer, volleyball) and tournaments (e.g., softball, volleyball, soccer, and baseball)
Unstructured:	Open play (e.g., baseball, softball, soccer)

14.G2 A monthly (or weekly) schedule of any activities to be held in each area should be posted outside the area in a conspicuous, appropriate place.

Staffing

14.G3 Outdoor recreational areas should be supervised by the staff on a regular basis.

14.G4 Playground areas should have adult supervision in accordance with federal, state, and local laws.

14.G5   A facility that provides organized competitive sports programs should provide umpires, referees, or officials who are certified by an appropriate governing body.

Safety

Many, if not most, of the guidelines presented in this section are governed by relevant laws, regulations, or published standards (e.g., the Consumer Products Safety Commission has published standards for surfacing materials for playground areas in *Handbook for Public Playgrounds,* volumes 1 and 2, 1981). These guidelines are therefore subject to Standard #6 in chapter 1. In the event that a relevant law, regulation, or previously published standard does not apply in a particular situation, the issue addressed should be considered as a guideline.

14.G6   Usage and spectator rules and policies should be clearly formulated and posted in an appropriate area adjacent to the outdoor recreational areas.

14.G7   All ball field and volleyball court users should comply with posted eye-guard and footwear requirements.

14.G8   Playground equipment should be located over protective, impact-absorbing surfaces that will minimize the dangers of injuries or abrasions due to falls from such equipment. It is important to note that such surfacing materials must comply with existing local and state laws, regulations, and published standards.

14.G9   If a playground includes a slide, an appropriate landing surface should be provided.

14.G10   Warnings should be posted in playground equipment areas to warn children, parents, and those supervising children of the potential dangers associated with scarves, hoods, coats, sweaters, sweatshirts, or shirts with collar strings, neck strings, drawstrings, or other materials that could be caught during activity on certain playground equipment, such as slides, and result in strangulation injury or death.

14.G11   All steps on playground equipment should have skid-resistant tread.

14.G12 All steps and ladders on playground equipment should have handrails or safety rails.

14.G13 All playground equipment should be free of all sharp, protruding surfaces, including those caused by welds, bolts, rivets, or joints.

14.G14 Fences around ball field areas should be padded and have a warning track system (a border of a differently textured surface between the ball field and the fence).

14.G15 All equipment and furnishings used on outdoor recreational areas should be cleaned on a regular basis.

14.G16 Playground equipment should be cleaned at least every month.

Facilities and Equipment

The guidelines in this section are divided into three areas: general guidelines, outdoor sports areas, and playground areas.

General Guidelines

14.G17 The surfaces of all outdoor recreational areas should be appropriate for the purpose and the specific function of each area (e.g., ball field games, court games, and play equipment).

14.G18 All outdoor lighting for outdoor recreational areas should use underground wiring.

14.G19 Each light source should be mounted at a height appropriate to the unique characteristics of that source, which will ensure proper uniformity of light distribution, low glare, reduction of light spill onto surrounding areas, and ease of maintenance.

14.G20 The surface for an outdoor recreational area should be selected on the basis of whether the space is for multipurpose or single-purpose use and whether the area is used seasonally or year round. In addition, each surface should be selected on the basis of its probable resistance to the general wear caused by users and to wear caused by outdoor weathering from sunlight, rain, freezing weather, dirt, and dust. Furthermore, each surface should be a clean and attractive material that will not discolor the users' clothing or be tracked into the adjacent health/fitness facility and should not require undue repair or upkeep.

14.G21 Rules and regulations for each outdoor activity area should be posted in an appropriate place adjacent to the area.

14.G22 It is recommended that fencing be placed around outdoor recreational areas.

Outdoor Sports Areas

14.G23 A sufficient quantity of light should be provided to all outdoor sports areas. The illumination level required for a ball field depends on the activities planned for the field. For example, 100 foot-candles (minimum) at the surface of the field is recommended for an area in which softball is played, whereas soccer requires about half that level (50 foot-candles). An outdoor volleyball court should have 50 foot-candles at the surface of the court. Additional information on illumination-related factors is presented in supplement 10 in appendix A.

14.G24   Outdoor court lighting should be provided by one or more of three primary sources: high-intensity discharge sources (e.g., mercury vapor, metal halide, or high-pressure sodium), incandescent bulbs (e.g., quartz or tungsten halogen), and fluorescent bulbs. Each source has its own unique qualities and requires a specific lighting design. Supplement 21 in appendix A presents an overview of the general advantages and disadvantages of each source.

14.G25   Light levels should be distributed as uniformly as possible within both the primary playing areas and the adjacent areas.

14.G26   Light sources for outdoor sports areas should be placed on the outside of the field and court areas so that the beams of light are directed across the areas.

14.G27   Light poles for outdoor sports areas should be located between the volleyball center-court net posts or immediately outside adjacent fences surrounding the ball field area (as needed); if such fences exist, they should be no closer than 10 feet to the sidelines.

14.G28   All freestanding light poles next to sports playing areas should be padded.

14.G29   All field areas should be properly graded (not greater than 2.5 percent grade) and should have proper drainage.

14.G30   All ball field areas should have either natural or artificial turf fields.

14.G31   A minimum of 1.2 acres of ground space should be allotted per softball field. Generally, softball fields use 1.2 to 1.7 acres. Supplement 29 in appendix A lists the specific recommended dimensions for a softball field.

14.G32   To the extent possible, softball fields should be placed in a north-south direction so that placement of home plate allows the pitcher to throw perpendicular to the direction of the sun, thereby preventing the batter from facing the sun.

14.G33   A minimum of 1.7 acres of ground space should be allotted per soccer field. The recommended dimensions for a soccer field are presented in supplement 30 in appendix A.

14.G34   The long axis of a soccer field should be oriented north-south.

14.G35   A volleyball court requires 4,000 square feet of ground space. Supplement 13 in appendix A presents the recommended dimensions of a volleyball court.

14.G36   The long axis of an outdoor volleyball court should be oriented north-south.

14.G37   Every area that is to be used for athletic competition (e.g., ball fields and volleyball courts) should be marked accordingly. Supplement 13 in appendix A presents the general markings for a volleyball court. The markings required for softball and soccer, probably the two most popular outdoor ball field activities, are illustrated in supplements 29 and 30, respectively, in appendix A.

14.G38   Outdoor sports areas should be remarked on a regular basis.

14.G39   Outdoor sports areas should be adequately equipped and furnished to meet the material requirements for all activities scheduled to be conducted in each particular area. Among the equipment that should be available are field-marking equipment, softballs, baseballs, soccer balls, volleyballs, nets, and cones.

14.G40   The outdoor sports areas (e.g., ball fields, volleyball court) should have readily accessible rest-room facilities.

14.G41   Storage rooms for any equipment and supplies used on the outdoor sports areas should be located adjacent to the specific sports area.

Playground Areas

14.G42   If playground areas are open for use in the hours of darkness, the playground should be well lighted. An illumination level of 100 foot-candles at the surface of play areas is recommended.

14.G43   Light sources for a playground should be placed in a location that will provide a well-lighted, safe environment.

14.G44   A playground should be readily accessible from the health/fitness facility.

14.G45   The specific layout and shape of each playground area should be governed by the existing site conditions and the activities to be provided.

14.G46   A playground should include several areas: a play lot for preschool children (up to 6 years of age); an enclosed playground equipment area for elementary school children (6 to 12 years of age); shaded areas for quiet activities; a paved, multipurpose area; an open, turfed area for active games; and circulation and buffer space.

14.G47   The play lot and the playground equipment area should be located adjacent to each other.

14.G48   Areas for quiet activities should be somewhat removed from active play space and should be close to shaded areas and other natural features of the site.

14.G49   If a playground has a paved, multipurpose area, it should be set off from other areas by supplemental plantings.

14.G50   If a playground has an open, turfed area for active play and shaded areas for quiet activities, they should be adjacent to the enclosed equipment area and should serve as buffer space around it.

14.G51   Arrangements should be made for natural or artificial shade to be placed over the sedentary play equipment in areas where children tend to play on hot days.

14.G52   A playground site should be fully landscaped. The landscape should enhance the area's activity control, traffic control, and aesthetic appearance.

14.G53   Immovable benches for use by staff, parents, and other interested individuals should be conveniently positioned to ensure excellent visibility and protection of the children at play.

14.G54   A neat, orderly appearance for the playground area should be enhanced through the placement of an appropriate number of trash containers.

14.G55   Walks, benches, and plantings should be laid out to encourage movement through the playground area in a safe, orderly manner.

14.G56   A playground site should have readily accessible toilet facilities, drinking fountains, and equipment storage areas.

14.G57 Drinking fountains should be strategically placed in playground areas for the convenience of both adults and children.

14.G58 A facility should equip its playground area with a variety of items, including swings; slides; merry-go-rounds; climbers; balancing equipment such as balance beams, leaping posts, and boxes; hanging equipment such as parallel bars, ladders, and horizontal bars; play walls; playhouses; sand area; and a variety of play sculpture forms. Examples of types of playground equipment and their dimensions are presented in supplement 31 in appendix A.

14.G59 Playground equipment should be selected and arranged with sufficient surrounding space in small, natural play groups.

14.G60 Playground equipment that permits large numbers of children to be involved (e.g., play sculpture and climbers) should be placed near the entrance of the play lot in a location that will not cause congestion.

14.G61 A portion of the sand area should be maintained free of equipment for general sand play.

14.G62 Swings and other moving equipment in the playground area should be placed near the outside of the equipment area and should be separated from the immediately adjacent area (by walls or fences) to prevent children from walking into equipment while it is moving.

14.G63 To the extent possible, swings should be placed in a north-south direction in the playground area so that children do not face the sun while using them.

14.G64 Sliding equipment in the playground area should face away from the sun.

14.G65 Equipment with metal surfaces in the playground area should be positioned in the shade.

14.G66 Ideally, all equipment in the playground area should require a minimum of direct supervision.

14.G67 All equipment in the playground area should be sufficiently durable to withstand normal play wear, should require a minimum of maintenance, and should be functionally designed, visually appealing (to stimulate the imagination of its users), aesthetically proportioned, and aesthetically harmonious with its surroundings.

15 Guidelines for Running Track Areas

Running track areas offer settings in which many different activities can be scheduled to serve a wide variety of the interests of a facility's users, including fitness walking/jogging programs, competitive athletics, and an array of special events. In addition, because of the substantial dimensions of a running track, the infield enclosed by both indoor and outdoor running tracks can provide a unique space in which other activities can be scheduled. Furthermore, although they are relatively expensive in terms of both space and installation charges, running track areas can represent a positive addition to a facility because of their relatively low upkeep and breadth of use. This chapter presents guidelines that address issues related to running track areas.

Programming

15.G1 A facility should provide a regularly scheduled program of both structured and unstructured activities for its running track areas that are appropriate for the needs, interests, and goals of the facility's users.

15.G2 A monthly (or weekly) schedule of any activities to be held on the running track areas should be posted in a conspicuous location adjacent to the areas.

Staffing

15.G3 The running track areas should be supervised on a regular basis.

Safety

15.G4 All activities conducted on running track areas should comply with nationally recognized guidelines for exercise (refer to *ACSM's Guidelines for Exercise Testing and Prescription*, fifth edition).

15.G5 All participants in activities conducted on running track areas should comply with footwear requirements.

15.G6 All activities on running track areas should be conducted in accordance with rules and guidelines that prohibit unsafe actions by the participants.

15.G7   A large, highly visible lap clock (preferably one with a 60-second sweep) should be located in the indoor running track area to facilitate self-monitoring during activity.

15.G8   A facility should change the running direction of an indoor running track on a daily basis. This change should be communicated to the track's users via the appropriate signage.

Facilities and Equipment

The guidelines in this section are divided into three areas: general guidelines, indoor tracks, and outdoor tracks.

General Guidelines

15.G9   Running track areas should be equipped and furnished to meet the material requirements for all activities scheduled to be conducted in the areas (e.g., a manually operated squeegee device for outdoor tracks, marking cones, hurdles, relay batons, wrist-worn pulse meters).

15.G10   Each running track (both indoor and outdoor) should have appropriate markings (e.g., running lanes, specific general distances, and starting and finishing line points for specific race distances if the track is to be used for competitive events). Supplement 32 lists the guidelines for marking running lanes for an outdoor track that will be used for competition, while supplement 33 provides the dimensions and markings for a standard 440-yard running track.

15.G11 Running tracks should be constructed with concrete foundations.

15.G12 The track surface (over the foundation of a track) should be made of a composite, synthetic material specifically engineered for running and walking. Furthermore, the surface materials (at least 3/8 inch thick) for a track should provide a durable, resilient, cushioned covering.

15.G13 A running track should be textured for superior traction.

15.G14 Both indoor and outdoor running tracks should be constructed with surfaces made of an all-weather synthetic material. (Note: Some outdoor tracks are covered with a crushed cinder surface, which is more difficult to maintain and does not have all-weather capabilities.) The materials used for surfacing a running track should permit vapor and moisture pressures to escape.

15.G15 Spectator and user safety guidelines for access to and egress from the running tracks should be posted.

15.G16 A facility should post a rules-and-regulations sign concerning actions of participants and spectators in the areas adjacent to the running tracks.

Indoor Tracks

15.G17 An indoor running track should have a maximum of 18 laps to the mile; 11 laps (or fewer) to the mile are recommended.

15.G18 The 180-degree turns on an indoor running track should have at minimum a 30-foot outside radius and a 20-foot inside radius.

15.G19 The height of banked (to the inside) curves on an indoor track should not exceed one inch per foot of track width.

15.G20 An indoor running track should have a width of at least six feet from one edge to the other.

15.G21 Appropriate temperature, humidity, and air circulation levels should be maintained in the indoor running track area. The following levels are recommended:

Temperature:	68 to 72 degrees Fahrenheit
Humidity:	60 percent or less
Air circulation:	8 to 12 exchanges per hour

Air exchanges should have the appropriate mix of outside and inside air. This mix is usually 10 percent outside air and 90 percent inside air, though a mix of 40 to 60, outside to inside, is preferred. The specific ratio of outside air to inside air (recirculated air) is most often governed by local engineering codes. These codes should be followed when any air-handling system is installed. Additional information on temperature-related factors is presented in supplement 9 in appendix A.

15.G22 The indoor running track area should have an appropriate source and level of light. Mercury vapor, metal halide, or fluorescent lights are recommended. The illumination level should be at least 50 foot-candles at the surface of the indoor running track. Additional information on illumination-related factors is presented in supplement 10 in appendix A.

15.G23   An indoor running track should have a bulletin board placed in a visible, adjacent area on which appropriate information and materials are posted (e.g., injury guidelines, running and aerobic tips, target heart zone information, instructions for measuring heart rate).

Outdoor Tracks

15.G24   An outdoor running track should be located adjacent to the main health/fitness facility building.

15.G25   The minimum amount of ground space that should be allotted for an outdoor running track area is 4.3 acres.

15.G26   An outdoor running track should be one-quarter mile in circumference. It should be noted that in response to the international emphasis on the metric system, some facilities have built outdoor running tracks that have 400-meter circumferences.

15.G27   When an outdoor running track of wider or narrower proportions or of a different length is required, the appropriate dimensions should be calculated from the following formula: $L = 2P + 2\pi R$, where L = length of track (meters), P = length of parallels or distance between centers of curves (meters), R = radius to the track side of the curb plus 300 millimeters, and $\pi = 3.1416$ (not 22/7). The radius of the semicircles should not normally be less than 32 meters or more than 42 meters for a 400-meter track.

15.G28   The inside radius to the face of the curb for an outside running track should be 106 feet. A track width of 32 feet accommodates eight 4-foot-wide lanes. The overall width and length of the track should be 276 feet and 600.02 feet, respectively.

15.G29   The maximum slopes for an outdoor track should be 2 percent (1:50) inward in the center of the curves, 1 percent (1:100) inward in the straightaway, and 0.1 percent (1:1,000) in the running direction.

15.G30   An outdoor track should be oriented so that the long axis lies in a sector from north-south to northwest-southeast.

15.G31   If an outdoor running track is to be used for competition, the finish line should be at the northern end.

15.G32   Two white posts should denote the extremities of the finish line and should be placed at least two feet from the edge of the outdoor running track.

15.G33   An outdoor running track area should have adequate drainage.

15.G34   A facility should consider developing outdoor turf-covered playing areas (e.g., soccer and touch football) in the center space of the outdoor running track area.

15.G35   Illumination for outdoor tracks should be provided by one or both of two primary sources: high-intensity discharge source (mercury vapor or metal halide) or incandescent source. The illumination level for outdoor running tracks should be at least 30 foot-candles at the surface of the track.

PART
IV

NONACTIVITY AREA GUIDELINES

This section of the book covers guidelines for those areas in a facility that allow users to enter and prepare to engage in physical activity program offerings. Referred to as nonactivity areas, these areas of entry and preparation have ongoing activity, but not programmed activity, that has been specifically designed to benefit the health, fitness, and leisure-time needs of users. Collectively, the guidelines in this section are intended to help a facility enhance its ability to deliver quality service and operate in a highly professional manner. It is important to note that these guidelines are not meant to be standards or give rise to duties of care.

For discussion and organizational purposes, the guidelines for each particular type of nonactivity area that is examined in this section are for the most part separated into the following components: staffing, safety, and facilities and equipment. Chapters 16 through 19 provide guidelines for four different nonactivity areas within a facility: external grounds (chapter 16); the control desk (chapter 17); the laundry (chapter 18); and the locker rooms (chapter 19).

Storage and office spaces have been omitted from this section because such areas are typically included in a facility's business operations. Because the total amount of storage space needed to operate efficiently is directly related to a facility's program offerings and to the geographical location of the facility, storage space requirements tend to vary from facility to facility and from one area of the country to another. The allocation of office space, on the other hand, usually depends on the facility's basic business structure. The more complex or layered the structure, the greater the need for more office space.

16 Guidelines for External Grounds

Although the inclusion of a chapter on the guidelines for the external grounds in a text on designing, developing, and operating a health/fitness facility may seem to be somewhat unusual, the fact that the external grounds of a facility can have a significant impact on the safety and satisfaction of its users makes such information relevant. The external grounds are those areas of a facility's property that are external to any building structure and are not used for recreational or sports activity. In most instances, the external grounds encompass parking lots, walkways, and lawns.

When considering guidelines for external grounds, the potential effect that properly designed and operated external grounds can have on the safety and satisfaction of the users of a facility should be taken into account. Facility staff members who have experienced the turmoil associated with inadequate parking or the legal repercussions of a user who trips on an uncared-for walkway, for example, can readily understand the need to address issues involved with external grounds. The two primary issues attendant to external grounds are safety and external space allocation and layout. This chapter presents guidelines that are designed to do more than address the issue of safety; they are intended to provide a basis for the safe and effective delivery of services to users before they step in the front door.

Safety

16.G1	A facility should keep all walkways, driveways, and lawn areas clear of hazards (e.g., ice, snow, excessive standing water). In addition, all damage to walkways and driveways that may endanger users should be promptly repaired. Until damage is repaired, posted warnings should be placed within view to adequately apprise users of the hazard.
16.G2	A facility should keep all lawn areas mowed regularly and free of excessive accumulation of leaves, trash, and so on.
16.G3	An adequate level of illumination should be provided for all external grounds. Guidelines for outdoor lighting are presented in supplement 1 in appendix A.

External Space Allocation

16.G4	To the extent possible, sufficient parking space should be made available for all facility users. Parking lot specifications usually require one parking space for every 200 to 300 square feet of facility space, or enough space for 15 percent of the facility's expected membership level. Depending on the location of a facility, specific requirements for allocating space for parking may be governed by federal, state, and local laws (including OSHA laws).
16.G5	A minimum of 108 square feet should be provided for each parking space unless federal, state, or local laws specify otherwise.
16.G6	Pedestrian walkways should be provided to bring users from either the street or parking lot to the entrance of the facility. These walkways should be a minimum of four feet wide and should be graded to prevent standing water. Exact specifications for pedestrian walkways are usually governed by state and local ordinances.

17 Guidelines for the Control Desk Area

The front desk or the reception desk is often referred to as the control desk. In health/fitness facilities, this area usually serves as the check-in point for all users. The primary function of a control desk is to serve as a focal point at which users are greeted, directed to their given activity areas, and provided with information. In most facilities, the control desk also serves as the central location for the entire facility's safety and emergency systems.

Because the control desk is the user's first stop inside the facility, it often has a significant impact on an individual's initial impression of a facility. User attitudes about a facility's level of professional operation, safety, security, service, and caring can be appreciably affected by the appearance of the control desk and by the appearance and actions of those who operate it. Accordingly, it is imperative that the control desk of a facility function in an optimal manner. This chapter presents guidelines that address designing and manning a control desk in an optimal manner, including

- staffing,
- safety, and
- facilities and equipment.

Staffing

17.G1 A facility should assign staff members to operate the control desk during all hours that the facility is open.

Safety

17.G2 A facility should provide a system at the control desk for checking in or signing in all users, guests, and visitors. As appropriate, some or all of the measures outlined in chapter 6 for preactivity participant screening should be incorporated into this system.

17.G3 A facility should develop and implement a system at the control desk for monitoring accidents and thefts.

Facilities and Equipment

17.G4 A facility should provide at least 30 square feet (e.g., a six-by-five-foot area) of floor space on the staff side of the control desk.

17.G5 A facility should build the control desk to accommodate a floor-to-writing-surface height of at least 42 inches on the user side and 36 inches on the staff side.

17.G6 A facility should provide sufficient space at the control desk for a computer, cash register, cabinets, and other necessary operating equipment.

17.G7 A facility should provide a ceiling height of at least eight feet above the control desk and a floor surface in front of and behind the desk area that is covered with antistatic carpeting, wood, or other material that is slip resistant.

17.G8 Appropriate temperature, humidity, and air circulation levels should be maintained at the control desk. The following levels are recommended:

Temperature:	72 to 78 degrees Fahrenheit
Humidity:	60 percent or less
Air circulation:	8 to 12 exchanges per hour

Air exchanges should have an appropriate mix of outside and inside air. This mix is usually 10 percent outside air and 90 percent inside air, though a mix of 40 to 60, outside to inside, is preferred. The specific ratio of outside air to inside air (recirculated air) is most often governed by local engineering codes. These local codes should be followed when any air-handling system is installed. Additional information on what constitutes appropriate temperature levels is provided in supplement 9 in appendix A.

17.G9 A facility should have an appropriate level of light at the control desk. The illumination level should be 50 foot-candles at the desk's writing surface. Additional information on what constitutes appropriate levels of illumination is provided in supplement 10 in appendix A.

18 Guidelines for the Laundry Room Area

One of the key areas for almost every health/fitness facility is its laundry. The laundry can play a positive role in enhancing the level of service that a facility offers to its users (e.g., by providing clean towels and uniforms). On the other hand, the laundry area involves several inherent conditions (e.g., chemicals, electrical hazards, heat) that can be dangerous if not controlled properly. This chapter presents guidelines that address several of the safety and user-satisfaction issues related to the laundry, including

- staffing,
- safety, and
- facilities and equipment.

Staffing

18.G1 A facility should assign a staff member to be responsible for the laundry area.

Safety

18.G2 A facility should provide appropriate safety equipment and clothing for handling chemicals in the laundry (e.g., rubber gloves, face masks).

18.G3 A facility should ensure that the dryers in its laundry room are vented outside the building structure.

18.G4 A facility should provide written operating policies for the laundry room area that are posted in a conspicuous place in the laundry. These policies should include the following:

- Information on load capacities for the washers and dryers
- Instructions for cycles for washers and dryers
- Instructions for chemicals to be used and levels at which they are to be used
- Instructions for cleaning and maintaining the equipment

Facilities and Equipment

18.G5 All wiring and electrical equipment should be inspected and approved for continued use at least annually by an electrical engineer or inspector.

18.G6 All equipment used in the laundry should be inspected periodically and promptly replaced if determined to be defective.

18.G7 A facility should provide a minimum of 150 to 300 square feet of floor space for the laundry area.

18.G8 A facility should provide an additional six- to eight-inch concrete pad on top of the existing floor of the laundry area for the washer extractor, particularly if the laundry area is located on an upper-level floor of the facility.

18.G9 Appropriate temperature, humidity, and air circulation levels should be maintained in the laundry area. The following levels are recommended:

Temperature:	72 to 78 degrees Fahrenheit
Humidity:	60 percent or less
Air circulation:	8 to 12 exchanges per hour

Air exchanges should have the appropriate mix of outside and inside air. This mix is usually 10 percent outside air and 90 percent inside air, though a mix of 40 to 60,

outside to inside, is preferred. The specific ratio of outside air to inside air (recirculated air) is most often governed by local engineering codes. These codes should be followed when any air-handling system is installed. Additional information on what constitutes appropriate temperature levels is provided in supplement 9 in appendix A.

18.G10 A facility should provide an appropriate level of light for the laundry. The illumination level should be 50 foot-candles at the floor surface. For more information about illumination, see supplement 10 in appendix A.

18.G11 A facility should provide a floor in its laundry room area that has a surface of either painted concrete or linoleum for easy care.

18.G12 The laundry area of a facility should have venting ducts, electrical wires, and gas lines that enter from the ceiling.

18.G13 The laundry area of a facility should have the following types of equipment:

- Washer extractors
- Dryers (two dryers minimum per washer extractor)
- Slop sink
- Folding tables

19 Guidelines for the Locker Room Area

One of the most-used areas in a health/fitness facility is the locker room. Statistics indicate that during a visit to a health/fitness facility, users will typically spend between one fourth to one third of their time in the locker rooms. Because locker rooms often serve many functions, they can have a substantial impact on both the safety and the satisfaction of the user. For example, they provide an area for showering, changing, dressing, and lounging. They can also serve as a location where such services as steam, sauna, massage, and shoe shines are offered.

Unfortunately, locker rooms also have the potential to expose users to undesirable conditions. For example, locker rooms are sometimes an environment of high traffic, high moisture, and unacceptable sanitary conditions, which can give rise to several types of safety issues. Accordingly, safety is a critical issue for locker room areas. This chapter presents guidelines that address several of the issues that affect user safety and satisfaction in the locker room, including

- staffing,
- safety, and
- facilities and equipment.

Note: While a few facilities cater to a single sex and therefore require only one locker room, most facilities serve both sexes. As a result, these facilities provide separate locker rooms for men and women. For presentation purposes, all guidelines discussed in this chapter apply to the locker rooms for both sexes.

Staffing

19.G1 A facility should assign staff the responsibility of monitoring and cleaning the locker rooms.

Safety

19.G2 A facility should ensure that all wet areas in the locker room area are cleaned and disinfected daily.

19.G3 A facility should ensure that all dry areas in the locker room area are vacuumed and that all debris is picked up daily.

19.G4 Staff should supervise the locker rooms on a regular basis (e.g., once an hour, once every two hours) during the facility's operational hours.

19.G5   A facility should provide clocks that are visible from any area of the locker room where overexposure to heat may cause safety problems (e.g., whirlpool, steam room).

Facilities and Equipment

19.G6   A facility should provide 10 to 20 square feet of space per person in the locker room area, based on the number of individuals that are expected to use the locker rooms at any given time. As a general rule, a facility should expect that no more than 50 percent of the individuals using a facility will occupy the locker rooms at any one time. In most instances, the total square footage allocated to the locker room area will be between 25 and 35 percent of the total space in a facility.

19.G7   A facility should separate the dry areas and wet areas of the locker room area with a physical barrier, such as a door or other structure that completely keeps the two areas apart.

19.G8   A facility should provide either daily-use or permanent lockers for users. If the facility provides daily-use lockers, there should be enough lockers to handle about 20 percent of the facility's users. If the facility provides permanent rental lockers, there should be enough lockers to handle 70 to 85 percent of the facility's users.

19.G9   A facility should provide an appropriate number of showers in the two locker room areas to handle the level of expected usage. As a general rule, the number of showers (for both locker room areas) should be based on a rate of approximately one shower each for one percent of the total membership of the facility (for example, there should be 20 showers for 2,000 members).

19.G10   Appropriate temperature, humidity, and air circulation levels should be maintained in both the dry and wet areas of the locker room. The following levels are recommended:

Temperature: 72 to 78 degrees Fahrenheit in both dry and wet areas

Humidity: 60 percent or less in both areas

Air circulation: 8 to 12 exchanges in dry areas, 20 to 30 exchanges in wet areas

Air exchanges should have an appropriate mix of outside and inside air. This mix is usually 10 percent outside air and 90 percent inside air, though a mix of 40 to 60, outside to inside, is preferred. The specific ratio of outside air to inside air (recirculated air) is usually governed by local engineering codes. These local codes should be followed when any air-handling system is installed. Additional information on what constitutes appropriate temperature levels is provided in supplement 9 in appendix A.

19.G11   The locker room area should have an appropriate level of light. The illumination level should be at least 50 foot-candles at the floor surface. Additional information on what constitutes appropriate illumination levels is presented in supplement 10 in appendix A.

PART

V

SPECIALTY AREA GUIDELINES

This section of the book presents guidelines for selected specialty areas within a health/fitness facility. Motivated by users who are demanding access to an increasing variety of amenities, services, and programs in addition to the traditional mainstream programming and nonactivity areas they normally receive, facilities are responding by offering an array of special services. The guidelines presented in this section are designed to enhance the ability of facilities to provide a high level of such services. It is important to note that these guidelines are not meant to be standards nor to give rise to duties of care.

For discussion and organizational purposes, the guidelines for the two special areas covered in this section are separated into the following components: programming, staffing, safety, and facilities and equipment. Chapters 20 and 21 provide guidelines for youth supervision areas and spa areas, respectively. Keep in mind that these two areas are not an exhaustive list of special services or programs that are offered or that can be offered by a facility. As the demand for such amenities continues to increase, the number and diversity of special services and programs offered by facilities will expand even further.

20 Guidelines for a Youth Supervision Area

Many individuals who exercise have relatively young children. As a consequence, these individuals may need to have access to child-care services in order to have the time to be able to exercise or participate in the other services available at health/fitness facilities. To accommodate these users, many health/fitness facilities have developed child-care areas supervised and operated by the facilities. Youth supervision areas in health/fitness facilities range from designated spaces where babysitting services are provided to full-service day-care centers. This chapter identifies and discusses guidelines for youth supervision areas covering only babysitting services. Babysitting services involve the supervision of a facility user's child while that user exercises at the facility. The requirements for this service are less stringent than those for day-care centers and, in many cases, are not regulated by municipality codes. Regardless of what youth supervision services a facility offers, the youth supervision area should be developed and operated in accordance with local regulations. Accordingly, a facility must ensure that in any youth supervision area in the facility, the safety, security, and well-being of the child is the facility's paramount concern. This chapter presents guidelines that address babysitting services provided at a health/fitness facility.

Programming

20.G1 A facility should have a written policy and procedure manual regarding the youth supervision area. This manual should be readily available to a facility's users.

Staffing

Please see Standard #5 in chapter 2 on p. 9.

Safety

20.G2 A facility should obtain a medical history form for each child who is to be supervised. This medical history form should elicit information that is required by federal, state, or local regulations.

20.G3 A facility should register each child in and out. The parent or legally sanctioned guardian of a child should sign the registration sheet each time the child is registered in or out.

20.G4   A facility should require the parent or legal guardian to remain on the facility's premises while the child is in the child-care area.

20.G5   A facility should ensure that all toys and other play objects in the youth supervision area meet federal, state, and local regulations for approved child-care use.

20.G6   A facility should ensure that an unobstructed entry to and exit from the youth supervision area exists and that this entry/exit is clearly marked for the children.

20.G7   Children within the area for child care should remain under the direct supervision of staff at all times.

Facilities and Equipment

20.G8   A facility should provide an enclosed lavatory area and sink within the youth supervision area. This enclosed lavatory should not lock from the inside.

20.G9   Safety caps should be provided for all electrical outlets in the youth supervision area.

20.G10   A facility should ensure that its youth supervision area has an appropriate level of visibility within the area and externally out of the area.

20.G11   A youth supervision area in a facility should be allotted between 15 and 20 square feet of space per child.

20.G12   Appropriate temperature, humidity, and air circulation levels should be maintained in the youth supervision area. The following levels are recommended:

Temperature:	72 to 78 degrees Fahrenheit
Humidity:	60 percent or less
Air circulation:	Four to six exchanges per hour

Air exchanges should have the appropriate mix of outside and inside air. This mix is usually 10 percent outside air and 90 percent inside air, though a mix of 40 to 60, outside to inside, is preferred. The specific ratio of outside air to inside air (recirculated air) is most often governed by local engineering codes. These codes should be followed when any air-handling system is installed. Additional information on temperature-related factors is presented in supplement 9 in appendix A.

20.G13   A facility should have an appropriate level of light in its youth supervision area. The illumination level should be 50 foot-candles at the floor surface. Additional information on illumination-related factors is presented in supplement 10 in appendix A.

20.G14   A facility should provide low-pile, antistatic carpets and washable vinyl walls in its youth supervision area.

20.G15   A facility should ensure that its youth supervision area has appropriate equipment and furnishings, including the following:

- Cribs
- Playpens
- Desks and chairs
- Changing tables
- Mats
- Approved toys
- VCR and television

21 Guidelines for Spa Areas

In an effort to increase the extent of their offerings to users, many health/fitness facilities have expanded the number of available on-site activities to include traditional health spa services. Health spa services provide a variety of soothing and relaxing amenities, including massage, sauna, steam room, and whirlpool (Jacuzzi), as well as a variety of salon body treatments, such as herbal wraps and mud baths. As a result of the growing demand for the wide array of spa services, many health/fitness facilities have undertaken efforts to develop spa areas and hire personnel to provide these services.

Unfortunately, spa areas—particularly those providing a sauna, steam room, and whirlpool—involve exposing users to an increased health risk due to the extreme temperatures in such areas and, in the case of steam rooms and whirlpools, as a result of relatively high levels of moisture. Such conditions expose users (particularly individuals with certain cardiovascular diseases and pregnant women) to both undesirably high levels of thermal stress and undue risk of infection from moisture-bound infectious agents. This chapter presents guidelines that address safety and operational issues for spa areas.

Programming

21.G1   A facility should have a sign-up or registration system available at the control desk for spa area services such as massage, herbal wraps, and other body-work treatments.

21.G2   A facility that offers massage services should make every effort to provide massage programs that meet the personal interests and needs of users. Specific types of massage programs that should be offered include (but are not limited to) Swedish, sports, reflexology, and deep muscle massage.

21.G3   A facility that offers salon services should make every effort to provide services that meet the personal interests and needs of users. Examples of salon services that can be offered include (but are not limited to) facials, hairstyling, manicures, and pedicures.

21.G4   A facility that offers spa area services should also consider providing the following services if an appropriate level of user demand exists: plunges (cold and warm), hydrotherapy, herbal wraps, mud baths, paraffin treatments, and similar services that are found in destination-type spas.

Staffing

21.G5 A facility that offers massage programs and services should employ a professionally trained massage therapist to provide such amenities. (Note: Most states require licensure of massage therapists.)

21.G6 A facility that provides other spa services such as facials, hairstyling, manicures, and herbal wraps should hire or contract the services of a trained specialist in that area. Such a provider should have state licensure, if required.

21.G7 A facility should ensure that its sauna, steam room, and whirlpool areas are supervised by a staff person on a regular basis.

Safety

21.G8 A facility should provide clocks that can be viewed from its sauna, steam room, and whirlpool areas to facilitate exertional self-monitoring.

21.G9 A facility should provide emergency systems for its sauna, steam room, and whirlpool areas that will automatically shut off the equipment when conditions unsafe to the user arise (e.g., a whirlpool should have a system that shuts off the drains). These emergency systems should be easily accessible by the user in the event of an emergency.

21.G10 A facility should provide thermometers in its sauna, steam room, and whirlpool areas to allow staff to monitor and maintain safe thermal conditions for users. (Note: This aspect is regulated in many localities and states.)

21.G11 The water chemical levels of whirlpools and other water therapy areas should be monitored on a regular basis (i.e., several times daily). Such a guideline is regulated in many localities and states.

21.G12 The temperature levels of the sauna, steam room, and whirlpool areas should be monitored on a regular basis. (Note: This aspect is regulated in many localities and states.)

21.G13 Individuals at high risk (pregnant women, individuals who take prescription medicine or use alcohol, and individuals with elevated blood pressure, diabetes, or heart disease) should be advised not to use the sauna, steam room, or whirlpool areas unless authorized by a physician.

21.G14 A facility should ensure that all whirlpools, hydrotherapy pools, and other modalities in its spa area in which users share a common area filled with water have the proper water chemistry. Subject to state or local laws and regulations, the following water chemical levels are recommended:

pH level:	7.2 to 7.6
Chlorine level:	1.0 to 3.0 parts per million
Bromine level:	1.0 to 3.0 parts per million
Alkalinity level:	80 to 200 parts per million

21.G15 A facility should ensure that its sauna, steam room, and whirlpool areas are kept at safe thermal levels. Subject to state or local laws, the following temperatures and humidity levels are recommended:

Sauna: Temperature: 170 to 180 degrees Fahrenheit; humidity: 5 percent relative

Steam room: Temperature: 100 to 110 degrees Fahrenheit; humidity: 100 percent relative

Whirlpool: Temperature: 102 to 105 degrees Fahrenheit

Facilities and Equipment

21.G16 The massage area should have a sink. If the room is to be used for herbal wraps or mud baths, a second sink will be needed in the massage area, as well as a shower. If wet treatments are provided, there should be a floor drain.

21.G17 The steam room should have a shower.

21.G18 Adequate space should be provided for the spa areas. The following minimum space allocations for the sauna, steam room, and whirlpool are recommended:

Sauna: 640 cubic feet (8 feet by 10 feet by 8 feet)

Steam room: 640 cubic feet (8 feet by 10 feet by 8 feet)

Whirlpool: 500 gallons (7 feet 6 inches by 5 feet 4 inches)

21.G19 The spa area should have an appropriate level of lighting. An illumination level of at least 50 foot-candles in the sauna, steam room, and whirlpool is recommended. Lighting sources in these areas should be surface mounted. Additional information on illumination-related factors is presented in supplement 10 in appendix A.

21.G20 A minimum of 120 square feet of floor space should be allotted for the massage room and other treatment rooms.

21.G21 The massage area should be equipped with a massage table that has the following features:

- Adjustable height (24 to 34 inches)
- Width of at least 30 inches
- Adjustable face cradle
- Double padding under double-stitched vinyl
- Cervical pillows and lumbar rolls

21.G22 The massage room should have an adequate level of illumination. A lighting system in the massage room that can adjust light levels from 0 foot-candles to 30 to 50 foot-candles at the surface of the floor is recommended. Ideally, this system should use indirect lighting sources. Additional information on illumination-related factors is presented in supplement 10 in appendix A.

21.G23   Appropriate temperature, humidity, and air circulation levels should be maintained in the massage area. The following levels are recommended:

Temperature: 72 to 78 degrees Fahrenheit

Humidity: 60 percent or less

Air circulation: 6 to 10 exchanges per hour

Air exchanges should have the appropriate mix of outside and inside air. This mix is usually 10 percent outside air and 90 percent inside air, though a mix of 40 to 60, outside to inside, is preferred. The specific ratio of outside air to inside air (recirculated air) is most often governed by local engineering codes. These codes should be followed when any air-handling system is installed. Additional information on temperature-related factors is presented in supplement 9 in appendix A.

21.G24   Nonferrous materials should be used in the construction of the steam room and sauna.

A Supplements

Some supplements have abbreviated credit lines. Please see page v for complete publication information.

1. Lighting Guidelines for Selected Outdoor Areas and Activities
2. Samples of Signage Used in a Health/Fitness Facility
3. Sample Preventive Maintenance Schedule—Resistance Equipment
4. Sample Preventive Maintenance Schedule—Cardiovascular Equipment
5. Outline for a Hazard Communication Program
6. Sample Organizational Chart
7. Sample Organizational and Staffing Structure
8. Acoustical Guidelines for a Health/Fitness Facility
9. Effects of Various Temperatures on Human Performance
10. General Illumination Guidelines
11. DIN Floor Standards
12. Dimensions and Markings for a Basketball Court
13. Dimensions and Markings for a Volleyball Court
14. Dimensions and Markings for a Badminton Court
15. Dimensions and Markings for a Racquetball/Handball Court
16. Dimensions and Markings for a Singles Squash Court
17. Dimensions and Markings for a Tennis Court
18. Dimensions and Markings for a Platform Tennis Court
19. Dimensions and Markings for a Paddle Tennis Court
20. Illumination Requirements for Different Competitive Levels of Indoor Tennis Play
21. Basic Comparative Advantages and Disadvantages of the Three Primary Sources of Lighting for Outdoor Courts
22. Illumination Requirements for Different Competitive Levels of Outdoor Tennis Play
23. Safety Checklist for Pool Areas
24. Dimensions and Markings for a 25-Yard Pool
25. Dimensions and Markings for a 50-Meter Pool
26. Recommended Diving Pool and Platform Dimensions for Competitive Swimming Programs
27. Advantages and Disadvantages of Selected Types of Pool Overflow Systems
28. Agencies That Offer Construction Standards for Aquatic Facilities and Associations That Serve the Field of Aquatics
29. Dimensions and Markings for a Softball Field for 12-Inch Softball
30. Dimensions and Markings for a Soccer Field
31. Playground Equipment Dimensions
32. Outdoor Running Track Lane-Marking Guidelines
33. Dimensions and Markings for a 440-Yard Running Track
34. Components of a First-Aid Kit
35. Peer Review Group for the Second Edition

Supplement 1
Lighting Guidelines for Selected Outdoor Areas and Activities

Considerations

The following factors must be considered when installing or renovating outdoor lighting systems:

1. In general, overhead lighting is more efficient and economical than low-level lighting.

2. Fixtures should provide an overlapping pattern of light at a height of about 7 ft.

3. Lighting levels should respond to site hazards such as steps, ramps, and steep embankments.

4. Posts and standards should be placed so that they do not create hazards for pedestrians or vehicles.

Notes

1. Because of their effect on light distribution, trees and shrubs at present height and growth potential should be considered in a lighting layout.

2. It is recommended that facilities use manufacturer-provided lighting templates sized for fixture type, wattage, pole height, and layout scale.

3. Facilities should consider color rendition when selecting light source. When possible, colors should be selected under proposed light source.

4. Light pollution to areas other than those to be illuminated should be avoided.

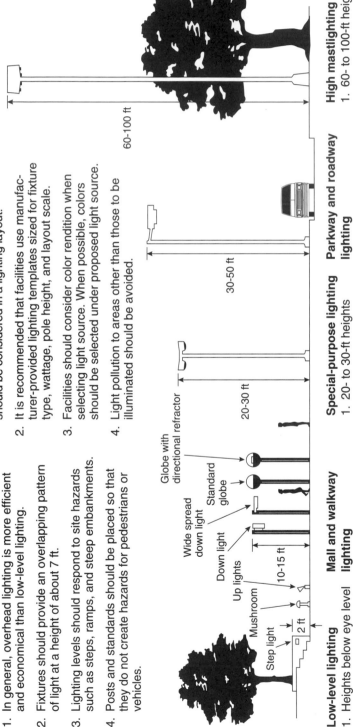

Low-level lighting

1. Heights below eye level
2. Very finite patterns with low wattage capabilities
3. Incandescent, fluorescent, and high-pressure sodium, 5- to 150-W lamps
4. Lowest maintenance requirements, but highly susceptible to vandals

Mall and walkway lighting

1. 10- to 15-ft heights average for multiuse areas; wide variety of fixtures and light patterns
2. Mercury, metal halide, or high-pressure sodium, 70- to 250-W lamps
3. Susceptible to vandals

Special-purpose lighting

1. 20- to 30-ft heights average
2. Recreational, commercial, residential, and industrial
3. Mercury, metal halide, or high-pressure sodium, 200- to 400-W lamps
4. Fixtures maintained by gantry

Parkway and roadway lighting

1. 30- to 50-ft heights average
2. Large recreational, commercial, and industrial areas, and highways
3. Mercury, metal halide, or high-pressure sodium, 400- to 1000-W lamps
4. Fixtures maintained by gantry

High mastlighting

1. 60- to 100-ft heights average
2. Large areas—parking and recreational areas and highway interchanges
3. Metal halide or high-pressure sodium, 1000-W lamps
4. Fixtures must lower for maintenance

Note.   Reprinted from Ramsey and Sleeper 1988.

Supplement 2
Samples of Signage Used in a Health/Fitness Facility

Sauna Policies

1. The sauna temperature is kept between 170 and 180 degrees Fahrenheit.
2. Limit yourself to a maximum of 10 minutes.
3. Due to high temperatures, the sauna can be dangerous to your health. We recommend that you consult your physician before you use the sauna. Those with medical conditions such as high blood pressure, heart disease, and respiratory problems, and those who are pregnant, should avoid exposure to high heat.
4. Allow yourself at least 5 minutes after exercising to cool down before entering.
5. No food or drink is allowed inside.
6. Please shower before entering.

Steam Room Policies

1. The steam room temperature is kept between 100 and 110 degrees Fahrenheit.
2. Limit yourself to a maximum of 10 minutes.
3. Due to high temperatures and humidity, the steam room can be dangerous to your health. We recommend that you consult your physician before you use the steam room. Those with medical conditions such as high blood pressure, heart disease, and respiratory problems, and those who are pregnant, should avoid exposure to high heat and humidity.
4. Allow yourself at least 5 minutes after exercising to cool down before entering.
5. No food or drink is allowed inside.
6. Please shower before entering.

Pool Policies

1. The pool temperature is kept between 78 and 84 degrees Fahrenheit and is posted daily.
2. Please shower before entering the pool.
3. No diving is allowed.
4. No food or drink is allowed in the pool area.
5. No running or playing is allowed on the pool deck.
6. Individuals with open wounds or sores should not enter the pool.

Racquetball Court Rules

1. Eye guards are required!
2. Black-soled shoes are not allowed on the court.
3. No food or drink is allowed on the court.

Court Numbers Signs

Racquetball Court 1	Squash Court 1
Racquetball Court 2	Squash Court 2
Racquetball Court 3	Squash Court 3

Cardiovascular Area Policies

1. Please limit yourself to 30 minutes on all cardiovascular equipment; 20 minutes during prime times.
2. Please use the sign-up board when all equipment is taken so people can use the equipment on a first come, first-served basis.
3. Please wipe off controls, seats, and railings when you are finished with your workout.
4. Please return cardiovascular equipment controls to their start position when your workout is completed.
5. We recommend you see the club's fitness staff before you start a training program.
6. Please warm up prior to using the equipment and cool down afterward
7. Please report any injuries to the facility staff.

Resistance Circuit Policies

1. We recommend you see the club's fitness staff before you start a training program.
2. During prime times, please limit yourself to a maximum of two sets per station. You may return after completing the rest of your circuit.
3. Please lower and raise the plates carefully.
4. Please wipe off the pads when your finish with a piece of equipment.

Free-Weight Area Policies

1. We recommend you see the club's fitness staff before you start a training program.
2. Due to the high risk of injury, we recommend you use a spotter when training with free weights.
3. Please replace all dumbbells and plates on the appropriate racks when finished with them.
4. Please remove plates from bars when you are finished with them.

Treadmill Policies

1. Start the treadmill before you step on the belt.
2. Increase the speed and elevation gradually.
3. After completing your workout, gradually reduce the speed to 3 miles per hour and the elevation to 0.
4. Please wipe off the control panel after completing your workout.

Pool Temperature

1. Pool temperature is _____.
   (The blank should be filled in with signage of temperature. Facility operators should create temperature figures from 78 to 86 degrees Fahrenheit.)

Whirlpool Policies

1. The whirlpool temperature is kept between 102 and 105 degrees Fahrenheit.
2. Limit yourself to a maximum of 10 minutes.
3. Due to high temperature and humidity, the whirlpool can be dangerous to your health. We recommend that you consult your physician before you use the whirlpool. Those with medical conditions such as high blood pressure, heart disease, and respiratory problems, and those who are pregnant, should avoid exposure to high heat and humidity.
4. Allow yourself at least 5 minutes after exercising to cool down before entering.
5. No food or drink is allowed in whirlpool.
6. Please shower before entering.

Equipment out of Order

This equipment is out of service. It will be repaired or in service by _____.

Note. Reprinted from Club Corporation of America 1995.

Supplement 3
Sample Preventive Maintenance
Schedule — Resistance Equipment

Equipment	Daily	Weekly	Monthly
Selectorized	Clean upholstery with cotton cloth and mild soap solution. Clean frames with cotton cloth and either warm mild detergent or all-purpose liquid cleaner. *Extra* Clean off dumbbell rack with warm mild detergent or all-purpose liquid cleaner.	Lubricate guide rods and linear bearings (wipe clean with dry cotton cloth, then wipe entire length with medium weight oil). Inspect and adjust the following: • Cables • Nuts/bolts • Torn upholstery Apply vinyl upholstery protectant. *Extra* Wipe off dumbbells and barbell plates. Check bolts on bars.	Wash grips in mild soap and water.
Pneumatic	Clean upholstery with cotton cloth and mild soap solution. Wipe off frames with cotton cloth. Release air pressure.	Polish chrome with cotton cloth and automotive chrome polish. Clean seat belts with mild soap. Every two weeks, switch the compressor pump. Apply vinyl upholstery protectant.	Lubricate cylinder rods with dry cotton cloth and lightweight machine oil. Lubricate pivot bearings. Wash rubber handgrips in mild soap and water.

Note.   Reprinted from Heart Healthy Fitness Center 1990.

Supplement 4
Sample Preventive Maintenance
Schedule — Cardiovascular Equipment

Equipment	Daily	Weekly	Monthly	Biannually
Rower	Clean monorail with nonabrasive pad. Wipe off seat and console with 100% cotton cloth using water and mild detergent (dilute).	Clean and lubricate chain using 100% cotton cloth and lightweight oil. Clean pads with vinyl protectant.	Inspect chain links. Adjust seat rollers. Inspect chain handle. Tighten shock cord.	Replace monitor batteries.
Arm/leg ergometer	Wipe off seat and console with 100% cotton cloth plus water and mild detergent. Rinse.	Clean and lubricate chain with cotton cloth and lightweight machine oil. Clean seat with vinyl protectant.	Inspect bolts.	
Computerized bike	Clean seat and console with 100% cotton cloth and mild soap with water (dilute). Clean housing with same materials.	Clean and lubricate chain with cotton cloth and lightweight machine oil. Clean pedals and lubricate. Wax seat post with auto wax. Clean shroud and seat with vinyl protectant.	Inspect bolts and screws.	
Mechanical stairclimber	Clean console and housing with cotton cloth and water with mild detergent. Wipe and clean pedals and grips with solution from above.	Clean and lubricate all bushings with lightweight machine oil. Clean machine with vinyl protectant.	Inspect housing, belts, and electrical components and repair as needed.	

Equipment	Daily	Weekly	Monthly	Biannually
Treadmill	Clean console and housing with cotton cloth and water with mild detergent solution.	Clean belt with cotton cloth and mild detergent solution. Must run belt at 2 mph while cleaning.	Inspect electrical components and bolts — calibrate if needed (see manual).	
Windtrainer	Clean bike frame and housing frame with mild detergent and cotton cloth. Clean seat with same materials. Calibrate (see manual). Check mounting screws.	Clean and lubricate bike chain with teflon spray. Check tire pressure and fill if necessary. Inspect chain and lubricate if needed.		
Recumbent bike	Clean housing, console, and seat with cotton cloth and mild soap. Charge battery overnight.	Inspect all bolts and chains and adjust as needed.		

Note. Reprinted from Heart Healthy Fitness Center 1990.

Supplement 5
Outline for a Hazard Communication Program

The OSHA Hazard Communication Standard requires you to develop a written hazard communications programs. The following is an outline of how to set up your hazard communication.

1. **General company policy**
   This must state the organization's intent to comply with OSHA Hazard Communication Standard, Title 29, Code of Federal Regulations 1920.1200. This section should provide an overview of the organization's policy.

2. **List of hazardous chemicals**
   This must list chemicals and their locations. It should also mention that lists of chemicals will be posted in the appropriate facility areas.

3. **Material safety data sheets**
   This must outline what the chemical compositions and safety hazards of a product are, how they will be posted, and who is in charge.

4. **Labels and other forms of warning**
   This section must clearly state that labels and other warnings will be posted on all hazardous materials.

5. **Nonroutine tasks**
   This section must describe precautions and training that will be required for nonroutine tasks.

6. **Training**
   This section must outline the organization's initial and ongoing training programs that pertain to use and handling of hazardous materials.

7. **Contractor employees**
   This section must outline policies for dealing with independent contractors.

8. **Additional information**
   This must direct employees to the appropriate information source for further data.

Note. Based on information from the Occupational Safety and Health Administration.

Supplement 6
Sample Organizational Chart

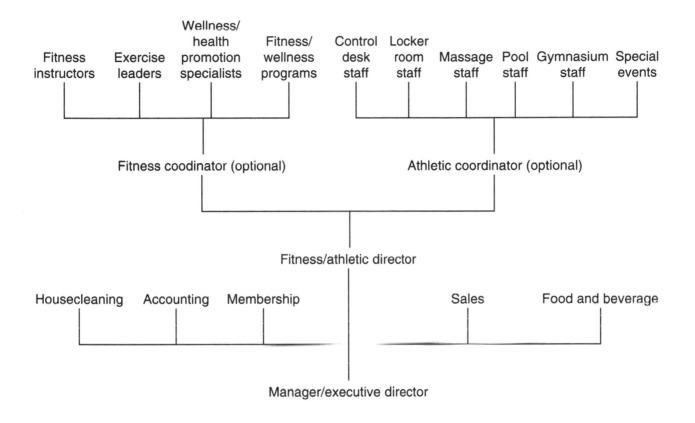

Supplement 7
Sample Organizational and Staffing Structure

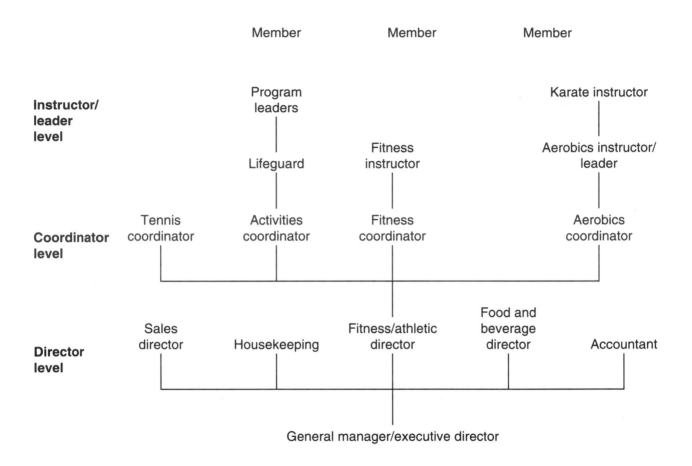

Note.   Support staff (e.g., massage therapists, locker room attendants, and control desk staff) will report to someone at the coordinator or director level. Specialty staff will usually report to someone at the director level.

Supplement 8
Acoustical Guidelines for a Health/Fitness Facility

Owners and managers of health/fitness facilities should incorporate the following noise guidelines into the design and operation of the health/fitness facility.

Area	STC rating	Measured reverberation time
Aerobic studio	45 to 55	.8 to 1.4 s
Control desk	45 to 50	.8 to 1.4 s
Cardiovascular training area	40 to 50	.8 to 1.4 s
Resistance training area	40 to 50	.8 to 1.4 s
Free-weight area	40 to 50	.8 to 1.4 s
Gymnasium	45 to 55	.8 to 1.4 s
Racquetball court	45 to 55	.8 to 1.4 s
Squash court	45 to 55	.8 to 1.4 s
Indoor pool	45 to 55	.8 to 1.4 s
Locker rooms	45 to 50	.8 to 1.4 s
Pro shop area	60 minimum	.8 to 1.4 s
Massage	45 to 55	.8 to 1.4 s
Sports/physical therapy	45 to 55	.8 to 1.4 s
Playroom	50 to 55	.8 to 1.4 s
Offices	50 to 55	.8 to 1.4 s
Storage	40 to 45	.8 to 1.4 s
Indoor tennis courts	45 to 55	.8 to 1.4 s
Laundry area	50 to 60	.8 to 1.4 s
Indoor track area	45 to 55	.8 to 1.4 s

Rationale
Sound Control Objectives

The primary reasons for attempting to control noise within the health/fitness facility involve either increasing the comfort level for facility employees and users or improving communications between occupants of the facility. Although little to no threat of hearing loss from sound abuses exists within the health/fitness facility, high noise levels do cause other problems. Noise can be disruptive and is usually irritating. Noise also hinders an individual's sense of privacy. Perhaps most importantly, noise can have negative effect on task performance.

Noise Standards

Noise is generally measured with sound-pressure meters that record sound in decibels (dB). Minimal acceptable standards for safe noise levels have been established by two federal regulatory agen-cies—the Occupational Safety and Health Administration (OSHA) and the Environmental Protection Agency. (EPA).

Noise Solutions

Excessive noise levels can be reduced to acceptable levels by specific actions defending upon the cause of the noise. The two primary sources of unwanted sound—high noise levels and excessive reverberation—can be dampened by adding acoustical absorbents in the affected areas. The degree of insulation of airborne sound provided by a given material is indicated by its sound transmission class (STC) rating. The higher the rating, the better the level of sound absorption. Other methods for diminishing unwanted sound include changing the shape or the layout of an area; using background sound to mask the noise; directly eliminating the cause of the noise (e.g., the stereo system may be too loud); and isolating either the sound or the vibration.

Recommended Maximum Background Noise Criterion Curves for Health and Fitness Facilities

Facility area	NC level	Facility area	NC level
Exercise classroom	35-40	Child care	25-35
Fitness floor	35-40	Racket courts	35-40
Gymnasium	35-40	Pools (indoor)	35-40
Locker rooms	35-40	Offices	30-35
Physical therapy	30-35		

Note. The noise criteria (NC) curves provide a convenient way of defining ambient noise level in terms of octave band sound pressure levels. The NC curves consist of a family of curves relating the spectrum of noise to an environment. Therefore, higher noise levels (decibels) may be allowed at lower frequencies because the ear is less sensitive to noise at lower frequencies.

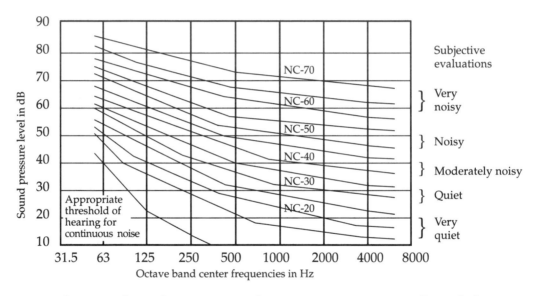

Noise Criteria Sound Pressure Level Table

NC curve	Sound pressure level, dB							
	63 Hz	125 Hz	250 Hz	500 Hz	1000 Hz	2000 Hz	4000 Hz	8000 Hz
NC-70	83	79	75	72	71	70	69	68
NC-65	80	75	71	68	66	64	63	62
NC-60	77	71	67	63	61	59	58	57
NC-55	74	67	62	58	56	54	53	52
NC-50	71	64	58	54	51	49	48	47
NC-45	67	60	54	49	46	44	43	42
NC-40	64	57	50	45	41	39	38	37
NC-35	60	52	45	40	36	34	33	32
NC-30	57	48	41	36	31	29	28	27
NC-25	54	44	37	31	27	24	22	21
NC-20	50	41	33	26	22	19	17	16
NC-15	47	36	29	22	17	14	12	11

Note. For convenience in using noise criteria data, the table lists the sound pressure levels in decibels for the NC curves from the above chart. This table and the above chart are reprinted from Ramsey and Sleeper 1988.

Supplement 9
Effects of Various Temperatures on Human Performance

Effective temperature (F°)*	Performance effects
90	Upper limit for continued occupancy over any reasonable period of time.
80-90	Expect universal complaints, serious mental and psychomotor performance decrement, and physical fatigue
80	Maximum for acceptable performance even of limited work; work output reduced as much as 40 to 50%; most people experience nasal dryness.
78	Regular decrement in psychomotor performance; individuals experience difficulty falling asleep and remaining asleep; optimum for bathing or showering.
75	Clothed subjects experience physical fatigue, become lethargic and sleepy, and feel warm; unclothed subjects consider this temperature optimum without some type of protective cover.
72	Preferred for year-round sedentary activity while subjects are wearing light clothing.
70	Midpoint for summer comfort; optimum for demanding visual-motor tasks.
68	Midpoint for winter comfort (heavier clothing) and moderate activity, but slight deterioration in kinesthetic response; people begin to feel cool indoors while performing sedentary activities.
66	Midpoint for winter comfort (very heavy clothing), while subjects are performing heavy work or vigorous physical exercise.
64	Lower limit for acceptable motor coordination; shivering occurs if individuals are not extremely active.
60	Hand and finger dexterity deteriorates, limb stiffness begins to occur, and shivering is positive.
55	Hand dexterity is reduced by 50%, strength is materially decreased, and there is considerable (probably uncontrolled) shivering.
50	Extreme stiffness; strength application accompanied by some pain; lower limit for unprotected exposure for more than a few minutes.

* These temperature effects are based on relatively still air and normal humidity (40 to 60%). Higher temperatures are acceptable if airflow is increased and humidity is lowered (a shift from 1 to 4°); lower temperatures are less acceptable if airflow increases (a shift upward of 1 to 2°).

Reprinted, by permission, from W.E. Woodson, 1981, *Human factors design handbook* (New York: McGraw-Hill, Inc.), 816.

Supplement 10
General Illumination Guidelines

Task requirements	Light level (FC)	Type of illumination
Small detail; low contrast; prolonged viewing; fast, error-free response	100	Supplementary lighting fixture located near visual task
Small detail, fair contrast, close but short duration work, speed not essential	50-100	Supplementary lighting and/or well-distributed and diffused general lighting
Typical office/desk activity	40-60	General lighting with diffusing fixture directly overhead
Sports (e.g., tennis and basketball) or indoor recreational games (e.g., Ping-Pong and billiards)	30-50	General lighting with sufficient number of fixtures to provide even court or table illumination
Recreational reading and letter writing	25-45	Supplementary lighting, positioned over reading so that page glare does not occur
Typical housekeeping activities	10-25	General lighting
Visibility for moving about, avoiding people and furniture, and negotiating standard stairs	5-10	General and/or supplementary lighting (with care taken not to allow supplementary sources to project in the user's eyes)

Note. These guidelines are only approximations. Foot-candle values are higher than some recommendations, not for seeing, but because these levels provide an additional psychological benefit as well. Levels relate to light levels measured at the primary seeing point (e.g., the desk or table surface on the floor or stair tread level). Brightness ratios between the seeing task and the immediate surroundings should not exceed 5:1; between the task and the remote surroundings, 20:1; and between the immediate work area and any other remaining visual environment, 80:1. Natural or white artificial light should be used regardless of the type of illumination (i.e., these levels do not apply to monochromatic light sources).

Reprinted, by permission, from W.E. Woodson, 1981, *Human factors design handbook* (New York: McGraw-Hill, Inc.), 434.

Supplement 11
DIN Floor Standards

The flooring for a multiuse exercise area should adhere to Deutsches Institut für Normung (DIN) standards. These standards require that a floor meet six criteria:

1. Shock absorption—a floor's ability to reduce the impact of contact with the floor surface. The greater the shock absorption, the more protective it is because it reduces impact forces. An aerobics floor, for example, would need more shock absorption than a basketball court.

2. Standard vertical deformation—the actual vertical deflection of the floor upon impact. The greater the deformation, the more the floor defects downward. Floors with minimal deformation are not good at absorbing impact forces.

3. Deflective indentation—the actual vertical deflection of the floor at a distance 50 cm from the point of impact. The greater the indentation, the more likely impact at one spot will cause deflection at a distant point.

4. Sliding characteristics—the surface friction of the finished floor. A floor with poor sliding characteristics would be inappropriate for aerobics or basketball.

5. Ball reflection (game-action response)—the response of a ball dropped on the floor compared to a ball dropped on concrete.

6. Rolling load—a floor's ability to withstand heavy weight without breaking or sustaining permanent damage.

These DIN criteria are then used to evaluate the effectiveness of a floor. A floor will have one of three functions:

1. Sports function—A floor that serves a sports function enhances athletic performance. Surface friction and ball reflection are important here.

2. Protective function—A floor that serves a protective function reduces the risk of injury (e.g., from a fall) during activity. Shock absorption is important here.

3. Material-technical function—A floor that serves a material-technical function meets the sports and protective functions.

In a health/fitness facility, the gymnasium and multipurpose floors are classified under sports function or material-technical function. The aerobics floor is classified under protective function, with some sports function characteristics.

A floor surface that has a material-technical function should meet the following DIN criteria:

Shock absorption	53% minimum
Standard vertical deformation	2.3 mm minimum
Deflective indentation	15% maximum
Sliding characteristics	0.5 to 0.7 range
Ball deflection	90% minimum
Rolling load	337.6 lb

Supplement 12
Dimensions and Markings for a Basketball Court

Court layout

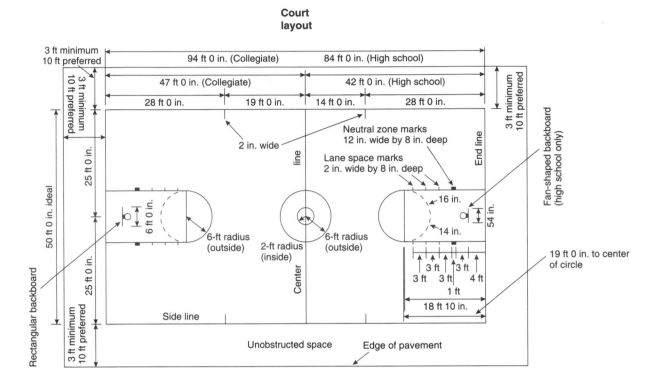

Fan-shaped backboard

Rectangular backboard

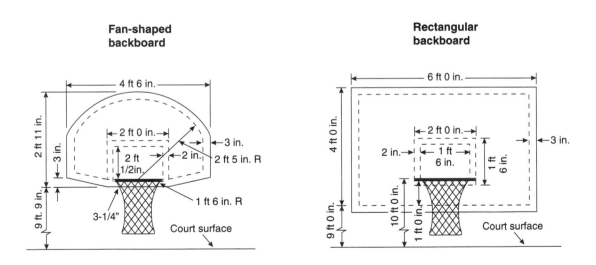

Note. A basketball court used in high school competition is generally 84 x 50 ft with a 10-ft unobstructed space on all sides (3-ft minimum). A basketball court used in colleges should be 94 ft x 50 ft, with a 10-ft unobstructed space on all sides (3-ft minimum). The color of the lane space marks and neutral zone marks should contrast with the color of the bounding lines. The mid-court marks should be the same color as the bounding lines. All lines should be 2-in. wide (neutral zone excluded). All dimensions are to inside edge of lines except as noted. The backboard should be of any rigid weather-resistant material. The front surface should be flat and painted white unless it is transparent. If the backboard is transparent, it should be marked with a 3-in.-wide white line around the border and an 18-in. x 24-in. target area bounded with a 2-in.-wide white line.

Reprinted, by permission, from J. DeChiara and J.H. Callendar, 1990, *Time-saver standards for building types*, 3rd ed. (New York: McGraw-Hill, Inc.), 1194.

Supplement 13
Dimensions and Markings for a Volleyball Court

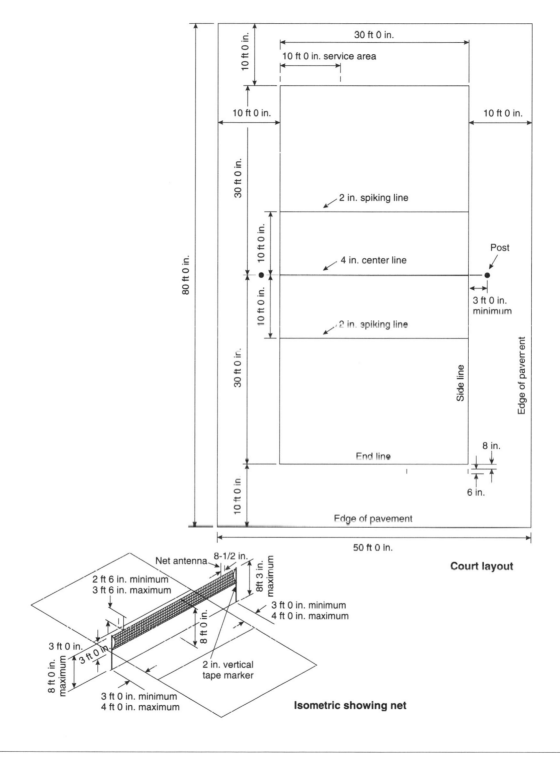

Court layout

Isometric showing net

Note. The recommended size of a volleyball court is 30 ft x 60 ft with a 10-ft unobstructed area on all sides (6 ft minimum). All measurements for court markings are to the outside of lines except for the centerline. All court markings to be 2 in. wide, except as noted. Net height at center should be as follows: men 8 ft 0 in., women 7 ft 4 in., high school 7 ft 0 in., elementary school 6 ft 6 in.

Reprinted, by permission, from J. DeChiara and J.H. Callendar, 1990, *Time-saver standards for building types*, 3rd ed. (New York: McGraw-Hill, Inc.), 1212.

Supplement 14
Dimensions and Markings for a Badminton Court

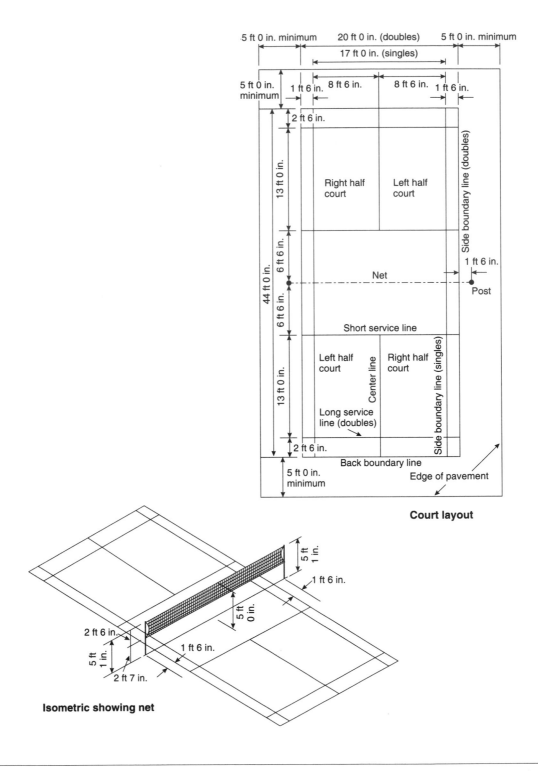

Court layout

Isometric showing net

Note. A singles court for badminton is 17 ft x 44 ft, whereas a doubles court is 20 ft x 44 ft. Both types of badminton courts should have a minimum unobstructed area of 5 ft on all sides. All measurements for court markings are to the outside of lines except for those involving the center service line, which is equally divided between right and left service courts. All court markings should be 1 1/2 in. wide and preferably white or in color. Minimum distance between sides of parallel courts should be at least 5 ft.

Reprinted, by permission, from J. DeChiara and J.H. Callendar, 1990, *Time-saver standards for building types*, 3rd ed. (New York: McGraw-Hill, Inc.), 1194.

Supplement 15
Dimensions and Markings for a Racquetball/Handball Court

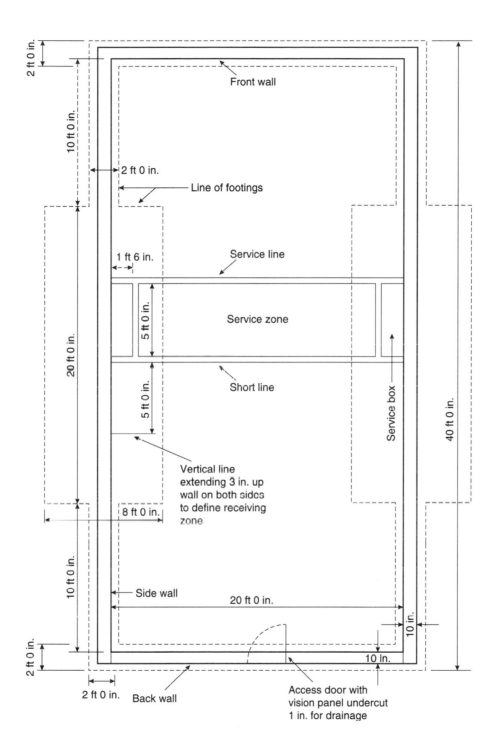

Front wall

2 ft 0 in.

10 ft 0 in.

2 ft 0 in.

Line of footings

1 ft 6 in.

Service line

5 ft 0 in.

Service zone

20 ft 0 in.

5 ft 0 in.

Short line

Service box

40 ft 0 in.

Vertical line extending 3 in. up wall on both sides to define receiving zone

8 ft 0 in.

10 ft 0 in.

Side wall

20 ft 0 in.

10 in.

2 ft 0 in.

10 in.

2 ft 0 in.

Back wall

Access door with vision panel undercut 1 in. for drainage

Note.   A standard-size, four-wall racquetball/handball court is 20 ft wide x 40 ft long x 20 ft high. All court markings should be 1 1/2 in. wide and painted white, red, or yellow.

Reprinted, by permission, from J. DeChiara and J.H. Callendar, 1990, *Time-saver standards for building types*, 3rd ed. (New York: McGraw-Hill, Inc.), 1200.

Supplement 16
Dimensions and Markings for a Singles Squash Court

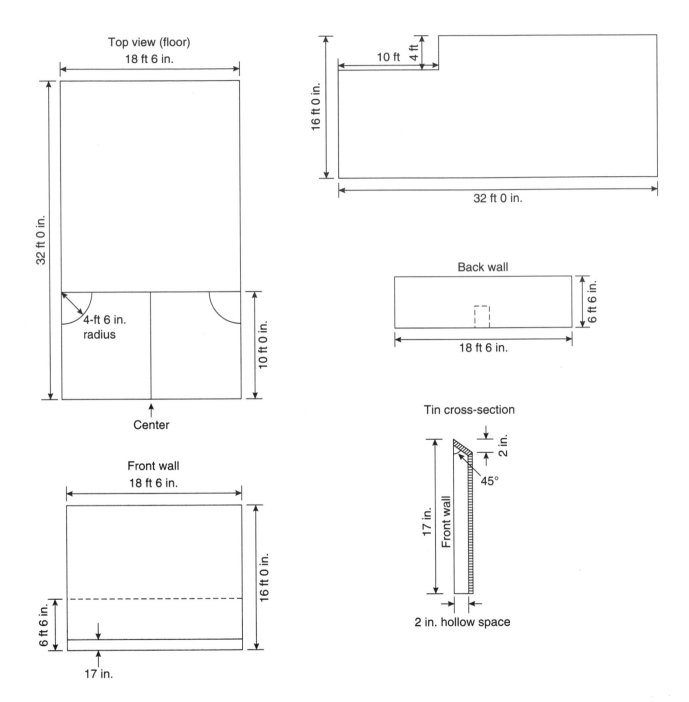

Note. All lines in squash are red. In hard ball and doubles, the line width is 1 in. In soft ball, the width of the line is 2 in. Tin should be made of 17-gauge or heavier sheet metal. Spacing between the tin and the front wall should not exceed 2 in. Approximately 2 in. of the top of the tin should be bevelled at 45° to meet the front wall at the prescribed height. In all courts, a minimum of 2 ft of height above court dimension is required. If light fixtures are flush mount, then a ceiling height of 2 ft above court height is the minimum standard. If light fixtures or other encumbrances hang or protrude from the ceiling into the court, the minimum clearance from that lowest hanging object is 2 ft from the height dimension of the court. The diagrams illustrate the dimensions of a court used almost exclusively in play and competition conducted in North America. An international squash court is 2 ft 6 in. wider and has a higher telltale and vastly different markings on the side wall. From the United States Squash Racquets Association, Bala-Cynwyd, PA.

Supplement 17
Dimensions and Markings for a Tennis Court

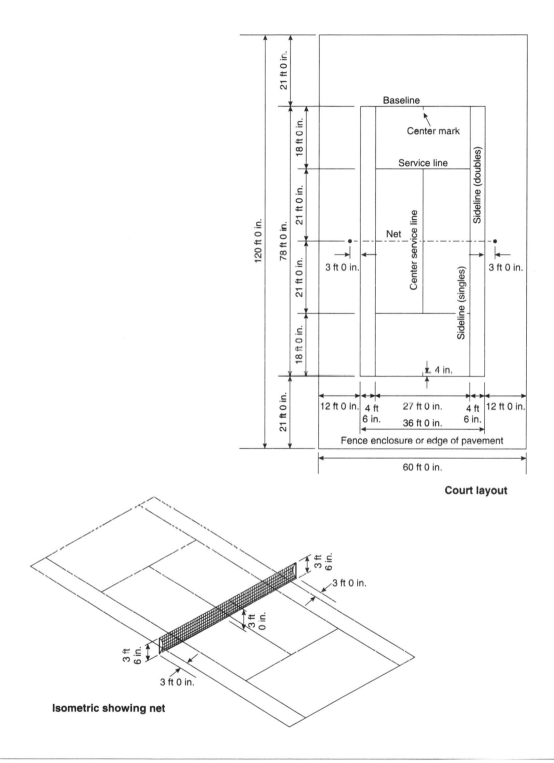

Court layout

Isometric showing net

Note. The playing area of a tennis court is 36 ft x 78 ft with at least 12 ft clearance on both sides or between a series of adjacent courts and 21 ft clearance on each end. All measurements for court markings are to the outside of lines except for those involving the center service line, which is equally divided between the right and left service courts. All court markings should be 2 in. wide. Fence enclosure, if provided, should be 10 ft high, 11-gauge, 1-3/4-in. mesh chain link.

Reprinted, by permission, from J. DeChiara and J.H. Callendar, 1990, *Time-saver standards for building types*, 3rd ed. (New York: McGraw-Hill, Inc.), 1210.

Supplement 18
Dimensions and Markings for a Platform Tennis Court

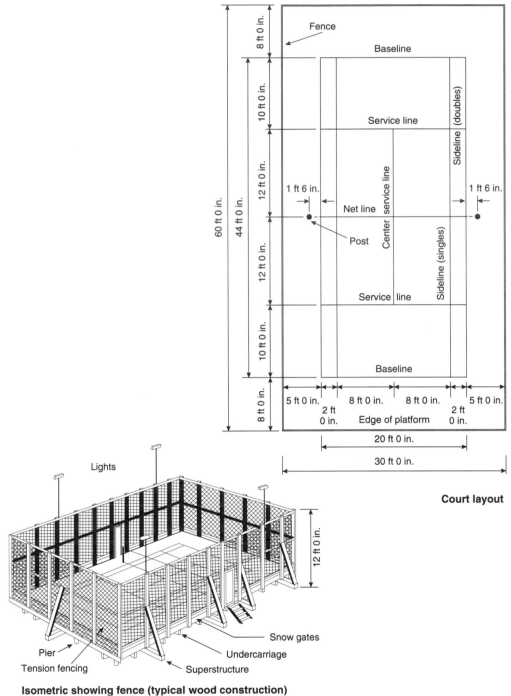

Court layout

Isometric showing fence (typical wood construction)

Note.   The playing area of a platform tennis court is 20 ft x 44 ft, with an 8-ft space on each end and a 5-ft space on each side. All measurements for court markings are to the outside of lines except for those involving the center service line, which is equally divided between the right and left service court. All court markings should be 2 in. wide. Fencing is required—12 ft high with 16-gauge hexagonal, galvanized 1-in. flat wire mesh fabric. The net should be 3 ft 1 in. high at posts and 2 ft 10 in. at the center court.

Reprinted, by permission, from J. DeChiara and J.H. Callendar, 1990, *Time-saver standards for building types,* 3rd ed. (New York: McGraw-Hill, Inc.), 1208.

Supplement 19
Dimensions and Markings for a Paddle Tennis Court

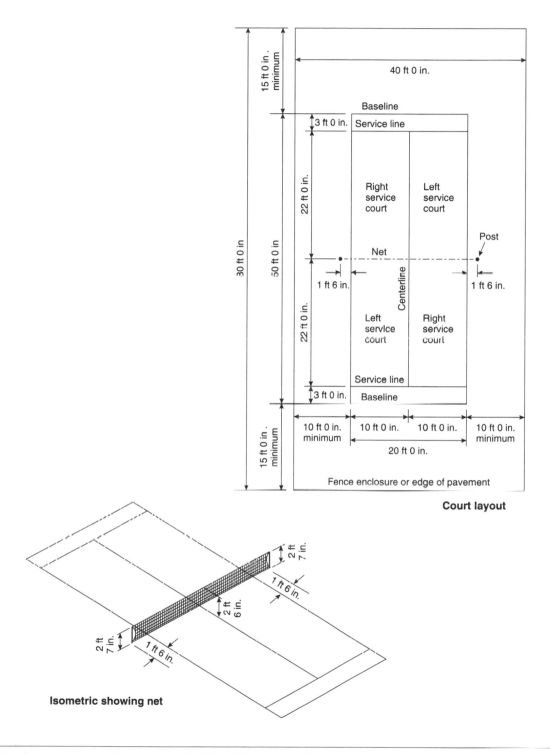

Court layout

Isometric showing net

Note. The playing area of a paddle tennis court is 20 ft x 50 ft, plus a 15-ft (minimum) space on each end and a 10-ft (minimum) space on each side or between an adjacent court. All measurements for court markings are to the outside of lines except for those involving the center service line, which is equally divided between right and left service court. All court markings should be 1 1/2 in. wide. Fence enclosure, if provided, should be 1 1/2-in. mesh, 11-gauge chain link.

Reprinted, by permission, from J. DeChiara and J.H. Callendar, 1990, *Time-saver standards for building types*, 3rd ed. (New York: McGraw-Hill, Inc.), 1209.

Supplement 20
Illumination Requirements for Different Competitive Levels of Indoor Tennis Play

		Illumination level for class of play			
		Tournament or championship			Nontournament
		I	II	III	IV
Description of the facility		Professional, international, national, college	Sectional, state, city, college, club	High school, club, instructional, parks	Recreational, social
Average maintained horizontal illumination within PPA (FC)		125	75	50	40
Minimum maintained horizontal illumination within PPA (FC)		100	60	35	30
Maximum uniformity ration within playing area (FC)	Within lines	1.2	1.5	1.7	2.0
	Within PPA	1.5	1.7	2.0	2.5

Note. Table courtesy of the Illuminating Engineering Society.

Supplement 21

Basic Comparative Advantages and Disadvantages of the Three Primary Sources of Lighting for Outdoor Courts

Source	Advantages	Disadvantages
High-intensity discharge	Long lamp life High efficiency	Fairly large and heavy Requires a warm-up time of 3 to 7 min to achieve maximum light output
Incandescent (e.g., quartz, iodine, tungsten, halogen)	Low initial cost High color acceptability Excellent light control Relatively small in size and weight Instantaneous starting Capability of using coin- or token-operated meters	Short lamp light High maintenance and operating costs due to low efficacy
Fluorescent	Daylight color Immediate relight time Lower mounting height for easy maintenance High efficiency	Undesirable glare Relatively low brightness Requires a ballast to operate

Supplement 22
Illumination Requirements for Different Competitive Levels of Outdoor Tennis Play

		Illumination level for class of play			
		Tournament or championship			Nontournament
		I	II	III	IV
Description of the facility		Professional, international, national, college	Sectional, state, city, college, club, residential	High school, club, instructional parks, residential	Recreational, social
Average maintained horizontal illumination within PPA (FC)		125	60	40	30
Minimum maintained horizontal illumination within PPA (FC)		100	40	30	30
Maximum uniformity ratio within playing area (FC)	Within lines	1.2	1.5	1.8	2.0
	Within PPA	1.5	2.0	2.5	3.0

Note.   Table courtesy of the Illuminating Engineering Society.

Supplement 23
Safety Checklist for Pool Areas

Inspection by _____ Date _____

Staff members are expected to report safety factors needing attention on a daily basis so that users are not exposed to unnecessary risks. Managers will make a complete written assessment of the condition of the facility on a regular basis.

Yes	No	
		Lifesaving equipment
___	___	Life guard stations are strategically located on decks near edge of pool.
___	___	Shepherd's crooks, spine boards, reaching poles, and ring buoys are consistently placed in a conspicuous and appropriate location.
		Pool and deck areas
___	___	All deck areas are in safe condition.
___	___	The decks are free of standing water.
___	___	The sunbathing area is free of any dangerous conditions.
___	___	The fence that encloses the pool area is in safe condition.
___	___	All rules and regulations are posted in high-traffic areas such as entrances to the locker rooms. Special rules and regulations such as those on using the diving boards are posted in appropriate locations.
___	___	All diving boards and stands are properly anchored and in good condition.
___	___	Water clarity is such that the main drain is clearly visible on the bottom of the pool from the pool deck.
___	___	All pool markings (depth/warning signs) are clearly visible.
___	___	All matting on guard platforms is fastened securely and is in safe condition.
___	___	Diving board steps and railings are fastened securely and are in safe condition.
___	___	All chairs, cots, and lounges are in safe condition.
		Guard room
___	___	A copy of the procedures for emergencies is posted next to the telephone.
___	___	Emergency phone numbers are also posted next to the telephone.
___	___	A first-aid kit with all the necessary emergency first-aid essentials is consistently stored in a conspicuous location.
		Filter and chlorinator rooms
___	___	All motor shafts and filter and soda ash pumps are covered with metal guards.
___	___	Fire extinguishers (Type B or C), filled and sealed and with current date tags, are kept in strategic locations.
___	___	All chemicals are stored according to the manufacturer's storage instructions.

_____ _____ Antichlorine gas mask is in operative condition. Mask is located immediately outside the entrance to the chlorine room. Canister element has a current, valid date.

_____ _____ All gas chlorine tanks are fastened to the wall.

_____ _____ Covers to powdered chemicals are fastened tightly and containers are neatly stored.

Locker rooms

_____ _____ All floors are kept as dry as possible and are inspected for possible slippery or unsafe conditions.

_____ _____ Basket/locker racks are secured to the wall or floor base and are in safe condition.

_____ _____ Baskets are in place in the racks.

_____ _____ All benches are secured to the wall. Bench tops are finished and free of any rough, splintered edges.

_____ _____ All bather signs for pool users are displayed on the walls at appropriate heights.

_____ _____ All shower-room plumbing is securely fastened to the walls, and is in safe and operable condition.

_____ _____ All walls and ceilings are in safe condition.

_____ _____ All lamps light when the switches are turned on.

Note. Completed checklists are valuable for several reasons. They are important tools for eliminating the avoidable injury. They also are tangible evidence that a pool manager has concern for the health and safety of pool patrons. In litigation alleging that an unsafe condition on the premises was the cause of the plaintiff's injuries, a completed checklist, signed and dated, could be invaluable. This checklist is incomplete. The items included are examples of safety checks that should be made. To be complete, the checklist should be tailored to a particular facility. Records of safety inspections should be kept indefinitely.

Reprinted from Arnold 1989.

Supplement 24
Dimensions and Markings for a 25-Yard Pool

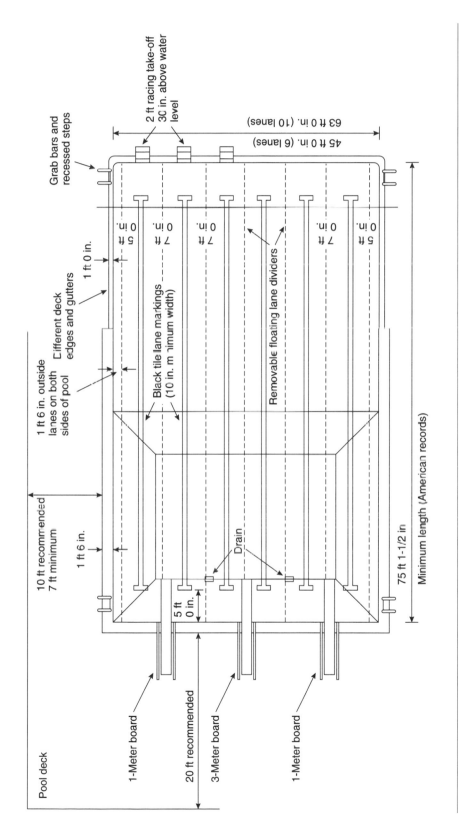

Note. Twenty-five yards is the minimum length pool for American records. In reality, the pool should be 76 ft 1-1/2 in. long to allow for electronic timing panels to be placed at one end. Twenty-five-yard pools should have a minimum of six lanes (45 ft wide), while 10 lanes (83 ft wide) are recommended.
Reprinted from Packard and Kliment 1989.

Supplement 25
Dimensions and Markings for a 50-Meter Pool

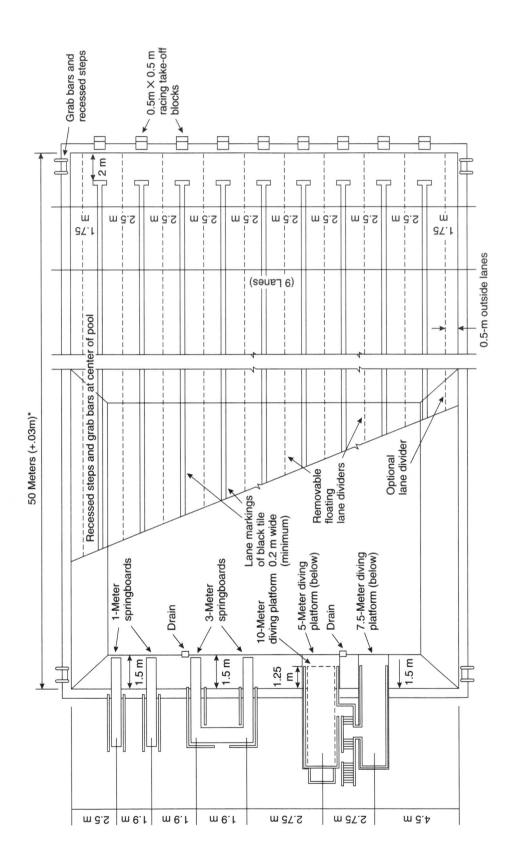

Note. The pool should actually be 50.03 m, allowing an extra 0.03 m to compensate for possible future structural defects, electrical timing devices, or tile facing. Fifty meters is the minimum pool length for world records.

Supplement 26
Recommended Diving Pool and Platform Dimensions for Competitive Swimming Programs

Board type	Board size Length	Board size Width	Height above water level	Distances* A — From edge of pool to end of board	Distances* B — From center of board to side of pool	Distances* C — From center of board to center of board	Distances* D — From end of board to wall ahead
1-meter springboard	16 ft	20 in.	3 ft 3 in.	A-1 7 ft 5 ft	B-1 10 ft 8 ft	C-1 8 ft 6 ft	D-1 28 ft 25 ft
3-meter springboard	16 ft	20 in.	9 ft 11 in.	A-3 7 ft 5 ft	B-3 15 ft 12 ft	C-3 10 ft 8 ft	D-3 33 ft 30 ft
5-meter platform	18 ft	7 ft	16 ft 5 in.	A-5 7 ft 5 ft	B-5 15 ft 12 ft	C-5 10 ft 8 ft	D-5 43 ft 35 ft
10-meter platform	20 ft / 20 ft	8 ft / 10 ft	32 ft 10 in.	A-10 8 ft 5 ft	B-10 20 ft 15 ft	C-10 10 ft 8 ft	D-10 52 ft 45 ft

Note. The dimensions in the accompanying table are based upon recommended Olympic requirements. Minimum requirements can be satisfied with a pool 35 ft × 45 ft but a somewhat larger size, for example, 60 ft × 60 ft, is recommended. A water-curling arrangement should be provided so that the diver can see exactly where the surface of the water is. If outdoors, the boards should be oriented so that the sun is not in the diver's eyes. Underwater observation parts are desirable. Diving does not require a very large pool, but it must be deep, with at least a 14-ft depth below a 10-m platform.

* Preferred dimensions appear in the left-hand side of a column, while the minimum safe dimensions are listed in the right-hand side of a column.

Reprinted, by permission, from J. DeChiara and J.H. Callendar, 1990, *Time-saver standards for building types*, 3rd ed. (New York: McGraw-Hill, Inc.), 1269.

Supplement 27

Advantages and Disadvantages of Selected Types of Pool Overflow Systems

Type	Advantages	Disadvantages
Fully recessed gutter	None	Old-fashioned system Most expensive to build Difficult to clean Contrary to efficient pool operation
Semirecessed gutter	Provides visible pool edge for competition Cuts down surface roughness when gutters are flooded Water surface closer to deck than in fully recessed gutter	Water level 5 or 6 inches below deck; difficult for users to climb out of pool Some cleaning difficulty Requires pipe tunnel for access Narrow edge of gutter lip provides precarious footing for diving off edge
Roll-out gutter	Comfortable pool use and egress Ideal for teaching and recreation Gives beginner swimmers feeling of security by allowing wide visibility Easy cleaning Low construction costs	Decks may flood if adequate number of drains not provided Pool edge not visible for competition; temporary turning boards can be used Requires pipe tunnel for access

Type	Advantages	Disadvantages
Deck-level or rimflow system	Trench serves as integral surge tank Minimum construction costs No pipe tunnel needed Comfortable pool use and egress Ideal for teaching and recreation Gives beginner swimmers feeling of security Easy cleaning	Deck can flood if not properly pitched Pool edge not visible for competition; temporary turning boards can be used Care needed in choosing cleaning materials for deck because some deck water enters pool recirulation system Bottom inlets in rimflow system inaccessible for servicing
Surface skimmers	No surge tank required Suitable for very small pools only	Continuing expense and nuisance of maintaining the moveable weirs Turbulence not eliminated in large pools
Prefabricated stainless steel recessed gutter	Pipe tunnel not required Large diameter return pipe is substituted by the manufacturer for a surge tank	Skimmer weirs need manual adjustments several times a day Waterline inlets disturb swimmers in end lanes Exposed rings for lane and lifelines

Supplement 28
Agencies That Offer Construction Standards
for Aquatic Facilities
and Associations That Serve the Field of Aquatics

The following associations and organizations outline criteria for the construction of aquatic facilities and have published architectural reference guidelines.

American National Standards Institute
1430 Broadway
New York, NY 10018

American Public Health Association
1015 15th St., NW
Washington, DC 20005

American Red Cross
17th and D St., NW
Washington, DC 20006

Council for National Cooperation in
 Aquatics (CNCA)
901 W. New York St.
Indianapolis, IN 46202

FINA
208-3540 West 41st Ave.
Vancouver, BC
Canada V6N E36

National Collegiate Athletic Association
 (NCAA)
P.O. Box 1906
Shawnee Mission, KS 66201

National Sanitation Foundation
P.O. Box 1468
Ann Arbor, MI 48106

National Spa and Pool Institute (NSPI)
2111 Eisenhower Ave.
Alexandria, VA 22314

U.S. Diving
901 W. New York St.
Indianapolis, IN 46202

U.S. Swimming and U.S. Synchronized
 Swimming
1750 E. Boulder St.
Colorado Springs, CO 80909

Supplement 29
Dimensions and Markings for a Softball Field for 12-Inch Softball

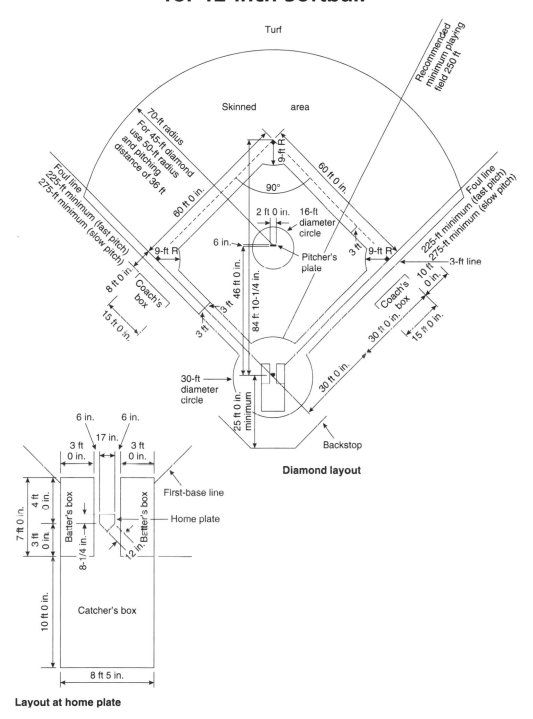

Diamond layout

Layout at home plate

Note. The recommended baselines are 60 ft for adults and 45 ft for juniors. Distances from home plate to the mound are 46 ft for men, 50 ft for women, and 35 ft for juniors. Juniors should use 45 ft between bases. A field for adult fast-pitch softball should have a 225-ft radius from home plate between the lines. A slow-pitch field has a 275-ft radius and a 250-ft radius for men and women, respectively. The backstop should be located at least 25 ft behind home plate. The foul lines; catcher's, batter's, and coach's boxes; and 3-ft lines should be marked with 2- to 3- in. chalk lines.

Reprinted, by permission, from J. DeChiara and J.H. Callendar, 1990, *Time-saver standards for building types*, 3rd ed. (New York: McGraw-Hill, Inc.), 1227.

Supplement 30
Dimensions and Markings for a Soccer Field

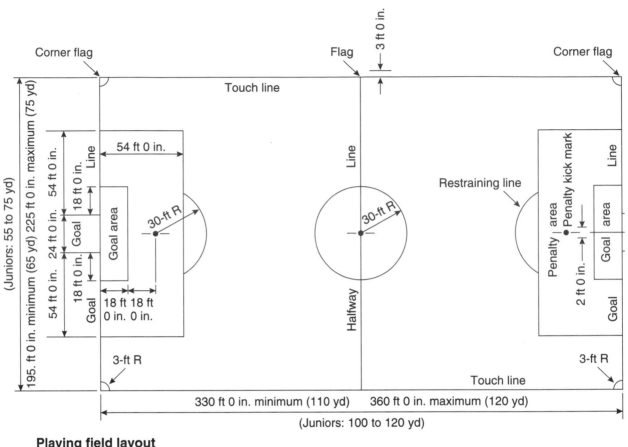

Playing field layout

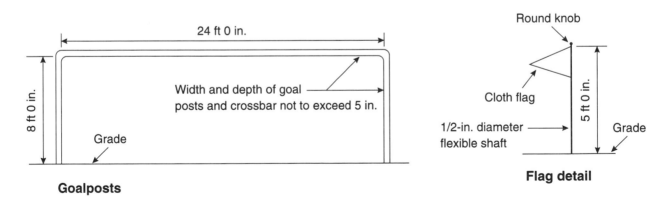

Goalposts

Flag detail

Note. A full-size soccer field is 195 to 225 ft wide by 330 to 360 ft long, with a minimum unobstructed area of 10 ft on all sides. A soccer field for juniors (and in some instances, women) is usually proportionally smaller. Goalposts should be pressure treated with a paintable, oil-borne preservative and painted above ground with three coats of white lead and oil. The goalposts and crossbar should present a flat surface to the playing field, not less than 4 in. or more than 5 in. in width. Nets should be attached to the posts, crossbar, and ground behind the goal. The top of the net must extend backward 2 ft level with the crossbar. All dimensions are to the inside edge of lines. All lines should be 2 in. wide and marked with a white, nontoxic material that is not injurious to the eyes or skin.

Reprinted, by permission, from J. DeChiara and J.H. Callendar, 1990, *Time-saver standards for building types*, 3rd ed. (New York: McGraw-Hill, Inc.), 1225.

Supplement 31
Playground Equipment Dimensions

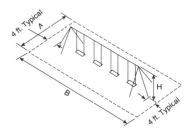

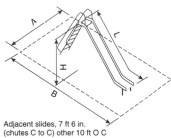

Adjacent slides, 7 ft 6 in.
(chutes C to C) other 10 ft O C

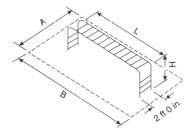

Swings

Swings	H(ft)	Safety zone A(ft)	Safety zone B(ft)
2	8	24	27
	10	28	27
	12	32	27
3	8	24	30
	10	28	30
	12	32	30
4	8	24	40
	10	28	40
	12	32	40
6	8	24	46
	10	28	46
	12	32	46
8	8	24	57
	10	28	57
	12	32	57
9	8	24	61
	10	28	61
	12	32	61

Slides

H	L	Safety zone A	Safety zone B
4	8	26	24
5	10	26	28
6	12	26	32
8	16	26	36

Horizontal ladder

H (ft, in.)	L (ft, in.)	Safety zone A (ft)	Safety zone B (ft)
6, 6	12, 6	14	25
7, 6	16, 0	14	30

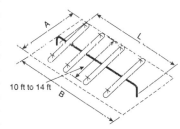

10 ft to 14 ft

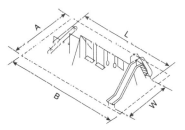

General planning information

Equipment	Area (Sq ft)	Capacity (Number of Children)
Slide	450	4–6
Low swing	150	1
High swing	250	1
Horizontal ladder	375	6–8
Seesaw	100	2
Junior climbing gym	180	8–10
General climbing gym	500	15-20

Seesaws

Boards	1	2	3	4	6
L	3	6	9	12	18
A	20	20	20	20	20
B	5	10	15	20	25

Combination units*

Enclosure limits

A = W + 12 ft 0 in
B = L + 0 ft 0 in.

*Types and number of units are variable

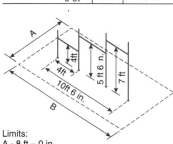

Limits:
A - 8 ft – 0 in.
B = L + 6 ft – 0 in. heights adjustable
Horizontal bars

Limits:
general 18 ft × 18 ft
junior: 10 ft × 12 ft

General:
8 ft 1-1/2 in.

Junior:
4 ft 6 in.

General:
6 ft 1-1/2 in.
Junior:
6ft 0 in.

General unit: 9 ft 0 in.
Junior unit: 6 ft 4 in.

N.Y.C Housing Authority standard
climbing gym

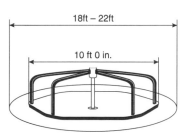

18ft – 22ft

10 ft 0 in.

10 ft diameter is considered standard
Other diameters 6 ft and 8 ft

Spin around

Note. Reprinted from Ramsey and Sleeper 1988.

Supplement 32
Outdoor Running Track Lane-Marking Guidelines

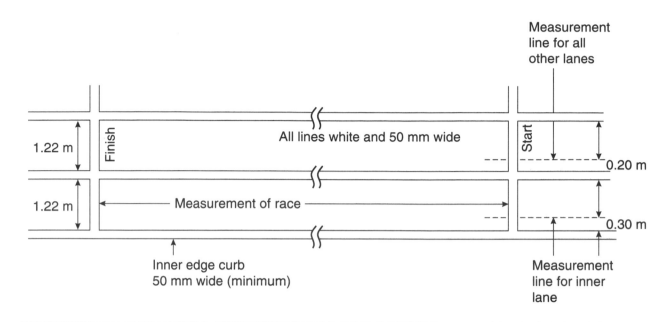

Note.   Each lane should be clearly marked and should be a minimum of 1.22 m and a maximum of 1.25 m wide. Each lane should be marked by lines 50 mm in width. The inside line of the inside lane should be measured from 0.30 m outward from the inner border of the track. All other lanes should be measured 0.20 m from the outer edge of the preceding line. Tracks used for competition should have a minimum of six lanes; if possible, eight lanes.

Reprinted from Packard and Kliment 1989.

Supplement 33
Dimensions and Markings for a 440-Yard Running Track

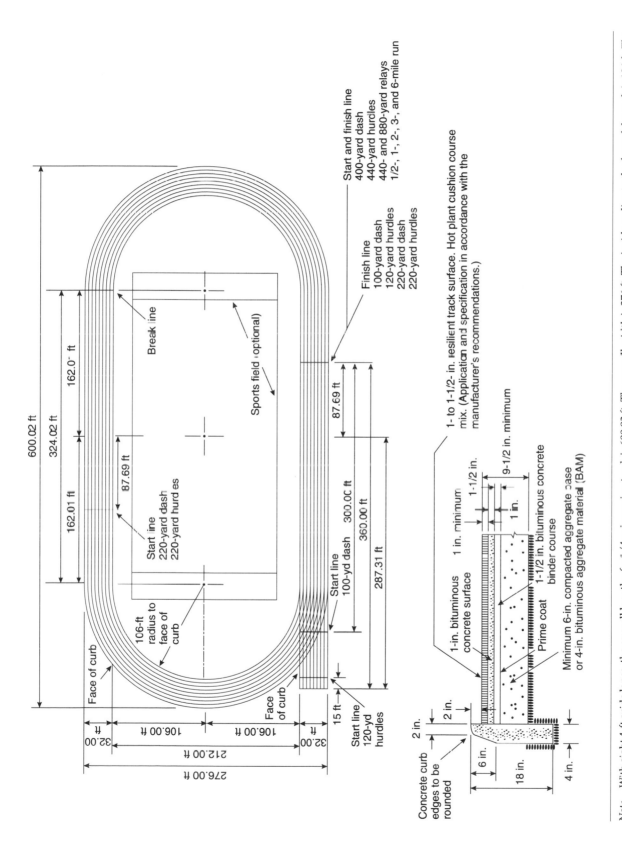

Note. With eight 4-ft-wide lanes, the overall length of a 1/4-mi running track is 600.02 ft. The overall width is 276 ft. The inside radius to the face of the curb is 106 ft. The width of the track is 32 ft. The field-space area inside the track could be marked and used for field sports (e.g., soccer or touch football). Reprinted, by permission, from J. DeChiara and J.H. Callendar. 1990, *Time-saver standards for building types,* 3rd ed. (New York: McGraw-Hill, Inc.), 1231.

Supplement 34

Components of a First-Aid Kit

At a minimum, a first-aid kit should include the following:

* Current first-aid manual

* Latex gloves (disposable)

* Scissors

* Tongue depressors

* Triangular bandages (at least six)

* Cotton swabs

* Bandages (variety of shapes and sizes)

* Sterile gauze pads (4 in. by 4 in. and 2 in. by 2 in.)

* Sterile eye pads

* Adhesive tape (1-in. rolls)

* Paper tape (1-in. rolls)

* 6-in. elastic wrap (at least 2)

* 4-in. elastic wrap (at least 2)

* 3-in. elastic wrap (at least 2)

* Blankets (at least 2)

* Cold packs (at least 6, or if ice is available, Ziploc bags)

* Safety pins

* First-aid creme or ointment

* Hydrogen peroxide solution

* Splints-air, metal, wood, variety of sizes

* Mouthpieces

* Household bleach and water solution (for cleaning up blood)

Supplement 35
Peer Review Group for the 2nd Edition
ACSM's Standards and Guidelines for Designing, Developing, and Operating a Health/Fitness Facility

BRENT ARNOLD
MID ATLANTIC CLUB MGMT ASSOC
12040 SOUTH LAKES DRIVE
RESTON VA 22091

CHRISTOPHER BRELEUX
BETHESDA INC
8044 MONTGOMERY ROAD
CINCINNATI OH 45236

MR. LOREN BRINK
FITNESS CORP OF AMERICA
3500 W 80TH STREET STE 200
MINNEAPOLIS MN 55431

GIL BROWN
AAHPERD
1900 ASSOCIATION DRIVE
RESTON, VA 22091-9989

PETER BROWN
ATHLETIC BUSINESS
1846 HOFFMAN STREET
MADISON WI 53704

PETER BROWN
FITNESS+
44 DIGBY MANSIONS LOWER MALL
HAMMERSMITH LONDON W6 9DF
UNITED KINGDOM

MS SHERYL MARKS BROWN
AMERICAN COUNCIL ON EXERCISE
5820 VENTURA BLVD STE 200
SHERMAN OAKS CA 91430

MR. JOHN BUTTERFIELD
INT'L INLINE SKATING ASSOCIATION
1130 SUGARLANDS BLVD STE 190
RIVIERA BEACH FL 33404

RICK CARO JR
MANAGEMENT VISION INC
217 EAST 85TH STREET STE 231
NEW YORK NY 10028

DR KENNETH COOPER
COOPER INSTITUTE FOR AEROBICS
12330 PRESTON ROAD
DALLAS TX 75230

MS TRACEY COX
PRESBYTERIAN HOSPITAL DALLAS
5721 PHOENIX DRIVE
DALLAS TX 75231-5204

MS KATHIE DAVIS
THE INTERNATIONAL ASSOC OF
FITNESS PROFESSIONALS
6190 CORNERSTONE CT STE 204
SAN DIEGO CA 92121

DR. JOANN EICKHOPF-SHEMER
SCHOOL OF HPER
UNIVERSITY OF NEBRASKA
LINCOLN NE 68588

GARY FROST
CANYON RANCH
8600 ROCKCLIFF ROAD
TUCSON AZ 85715

SCOTT GARRETT
MIDTOWN ATHLETIC CLUB
4100 PROSPECT AVE
ALBERQUERQUE NM 87110

MS LAURA GLADWIN
AEROBICS & FITNESS ASSOC
15250 VENTURA BLVD STE 310
SHERMAN OAKS CA 91403

DR BERNIE GOLDFINE
KENNESAW STATE COLLEGE
1000 CHASTAIN RD DEPT. HPER
KENNESAW GA 30144

BOB GRAY
NATIONAL ATHLETIC TRAINERS ASSOC
168 TIMBERLINE DRIVE
ELYRIA OH 44035

JOHN GREEN
ASSOCIATION OF HOSPITAL
HEALTH & FITNESS
PO BOX 6280
EVANSTON IL 60604

WILL HOLSBERRY
NATIONAL INTRAMURAL
RECREATIONAL SPORTS ASSOC
850 SW FIFTEENTH ST
CORVALLIS OR 97333

MS SUSAN KALISH
NATIONAL ASSOCIATION FOR
SPORT & PHYSICAL EDUCATION
1900 ASSOCIATION DRIVE
RESTON VA 22091

MS PAULA KAHN
AMERICAN RUNNING & FITNESS
4405 E WEST HIGHWAY
BETHESDA MD 20814

BOB KARCH
NATIONAL FITNESS LEADERS ASSOC
7929 WESTPARK DRIVE STE 200
MCLEAN VA 22102

STEVE KASS
AMERICAN LEISURE
20 SQUADRON BLVD STE 370
NEW CITY NY 10956

Dr Richard Keelor
Congress For National
Health and Fitness
PO Box 97667
Raleigh NC 27624

Ms Jill Kinney
Club Source
380 Pine Street 6th Floor
San Francisco CA 94104

Dr Richard Larue
18 Chalk Pond Road
Newbury NH 03255

Hervey Lavoie
Ohlson Lavoie Corporation
1860 Blake St Ste 300
Denver CO 80202-1262

Herbert Lipsman
The Houstian Club
111 N Post Oak Lane
Houston TX 77240

Jim Liston
National Assoc of Governors
Council on Phy Fitness Sports
Pan American Plaza
Indianapolis IN 46225

Ms Martha Livingston
American Assoc of Card & Pul
Central Dupage Hospital
25 N Winfield Rd
Winfield IL 60190

Glen Meredith PhD
National Operating Committee
on Standards for Ath Equip
11724 NW Plaza Circle
Kansas City MO 64195

Dennis Monroe
Oregon State University
Dept of Recreational Sports
Corvallis OR 97333

Ms Linda Pelchar
H & H Solutions
PO Box 266
Lincoln MA 01773

Ms Barbara Pelz
NIRSA
850 SW 15th Street
Corvalllis OR 97333

Ms Sandy Perlmudder
President's Council on
Physical Fitness & Sports
701 Penn Ave NW Ste 250
Washington DC 20004

Tim Richardson
Boys & Girls Clubs of
America
1230 W Peachtree St NW
Atlanta GA 30309

Bud Rockhill
Club Sports International
1700 Broadway Ste 1900
Denver CO 80290

Joseph Samson
Association for Worksite
Health Promotion
60 Revere Drive Ste 500
Northbrook IL 60062

Dr Todd Seidler
206 Matthaei Bldg
Wayne State University
Detroit MI 48202

Mrs Jenny Silberman
Jewish Community Center
15 East 26th Street
New York NY 10010

Wayne Smith
Int'l Spa & Fitness Assoc
1300 L Street NW Ste 1050
Washington DC 20007

Mike Spezzano
National Health Fitness Dir
YMCA of the USA
101 N Wacker Drive
Chicago IL 60606

Patrick B Stinson
National Employee Services and
Recreation Assoc
2211 York Road Ste 207
Oakbrook IL 60521

Dean Tice
National Recreation and Parks
Association
3101 Park Center Drive
Alexandria VA 22302

Steve Tidrick
Club Managers Association of
America
1733 King Street
Alexandria VA 22314

United States Olympic
Committee
1 Olympic Plaza
Colorado Springs CO 80909

Larry Vorbrich
National Spa and Pool Assoc
2111 Eisenhower Ave
Alexandria VA 22314

Ms Kelly Walker
National Club Association
3050 K St NW Ste 330
Washington DC 20007

Neil Wolkodoff
Exertrends
800 Washington St Ste 309
Denver CO 80203

Ric Zimmerman
Athletic Clubs Inc
4020 West Chase Blvd Ste 425
Raleigh NC 27607

B Forms

This appendix contains sample forms for use in health/fitness facilities. The law varies from state to state—no form should be adopted or used by any program without individualized legal advice. Some forms have abbreviated credit lines. Please see page v for complete publication information.

1. Physical Activity Readiness Questionnaire (PAR-Q)
2. Health History Questionnaire (Fitcorp)
3. Guest Health History Questionnaire (Fitcorp)
4. Physician's Statement and Clearance Form (Fitcorp)
5. Physician's Approval Form
6. Agreement and Release of Liability Form
7. Informed Consent Agreement
8. Informed Consent for Participation in a Personal Fitness Training Program for Apparently Healthy Adults (Without Known or Suspected Heart Disease)
9. Informed Consent for Exercise Testing of Apparently Healthy Adults (Without Known or Suspected Heart Disease)
10. Informed Consent for Participation in an Exercise Program for Apparently Healthy Adults (Without Known or Suspected Heart Disease)
11. Express Assumption of Risk Form
12. Physician's Release for Exercise Form (East Side Athletic)
13. Guest Agreement and Waiver with Brief Medical History (Heart Healthy Fitness Center)
14. Emergency Medical Authorization Form
15. Fitness Evaluation Form
16. Fitness Integration Tracking Form (East Side Athletic)
17. Cardiovascular Assessment Data Sheet
18. Release of Information Form
19. Progress Notes (Fitcorp)
20. Incident Report Form
21. Theft Report Form
22. Special Event Sign-Up Sheet
23. Appointment Sheet
24. Sample Exercise Card
25. Physical Activity Readiness Medical Exam Form (PARmed-X)
26. Sample of an Emergency Procedure Sheet

Form 1

Physical Activity Readiness Questionnaire (PAR-Q) and You

Regular physical activity is fun and healthy, and increasingly more people are starting to become more active every day. Being more active is very safe for most people. However, some people should check with their doctor before they start becoming much more physically active.

If you are planning to become much more physically active than you are now, start by answering the seven questions in the box below. If you are between the ages of 15 and 69, the PAR-Q will tell you if you should check with your doctor before you start. If you are over 69 years of age, and you are not used to being very active, check with your doctor.

Common sense is your best guide when you answer these questions. Please read the questions carefully and answer each one honestly:

Check YES or NO

YES	NO		
☐	☐	1.	Has your doctor ever said that you have a heart condition <u>and</u> that you should only do physical activity recommended by a doctor?
☐	☐	2.	Do you feel pain in your chest when you do physical activity?
☐	☐	3.	In the past month, have you had chest pain when you were not doing physical activity?
☐	☐	4.	Do you lose your balance because of dizziness or do you ever lose consciousness?
☐	☐	5.	Do you have a bone or joint problem that could be made worse by a change in your physical activity?
☐	☐	6.	Is your doctor currently prescribing drugs (for example, water pills) for your blood pressure or heart condition?
☐	☐	7.	Do you know of <u>any other reason</u> why you should not do physical activity?

If

you

answered

YES to one or more questions

Talk to your doctor by phone or in person BEFORE you start becoming much more physically active or BEFORE you have a fitness appraisal. Tell your doctor about the PAR-Q and which questions you answered YES.

- You may be able to do any activity you want—as long as you start slowly and build up gradually. Or, you may need to restrict your activities to those which are safe for you. Talk with your doctor about the kinds of activities you wish to participate in and follow his/her advice.
- Find out which community programs are safe and helpful for you.

NO to all questions

If you answered NO honestly to <u>all</u> PAR-Q questions, you can be reasonably sure that you can:

- start becoming much more physically active—begin slowly and build up gradually. This is the safest and easiest way to go.
- take part in a fitness appraisal—this is an excellent way to determine your basic fitness so that you can plan the best way for you to live actively.

Delay becoming much more active:

- if you are not feeling well because of a temporary illness such as a cold or a fever—wait until you feel better; or
- if you are or may be pregnant—talk to your doctor before you start becoming more active.

Please note: If your health changes so that you then answer YES to any of the above questions, tell your fitness or health professional. Ask whether you should change your physical activity plan.

Informed use of the PAR-Q: The Canadian Society for Exercise Physiology, Health Canada, and their agents assume no liability for persons who undertake physical activity, and if in doubt after completing this questionnaire, consult your doctor prior to physical activity.

I have read, understood and completed this questionnaire. Any questions I had were answered to my full satisfaction.

Name _____

Signature _____   Date _____

Signature of Parent _____   Witness _____
or Guardian (for participants under the age of majority)

Note.   The law varies from state to state. No form should be adopted or used by any program without individualized legal advice.

Reprinted from the Canadian Society for Exercise Physiology, Inc., 1994.

Form 2

Health History Questionnaire

Name_____ Company_____

Home address_____

Position_____

Telephone home_____ work_____

Height_____ Weight_____

Gender_____ Birth date_____ Age_____

Regular physical activity is safe for most people. However, some individuals should check with their doctor before they start an exercise program. To help us determine if you should consult with your doctor before starting to exercise with (your organization), please read the following questions carefully and answer each one honestly. All information will be kept confidential. Please check YES or NO:

YES	NO		
❏	❏	1.	Do you have a heart condition?
❏	❏	2.	Have you ever experienced a stroke?
❏	❏	3.	Do you have epilepsy?
❏	❏	4.	Are you pregnant?
❏	❏	5.	Do you have diabetes?
❏	❏	6.	Do you have emphysema?
❏	❏	7.	Do you feel pain in your chest when you engage in physical activity?
❏	❏	8.	Do you have chronic bronchitis?
❏	❏	9.	In the past month, have you had chest pain when you were not doing physical activity?
❏	❏	10.	Do you ever lose consciousness or do you ever lose control of your balance due to chronic dizziness?
❏	❏	11.	Are you currently being treated for a bone or joint problem that restricts you from engaging in physical activity?
❏	❏	12.	Has a physician ever told you or are you aware that you have high blood pressure?
❏	❏	13.	Has anyone in your immediate family (parents/brothers/sisters) had a heart attack, stroke, or cardiovascular disease before age 55?
❏	❏	14.	Has a physician ever told you or are you aware that you have a high cholesterol level?
❏	❏	15.	Do you currently smoke?
❏	❏	16.	Are you a male over 44 years of age?
❏	❏	17.	Are you a female over 54 years of age?

YES   NO

❑   ❑   18.   Are you currently exercising *LESS* than 1 hour per week? If you answered no, please list your activities.
_____

❑   ❑   19.   Are you currently taking any medication?
Please list the medication and its purpose _____

What are your specific fitness goals at (your organization)? (Indicate all that apply)

❑   Increase strength and endurance   ❑   Improve flexibility
❑   Improve cardiovascular fitness   ❑   Improve muscle tone
❑   Reduce body fat   ❑   Increase muscle mass
❑   Exercise regularly   ❑   Injury Rehabilitation
❑   Sports conditioning   ❑   Other _____

What are your specific health goals at (your organization)? (Indicate all that apply)

❑   Reduce stress   ❑   Improve nutritional habits
❑   Control blood pressure   ❑   Control cholesterol
❑   Stop smoking   ❑   Achieve balance in life
❑   Improve productivity   ❑   Reduce back pain
❑   Feel better overall   ❑   Increase my health awareness
❑   Other (please be specific) _____

What motivated you to join (your organization)? (Indicate all that apply)

❑   Convenience/location
❑   Membership promotion
❑   Attended a (your organization) health promotion event at work
❑   Peer support
❑   Medical reasons
❑   Tried (your organization) as a guest
❑   Corporate membership
❑   Other _____

I have read, understood, and completed this questionnaire. Any questions that I had were answered to my full satisfaction.

Name _____   Date _____

Signature _____

Staff Use Only

Cleared to exercise _____ **Not cleared to exercise** _____

Reason_____

Staff Signature_____   **Date**_____

Resting Heart Rate_ _____

Resting Blood Pressure_____

EP_____

Note.   Reprinted from Fitcorp 1990.

Form 3

Guest Health History Questionnaire

Name_____   Date _____

Date of Birth _____

Employer _____

Title _____

Home address _____   City _____ Zip _____

Phone (home)_____   (work)_____

Gender   (Please circle)   M   F

Guest of _____

Health insurance provider _____

In case of emergency contact _____   #_____

Regular physical activity is safe for most people. However, some individuals should check with their doctor before they start an exercise program. To help us determine if you should consult with your doctor before starting to exercise with (your organization), please read the following questions carefully and answer each one honestly. All information will be kept confidential.

Please check YES or NO:

YES	NO		
❏	❏	1.	Do you have a heart condition?
❏	❏	2.	Have you ever experienced a stroke?
❏	❏	3.	Do you have epilepsy?
❏	❏	4.	Are you pregnant?
❏	❏	5.	Do you have diabetes?
❏	❏	6.	Do you have emphysema?
❏	❏	7.	Do you feel pain in your chest when you engage in physical activity?
❏	❏	8.	Do you have chronic bronchitis?
❏	❏	9.	In the past month, have you had chest pain when you were not doing physical activity?
❏	❏	10.	Do you ever lose consciousness or do you ever lose control of your balance due to chronic dizziness?
❏	❏	11.	Are you currently being treated for a bone or joint problem that restricts you from engaging in physical activity?
❏	❏	12.	Has a physician ever told you or are you aware that you have high blood pressure?

YES   NO

☐   ☐   13. Has anyone in your immediate family (parents/brothers/sisters) had a heart attack, stroke, or cardiovascular disease before age 55?

☐   ☐   14. Has a physician ever told you or are you aware that you have a high cholesterol level?

☐   ☐   15. Do you currently smoke?

☐   ☐   16. Are you a male over 44 years of age?

☐   ☐   17. Are you a female over 54 years of age?

☐   ☐   18. Are you currently exercising *LESS* than 1 hour per week? If you answered no, please list your activities.
_____

☐   ☐   19. Are you currently taking any medication?
Please list the medication and its purpose _____

How did you hear about (your organization)?

_____ Employer   _____ Yellow Pages   _____ Friend
_____ Television   _____ Newspaper   _____ Radio
_____ Co-worker   _____ Health ins. plan   _____ Worksite event

Are you interested in joining (your organization)?   Y   or   N

Are you interested in learning how (your organization) can develop a corporate fitness and wellness benefit for your organization?   Y   or   N

I understand that any exercise program I undertake may create physical stress and subsequent harmful effects. I agree that it is solely my responsibility and not the responsibility of (your organization) to require me to consult with a physician prior to commencing any exercise program, to remain under medical supervision if that is indicated, and to seek medical assistance in the event of an injury. I recognize that the use of the equipment entails some risk of accidental injury to myself and to others and I agree that I will use such equipment and facilities with due care.

_____   _____
Signature   Date

Staff Use Only

☐ **Cleared to exercise**   ☐ **Not cleared to exercise**   **Guest #**_____

Reason _____

Staff Signature _____   **Date** _____

Visit Date/Time _____   **Visit Date/Time** _____

Visit Date/Time _____   **Visit Date/Time** _____

Visit Date/Time _____   **Visit Date/Time** _____

Note.   Reprinted from Fitcorp 1990.

Form 4

Physician's Statement and Clearance Form

At (your organization), your safety is our primary concern. For that reason, we comply with the health and fitness standards of the American College of Sports Medicine and the International Health, Racquet and Sportsclub Association.

On the Health History Questionnaire you just completed, you identified that you have one or more coronary and/or other medical risk factors which may impair your ability to exercise safely. For this reason, you need to have a physician complete and return this medical clearance form before you can begin exercising at (your organization).

We recognize that you are eager to start your fitness program, and we sincerely regret any inconvenience that this may cause you. However, please keep in mind that we want your exercise experience at Fitcorp to be as safe as possible.

In order to expedite this process, we will gladly fax this form directly to the physician of your choice. If the doctor is aware of your medical history, he/she may be able to complete this form and fax it right back to us. In many cases the delay is only one day.

I hereby give my physician permission to release any pertinent medical information from any medical records to the staff at (your organization). All information will be kept confidential.

Patient's signature _____ **Date** _____

Information requested for _____

Reason for medical clearance _____

Physician's name _____ Phone _____ Fax _____

Address _____ _____

For Physician Use Only

Please check one of the following statements:

❑   I concur with my patient's participation with no restrictions.

❑   I concur with my patient's participation in an exercise program if he/she restricts activities to:

_____

_____

❑   I do not concur with my patient's participation in an exercise program (if checked, the individual will not be allowed to join (your organization))

Reason _____

Physician's name (type or print) _____

Physician's signature ___ _____ Date _____

Please return fax to:
General Manager,
Phone   **Fax**

Note. Reprinted from Fitcorp 1990.

Form 5

Physician's Approval Form

_____ has medical approval to participate in fitness programs and in the use of exercise equipment at various sites, including home or office, that may be provided by and/or recommended by _____.

The following restrictions apply (if none, so state):

_____

Physician's signature

_____

Physician's name

_____

Street address

_____   _____   _____

City   State   Zip

_____

Phone

_____

Date

*** Please attach a copy of the results of the
latest physical examination.

Note.   The law varies from state to state. No form should be adopted or used by any program without individualized legal advice.

Reprinted from Koeberle 1990.

Form 6

Agreement and Release of Liability

1.   In consideration of gaining membership or being allowed to participate in the activities and programs of _____ and to use its facilities, equipment, and machinery in addition to the
payment of any fee or charge, I do hereby waive, release and forever discharge _____ and
its officers, agents, employees, representatives, executors, and all others from any and all responsibilities or
liability for injuries or damages resulting from my participation in any activities or my use of equipment or
machinery in the above-mentioned facilities or arising out of my participation in any activities at said
facility. I do also hereby release all of those mentioned and any others acting upon their behalf from any
responsibility or liability for any injury or damage to myself, including those caused by the negligent act or
omission of any of those mentioned or others acting on their behalf or in any way arising out of or connected
with my participation in any activities of _____ or the use of any equipment at
_____ . **(Please initial _____)**

2.   I understand and am aware that strength, feasibility, and aerobic exercise, including the use of equipment, is a potentially hazardous activity. I also understand that fitness activities involve a risk of injury and
even death and that I am voluntarily participating in these activities and using equipment and machinery
with knowledge of the dangers involved. I hereby agree to expressly assume and accept any and all risks of
injury or death. **(Please initial _____)**

3.   I do hereby further declare myself to be physically sound and suffering from no condition, impair-
ment, disease, infirmity, or other illness that would prevent my participation in any of the activities and
programs of _____ or use of equipment or machinery except as hereinafter stated. I do
hereby acknowledge that I have been informed of the need for a physician's approval for my participation
in an exercise/fitness activity or in the use of exercise equipment and machinery. I also acknowledge that it
has been recommended that I have a yearly or more frequent physical examination and consultation with
my physician as to physical activity, exercise, and use of exercise and training equipment so that I might
have recommendations concerning these fitness activities and equipment use. I acknowledge that I have
either had a physical examination and have been given any physician's permission to participate, or that I
have decided to participate in activity and/or use of equipment and machinery without the approval of my
physician and do hereby assume all responsibility for my participation and activities, and utilization of
equipment and machinery in my activities. **(Please initial _____)**

Date _____   Signature _____

Note.   The law varies from state to state. No form should be adopted or used by any program without individualized legal advice.

Reprinted from Herbert 1989.

Form 7

Informed Consent Agreement

Thank you for choosing to use the facilities, services, or programs of _____ . We request your understanding and cooperation in maintaining both your and our safety and health by reading and signing the following informed consent agreement.

I, _____ , declare that I intend to use some or all of the activities, facilities, programs, and services offered by _____ and I understand that each person, (myself included), has a different capacity for participating in such activities, facilities, programs, and services. I am aware that all activities, services, and programs offered are either educational, recreational, or self-directed in nature. I assume full responsibility, during and after my participation, for my choices to use or apply, at my own risk, any portion of the information or instruction I receive.

I understand that part of the risk involved in undertaking any activity or program is relative to my own state of fitness or health (physical, mental, or emotional) and to the awareness, care, and skill with which I conduct myself in that activity or program. I acknowledge that my choice to participate in any activity, service, and program of _____ brings with it my assumption of those risks or results stemming from this choice and the fitness, health, awareness, care, and skill that I possess and use.

I further understand that the activities, programs, and services offered by _____ are sometimes conducted by personnel who may not be licensed, certified, or registered instructors or professionals. I accept the fact that the skills and competencies of some employees and/or volunteers will vary according to their training and experience and that no claim is made to offer assessment or treatment of any mental or physical disease or condition by those who are not duly licensed, certified, or registered and herein employed to provide such professional services.

I recognize that by participating in the activities, facilities, programs, and services offered by _____ , I may experience potential health risks such as transient light-headedness, fainting, abnormal blood pressure, chest discomfort, leg cramps, and nausea and that I assume willfully those risks. I acknowledge my obligation to immediately inform the nearest supervising employee of any pain, discomfort, fatigue, or any other symptoms that I may suffer during and immediately after my participation. I understand that I may stop or delay my participation in any activity or procedure if I so desire and that I may also be requested to stop and rest by a supervising employee who observes any symptoms of distress or abnormal response.

I understand that I may ask any questions or request further explanation or information about the activities, facilities, programs, and services offered by _____ at any time before, during, or after my participation.

I declare that I have read, understood, and agree to the contents of this informed consent agreement in its entirety.

Signature _____

Date of signing _____

Witness _____

Note.   The law varies from state to state. No form should be adopted or used by any program without individualized legal advice.

Form 8

Informed Consent for Participation in a Personal Fitness Training Program for Apparently Healthy Adults (Without Known or Suspected Heart Disease)

Name _____

1. Purpose and explanation of procedure

I hereby consent to voluntarily engage in an acceptable plan of personal fitness training. I also give consent to be placed in personal fitness training program activities that are recommended to me for improvement of my general health and well-being. These may include dietary counseling, stress management, and health/fitness education activities. The levels of exercise I perform will be based upon my cardiorespiratory (heart and lungs) and muscular fitness. I understand that I may be required to undergo a graded exercise test as well as other fitness tests prior to the start of my personal fitness training program in order to evaluate and assess my present level of fitness. I will be given exact personal instructions regarding the amount and kind of exercise I should do. I agree to participate 3 times per week in the formal program sessions. Professionally trained personal fitness trainers will provide leadership to direct my activities, monitor my performance, and otherwise evaluate my effort. Depending upon my health status, I may or may not be required to have my blood pressure and heart rate evaluated during these sessions to regulate my exercise within desired limits. I understand that I am expected to attend every session and to follow staff instructions with regard to exercise, diet, stress management, and other health/fitness-related programs. If I am taking prescribed medications, I have already so informed the program staff and further agree to so inform them promptly of any changes my doctor or I make with regard to use of these. I will be given the opportunity for periodic assessment and evaluation at regular intervals after the start of my program.

I have been informed that during my participation in this personal fitness training program, I will be asked to complete the physical activities unless symptoms such as fatigue, shortness of breath, chest discomfort, or similar occurrences appear. At that point, I have been advised that it is my complete right to decrease or stop exercise and that it is my obligation to inform the personal fitness training program personnel of my symptoms. I hereby state that I have been so advised and agree to inform the personal fitness training program personnel of my symptoms, should any develop.

I understand that while I exercise, a personal fitness trainer will periodically monitor my performance and perhaps measure my pulse and blood pressure or assess my feelings of effort for the purposes of monitoring my progress. I also understand that the personal fitness trainer may reduce or stop my exercise program when any of these findings so indicate that this should be done for my safety and benefit.

I also understand that during the performance of my personal fitness training program, physical touching and positioning of my body may be necessary to assess my muscular and bodily reactions to specific exercises, as well as ensure that I am using proper technique and body alignment. I expressly consent to the physical contact for these reasons.

2. Risks

I understand and have been informed that there exists the remote possibility of adverse changes occurring during exercise including, but not limited to, abnormal blood pressure, fainting, dizziness, disorders of heart rhythm, and very rare instances of heart attack, stroke, or even death. I further understand and I have been informed that there exists the risk of bodily injury including, but not limited to, injuries to the muscles, ligaments, tendons, and joints of the body. I have been told that every effort will be made to minimize these

(continued)

occurrences by proper staff assessments of my condition before each exercise session, by staff supervision during exercise, and by my own careful control of exercise efforts. I fully understand the risks associated with exercise, including the risk of bodily injury, heart attack, stroke, or even death, but knowing these risks, it is my desire to participate as herein indicated.

3. Benefits to be expected and available alternatives to exercise

I understand that this program may or may not benefit my physical fitness or general health. I recognize that involvement in the exercise sessions and personal fitness training sessions will allow me to learn proper ways to perform conditioning exercises, use fitness equipment, and regulate physical effort. These experiences should benefit me by indicating how my physical limitations may affect my ability to perform various physical activities. I further understand that if I closely follow the program's instructions, I will likely improve my exercise capacity and fitness level after a period of 3 to 6 months.

4. Confidentiality and use of information

I have been informed that the information obtained in this personal fitness training program will be treated as privileged and confidential and will consequently not be released or revealed to any person without my express written consent. I do, however, agree to the use of any information that is not personally identifiable with me for research and statistical purposes so long as same does not identify me or provide facts that could lead to my identification. I also agree to the use of any information for the purpose of consultation with other health/fitness professionals, including my doctor. Any other information obtained, however, will be used by the program staff in the course of prescribing exercise for me and evaluating my progress in the program.

5. Inquiries and freedom of consent

I have been given an opportunity to ask certain questions as to the procedures of this program. Generally, these requests have been noted by the interviewing staff with his/her responses as follows:

_____

_____

_____

I further understand that there are also other remote risks that may be associated with this personal fitness training program. Despite the fact that a complete accounting of all these remote risks has not been provided to me, it is still my desire to participate.

I acknowledge that I have read this document in its entirety or that it has been read to me if I have been unable to read same.

I expressly consent to the rendition of all services and procedures as explained herein by all program personnel.

Date _____

_____
Client's signature

By _____
Authorized representative

Note.   The law varies from state to state. No form should be adopted or used by any program without individualized legal advice.

Reprinted from Koeberle 1990.

Form 9

Informed Consent for Exercise Testing of Apparently Healthy Adults (Without Known or Suspected Heart Disease)

Name _____

1. Purpose and explanation of test

I hereby consent to voluntarily engage in an exercise test to determine my circulatory and respiratory fitness. I also consent to the taking of samples of my exhaled air during exercise to properly measure my oxygen consumption. I also consent, if necessary, to have a small blood sample drawn by needle from my arm for blood chemistry analysis and to the performance of lung function and body fat (skin fold pinch) tests. It is my understanding that the information obtained will help me evaluate future physical activities and sports activities in which I may engage.

Before I undergo the test, I certify to the program that I am in good health and have had a physical examination conducted by a licensed medical physician within the last _____ months. Further, I hereby represent and inform the program that I have completed the pretest history interview presented to me by the program staff and have provided correct responses to the questions as indicated on the history form or as supplied to the interviewer. It is my understanding that I will be interviewed by a physician or other person prior to my undergoing the test who will in the course of interviewing me determine if there are any reasons which would make it undesirable or unsafe for me to take the test. Consequently, I understand that it is important that I provide complete and accurate responses to the interviewer and recognize that my failure to do so could lead to possible unnecessary injury to myself during the test.

The test I will undergo will be performed on a motor-driven treadmill or bicycle ergometer with the amount of effort gradually increasing. As I understand it, this increase in effort will continue until I feel and verbally report to the operator any symptoms such as fatigue, shortness of breath, or chest discomfort which may appear. It is my understanding and I have been clearly advised that it is my right to request that a test be stopped at any point if I feel unusual discomfort or fatigue. I have been advised that I should immediately upon experiencing any such symptoms, or if I so choose, inform the operator that I wish to stop the test at that or any other point. My wishes in this regard shall be absolutely carried out.

It is further my understanding that prior to beginning the test, I will be connected by electrodes and cables to an electrocardiographic recorder, which will enable the program personnel to monitor my cardiac (heart) activity. It is my understanding that during the test itself, a trained observer will monitor my responses continuously and take frequent readings of blood pressure, the electrocardiogram, and my expressed feelings of effort. I realize that a true determination of my exercise capacity depends on progressing the test to the point of my fatigue.

Once the test has been completed, but before I am released from the test area, I will be given special instructions about showering and recognition of certain symptoms that may appear within the first 24 hours after the test. I agree to follow these instructions and promptly contact the program personnel or medical providers if such symptoms develop.

2. Risks

I understand and have been informed that there exists the possibility of adverse changes during the actual test. I have been informed that these changes could include abnormal blood pressure, fainting, disorders of heart rhythm, stroke, and very rare instances of heart attack or even death. I have been told that every effort will be made to minimize these occurrences by preliminary examination and by precautions and observations taken during the test. I have also been informed that emergency equipment and personnel are readily available to deal with these unusual situations should they occur. I understand that there is a risk of injury, heart attack , or even death as a result of my performance of this test, but knowing those risks, it is my desire to proceed to take the test as herein indicated.

3. Benefits to be expected and available alternatives to the exercise testing procedure

The results of this test may or may not benefit me. Potential benefits relate mainly to my personal motives for taking the test, that is, knowing my exercise capacity in relation to the general population, understanding my fitness for certain sports and recreational activities, planning my physical conditioning program, or evaluating the effects of my recent physical activity habits. Although my fitness might also be evaluated by alternative means, for example, a bench step test or an outdoor running test, such tests do not provide as accurate a fitness assessment as the treadmill or bike test nor do those options allow equally effective monitoring of my responses.

4. Confidentiality and use of information

I have been informed that the information obtained in this exercise test will be treated as privileged and confidential and will consequently not be released or revealed to any person without my express written consent. I do, however, agree to the use of any information for research or statistical purposes so long as same does not provide facts that could lead to my identification. Any other information obtained, however, will be used only by the program staff to evaluate my exercise status or needs.

5. Inquiries and freedom of consent

I have been given an opportunity to ask certain questions as to the procedures. Generally these requests, which have been noted by the testing staff, and their responses are as follows:

_____

_____

_____

_____

I further understand that there are also other remote risks that may be associated with this prodedure. Despite the fact that a complete accounting of all these remote risks has not been provided to me, I still desire to proceed with the test.

I acknowledge that I have read this document in its entirety or that it has been read to me if I have been unable to read same.

I consent to the rendition of all services and procedures as explained herein by all program personnel.

Date _____   _____

                                                Participant's signature

_____

Witness's signature

_____

Test supervisor's signature

Note.   The law varies from state to state. No form should be adopted or used by any program without individualized legal advice.

Reprinted from Herbert 1994.

Form 10

Informed Consent for Participation in an Exercise Program for Apparently Healthy Adults (Without Known or Suspected Heart Disease)

Name_____

1. Purpose and explanation of procedure

I hereby consent to voluntarily engage in an acceptable plan of exercise conditioning. I also give consent to be placed in program activities that are recommended to me for improvement of my general health and well-being. These may include dietary counseling, stress reduction, and health education activities. The levels of exercise I will perform will be based upon my cardiorespiratory (heart and lungs) fitness as determined through my recent laboratory graded exercise evaluation. I will be given exact instructions regarding the amount and kind of exercise I should do. I agree to participate 3 times per week in the formal program sessions. Professionally trained personnel will provide leadership to direct my activities, monitor my performance, and otherwise evaluate my effort. Depending upon my health status, I may or may not be required to have my blood pressure and heart rate evaluated during these sessions to regulate my exercise within desired limits. I understand that I am expected to attend every session and to follow staff instructions with regard to exercise, diet, stress management, and smoking cessation. If I am taking prescribed medications, I have already so informed the program staff and further agree to so inform them promptly of any changes my doctor or I make with regard to use of these. I will be given the opportunity for periodic assessment with laboratory evaluations at 6 months after the start of my program. Should I remain in the program thereafter, additional evaluations will generally be given at 12 month intervals. The program may change the foregoing schedule of evaluations, if this is considered desirable for health reasons.

I have been informed that during my participation in exercise, I will be asked to complete the physical activities unless symptoms such as fatigue, shortness of breath, chest discomfort, or similar occurrences appear. At that point, I have been advised it is my complete right to decrease or stop exercise and that it is my obligation to inform the program personnel of my symptoms. I hereby state that I have been so advised and agree to inform the program personnel of my symptoms, should any develop.

I understand that, while I exercise, a trained observer will periodically monitor my performance and perhaps measure my pulse and blood pressure or assess my feelings of effort for the purposes of monitoring my progress. I also understand that the observer may reduce or stop my exercise program when any of these findings so indicate that this should be done for my safety and benefit.

2. Risks

I understand and have been informed that there exists the remote possibility during exercise of adverse changes including abnormal blood pressure, fainting, disorders of heart rhythm, and very rare instances of heart attack or even death. I have been told that every effort will be made to minimize these occurrences by proper staff assessment of my condition before each exercise session, by staff supervision during exercise, and by my own careful control of exercise efforts. I have also been informed that emergency equipment and personnel are readily available to deal with unusual situations should these occur. I understand that there is a risk of injury, heart attack, or even death as a result of my exercise, but knowing those risks, I desire to participate as herein indicated.

3. Benefits to be expected and alternatives available to exercise

I understand that this program may or may not benefit my physical fitness or general health. I recognize that involvement in the exercise sessions will allow me to learn proper ways to perform conditioning exercises, use fitness equipment, and regulate physical effort. These experiences should benefit me by indicating how my physical limitations may affect my ability to perform various physical activities. I further understand that if I closely follow the program instructions, I will likely improve my exercise capacity after a period of 3 to 6 months.

4. Confidentiality and use of information

I have been informed that the information obtained in this exercise program will be treated as privileged and confidential and will consequently not be released or revealed to any person without my express written consent. I do, however, agree to the use of any information that is not personally identifiable with me for research and statistical purposes so long as same does not identify me or provide facts that could lead to my identification. Any other information obtained, however, will be used only by the program staff in the course of prescribing exercise for me and evaluating my progress in the program.

5. Inquiries and freedom of consent

I have been given an opportunity to ask certain questions as to the procedures of this program. Generally these requests have been noted by the interviewing staff member, and his/her responses are as follows.

_____

_____

I further understand that there are also other remote risks that may be associated with this program. Despite the fact that a complete accounting of all these remote risks has not been provided to me, I still desire to participate.

I acknowledge that I have read this document in its entirety or that it has been read to me if I have been unable to read same.

I consent to the rendition of all services and procedures as explained herein by all program personnel.

Date _____   _____

                                                   Participant's signature

_____

Witness's signature

_____

Test supervisor's signature

Note.   The law varies from state to state. No form should be adopted or used by any program without individualized legal advice.

Reprinted from Herbert 1994.

Form 11

Express Assumption of Risk Form

I, the undersigned, hereby expressly and affirmatively state that I wish to participate in _____. I realize that my participation in this activity involves risks of injury, including but not limited to _____ (list) _____ and even the possibility of death. I also recognize that there are many other risks of injury, including serious disabling injuries, that may arise due to my participation in this activity and that it is not possible to specifically list each and every individual injury risk. However, knowing the material risks and appreciating, knowing, and reasonably anticipating that other injuries and even death are a possibility, I hereby expressly assume all of the delineated risks of injury, all other possible risk of injury, and even risk of death, which could occur by reason of my participation.

I have had an opportunity to ask questions. Any questions I have asked have been answered to my complete satisfaction. I subjectively understand the risks of my participation in this activity, and knowing and appreciating these risks I voluntarily choose to participate, assuming all risks of injury or even death due to my participation.

_____
Witness

Participant

Dated _____

Notes of questions and answers

_____

_____

_____

This is, as stated, a true and accurate record of what was asked and answered.

_____
Participant

To be checked by program staff

		Checked	Initials
I.	Risks were orally discussed.	_____	_____
II.	Questions were asked, and the participant indicated complete understanding of the risks.	_____	_____
III.	Questions were not asked, but an opportunity to ask questions was provided and the participant indicated complete understanding of the risks.	_____	_____

_____
Staff member

Dated _____

Note. The law varies from state to state. No form should be adopted or used by any program without individualized legal advice.

Reprinted from Herbert and Herbert 1993.

Form 12

Physician's Release for Exercise Form

Health Care Professional:

Dr. _____

Please REMIT TO:

_____

_____   Attn. FITNESS DIRECTOR:

_____   _____

PHYSICIAN'S RELEASE FOR EXERCISE

It is my understanding that _____ will be participating in a fitness evaluation and/or exercise program. I understand that aspects of the program include the following activities:

1.   A submaximal (bicycle ergometer) test.
      This test is used to estimate the member's maximal oxygen consumption ($\dot{V}O_2$ max). Blood pressure and pulse rate will be carefully monitored and the test will be terminated either by voluntary consent or by criteria established by the American College of Sports Medicine.

2.   Other physiological tests include:
      A.   Resting heart rate, resting blood pressure
      B.   Body composition (skinfolds)
      C.   Abdominal strength; sit-ups in one minute
      D.   Flexibility; sit and reach
      E.   Other _____

3.   Exercise program including:

      A.   Weights
      B.   Cardiovascular exercise
      C.   Other _____

As the individual's attending physician, I am not aware of any medical condition which would prevent him/her from participating in the exercises outline above.

Signed _____   Date _____

Note: If there are any contradictions to this fitness evaluation and exercise program, please list in the remaining spaces below.

_____

_____

_____

_____

Note.   Courtesy of East Side Athletic Club.

Form 13

Guest Agreement and Waiver
With Brief Medical History

Date ⎯⎯⎯⎯⎯

Name ⎯⎯⎯⎯⎯⎯⎯⎯⎯⎯⎯⎯⎯⎯⎯⎯⎯⎯⎯⎯⎯⎯⎯

Company name ⎯⎯⎯⎯⎯⎯⎯⎯⎯⎯⎯⎯⎯⎯⎯⎯⎯⎯⎯

Mailing address ⎯⎯⎯⎯⎯⎯⎯⎯⎯⎯⎯⎯⎯⎯⎯⎯⎯⎯

City ⎯⎯⎯⎯⎯⎯⎯⎯⎯⎯⎯⎯⎯⎯⎯ State ⎯⎯⎯⎯⎯⎯⎯ Zip ⎯⎯⎯⎯

Phone: (W) ⎯⎯⎯⎯⎯⎯⎯⎯⎯⎯⎯ (H) ⎯⎯⎯⎯⎯⎯⎯⎯⎯⎯⎯⎯

Guest of: ⎯⎯⎯⎯⎯⎯⎯⎯⎯⎯⎯⎯⎯⎯⎯⎯⎯⎯⎯⎯⎯

Please answer the following seven questions

YES	NO		
❏	❏	1.	Has your doctor ever said you have heart trouble?
❏	❏	2.	Do you frequently have pains in your heart and chest?
❏	❏	3.	Do you often feel faint or have spells of severe dizziness?
❏	❏	4.	Has a doctor ever said your blood pressure was too high?
❏	❏	5.	Has you doctor ever told you that you have a bone or joint problem such as arthritis that has been aggravated by exercise or might be made worse by exercise?
❏	❏	6.	Is there any good physical reason not mentioned here why you should not follow an activity program even if you wanted to?
❏	❏	7.	Are you over age 65 and not accustomed to vigorous exercise?

Guest Agreement/Waiver

The undersigned guest agrees to abide by the rules of the Club, including the completion of the above medical questionnaire.

The undersigned guest agrees that all use of the Club's facilities, services and programs shall be undertaken at his (her) sole risk and the Club shall not be liable for any injuries, accidents or deaths occurring to guest, arising either directly or indirectly out of utilizing the Club's facilities, services and programs. The guest, for himself (herself) and on behalf of his (her) executors, administrators, heirs and assigns, does hereby expressly release, discharge, waive, relinquish, and covenants not to sue Club, it officers and agents for all such claims, demands, injuries, damages or cause of action, with respect to use of the Club's facilities, programs and services.

The undersigned guest declares that they have completed the enclosed medical questionnaire as required by the Club and that they declare they are physically able to participate in physical activity. Furthermore, guest declares that the Club has advised guest to obtain a medical clearance in the event they answer yes to any of the medical history questions, or if they are unsure of their physical health and that guest maintains that he (she) is physically capable of pursuing physical activity in the Club without such steps being taken or has done so.

Guest signature ⎯⎯⎯⎯⎯⎯⎯⎯⎯⎯⎯⎯⎯⎯⎯⎯⎯⎯⎯

Date ⎯⎯⎯⎯⎯⎯⎯⎯⎯⎯⎯⎯⎯⎯⎯⎯⎯⎯⎯⎯⎯⎯

Form 14

Emergency Medical Authorization

I/we, the undersigned, am/are the father and mother of _____, minor(s).

Consent

I/we hereby give consent, in the event I/we cannot be contacted within a reasonable time, for (1) the administration of any treatment deemed necessary for my/our children by Dr. _____, or any of his/her associates, the preferred physician, or Dr. _____, or any of his/her associates, the preferred dentist, or in the event the appropriate preferred practitioner is not available, by another licensed, qualified physician or dentist; and (2) the transfer of any of my/our children to _____ Hospital, the preferred hospital, or any hospital reasonably accessible.

Major Surgery

This authorization does not cover nonemergency major surgery unless the medical opinions of two other licensed physicians or dentists concurring in the necessity for such surgery are obtained prior to the performance of such surgery and unless all reasonable attempts to contact me/us have been unsuccessful, defining such period for nonemergency surgery as 24 hours.

Medical Data

The following is needed by any hospital or practitioner not having access to my/our children's medical history:

Allergies: _____

Medication being taken: _____

Physical impairments: _____

Other pertinent facts to which physician should be alerted:

_____

Medical insurance coverage: _____

I/we, the undersigned parent(s), also do by these premises appoint and constitute _____ and _____ and/or _____ as temporary custodians of my/our children above mentioned, for the period of _____,19____, through and including_____, 19____, and do hereby authorize them to obtain any x-ray examination, anesthesia, medical or surgical diagnosis or treatment, and hospital care to be rendered to my/our children in our absence, under the general or special supervision, and on the advice of, a licensed physician, surgeon, anesthesiologist, dentist, or other qualified personnel acting under their supervision.

Witnesses

_____

_____

State of _____

SS:

_____ County

Note. The law varies from state to state. No form should be adopted or used by any program without individualized legal advice.

Reprinted from Herbert 1994.

Form 15
Fitness Evaluation Form

Date _____ / _____ / _____

Member name _____ Membership number _____

Member address _____ City _____ State _____ (Zip) _____ Member phone number

Physician's name _____

Physician's address _____ City _____ State _____ (Zip) _____ Physician's phone number

I. General physiological information   Birthdate _____ / _____ / _____
   1. Age _____ 2. Sex M☐ F☐ 3. Risk category _____ 4. Height _____ ft _____ in.
   5. Weight _____ 6. RHR _____ 7. RBP _____ 8. Predicted Max HR _____
   Medications _____
   Exercise history _____

II. Cardiovascular assessment
   1. RHR supine _____
   2. RBP supine _____
   3. RBP standing _____
   4. Predicted heart rate

      Max _____
      90% _____
      80% _____
      70% _____

   5. HVHR _____
   Protocol _____
   Equipment _____
   Max HR _____ Max BP ____/____
   Max met _____

Stage	Time	Speed KPM	Grade	HR	BP	DP	ST	Comments
1	1							
	2							
	3							
2	1							
	2							
	3							
3	1							
	2							
	3							
4	1							
	2							
	3							
5	1							
	2							
	3							
Rest	1							
	3							
	6							
	9							

III. Lung capacity
   1. Vital capacity ___/___ % Pred.
   2. FEV ___/___ % Pred.

IV. Flexibility
   1. Sit'n'reach ___ ___ ___ in.

V. Muscular strength and endurance
   1. Grip ___ / ___ / ___ KgR ___/___/___ KgL
   2. Trunk curl/sit-up _____ # _____ Time
   3. _____ _____

VI. Body composition
   A. Skin folds   1   2   Avg.
      1. Chest _____ _____ _____
      2. Subscapula _____ _____ _____
      3. Suprailliac _____ _____ _____
      4. Umbilical _____ _____ _____
      5. Tricep _____ _____ _____
      6. Ant. thigh _____ _____ _____
            Total skin folds _____

   B. Body fat
      1. Percent fat _____ %
      2. Fat wt. _____ lb
      3. Lean wt. _____ lb
      4. Ideal percent fat _____ %
      5. Ideal wt. _____ lb

   C. Girths
      1. Neck _____   6. Thigh ___ R ___ L
      2. Shoulder _____   7. Calf ___ R ___ L
      3. Chest _____   8. Bicep ___ R ___ L
      4. Waist _____   9. Forearm ___ R ___ L
      5. Hips _____

   VII. Blood chemistry
      1. Cholesterol _____
      2. Chol./HDL _____
      3. LDL/HDL _____
      4. Triglycerides _____
      5. Glucose _____
      6. Hematocrit _____

Note: RHR = resting heart rate; RBP = resting blood pressure; MET = unit of metabolic measurement; HVHR = hyperventilating heart rate; FEV = forced expiratory volume; HR = heart rate; BP = blood pressure; DP = double product; ST = S-T segment; KgR = kilogram right hand; KgL = kilogram left hand. The law varies from state to state. No form should be adopted or used by any program without individualized legal advice.

Reprinted from Club Corporation of America 1995.

Form 16

Fitness Integration Tracking Form

Member's name_____ Age _____ Acct.# _____ Acct. type _____

Consultation appt.   Date/time _____ Fit specialist _____ Coach _____

Reasons		Interests		
(check) (rank)		❏ lose body fat	❏ karate	❏ personal training
❏ Lose body fat _____		❏ weight training	❏ massage	❏ child care
❏ Stress release _____		❏ swimming	❏ water exerc. classes	❏ physical therapy
❏ Meet similar folk _____		❏ exerc. group classes	❏ fitness evaluation	❏ nutrition
❏ Family recreation _____		❏ youth activities	❏ swim lessons	❏ social events
❏ Strengthen/Tone _____		❏ racquetball	❏ sports leagues	❏ volleyball
❏ Self-esteem increase _____		❏ basketball	❏ fitness leagues	❏ _____
❏ Energy level increase _____		❏ sauna/steam	❏ jacuzzi	❏ _____
❏ _____ _____				

Success Plan

1. My MAIN objective is: _____

2. Why?_____

3. How will this accomplishment make you feel? _____

4. When would you like to accomplish this? _____

5. Why by then? _____

6. Baby Steps:_____

7. Will you need support in accomplishing these steps or changes? yes/no _____

   From whom? (family, training coach, social group, work peers, etc.) _____

8. What days of the week do you see yourself using the Club (circle) S   M   T   W   Th   F   S

9. Time of day?_____ # of Club visits per week? _____

10. Are #8 and #9 above realistic for you?   yes/no _____

11. If you consistently follow through on Baby Steps, how will you feel? _____

12. Do you foresee any potential obstacle or distractions? _____

13. How can I assist you in accomplishing your goals? _____

14. What type of coaching/support would benefit you most? _____

    _____

15. Notes:

Form 17

Cardiovascular Assessment Data Sheet

Name _____ Date _____ Age _____

Weight (kg) _____ Resting heart rate _____

Age-predicted max heart rate _____

60% _____ 65% _____ 70% _____ 90% _____

Mode of cardiovascular evaluation: bike RPMs _____, treadmill (please circle one)

I.   Warm-up workload: _____

    1 min _____   RPE _____

    2 min _____   BP _____

    3 min _____

    4 min _____

II. Target workload #1:   _____

    1 min _____   RPE _____

    2 min _____   BP _____

    3 min _____

    4 min _____

III. Target workload #2 (if indicated):   _____

    1 min _____   RPE _____

    2 min _____   BP _____

    3 min _____

    4 min _____

IV. Cool-down workload: _____

    1 min _____   RPE _____

    2 min _____   BP _____

V. $\dot{V}O_2$ max calculation conversion to METs: _____

    Predicted $\dot{V}O_2$ max (L/min)_____ × age factor_____ = maximum $\dot{V}O_2$ (L/min) _____

    $\dot{V}O_2$ max (ml/min)_____ – wt (kg)_____ = $\dot{V}O_2$max (ml/kg/min) _____

    $\dot{V}O_2$ max (ml/kg/min_____ – 3.5 = predicted maximal capacity in METs

VI. Summary

- Predicted maximal capacity (METs) _____
- Recommended training range (METs) _____
- Recommended training range (heart rate) _____

Note. BP = blood pressure; MET = unit of metabolic measurement; RPM = rotations per minute; RPE = rating of perceived exertion. The law varies from state to state. No form should be adopted or used by any program without individualized legal advice.

Reprinted from Fitcorp 1990.

Form 18

Release of Information Form

To whom it may concern:

Please be advised that (_____) and any member, associate, or designee of that firm are hereby authorized to inspect and copy or be furnished copies of any and all hospital, dental, or medical records of any sort as well as charts, notes, medical bills, dental bills, x-rays, lab reports, and prescriptions and are to be furnished any and all other information without limitations pertaining to any confinement, examination, treatment, or condition of myself, including medical, dental, psychological, or other treatment; examinations; or counseling for any medical, dental, or psychological condition.

This authorization shall be considered as continuing and you may rely on it in all respects unless you have previously been advised by me in writing to the contrary. It is expressly understood by the undersigned and you are hereby authorized to accept a copy or photocopy of this medical authorization with the same validity as though an original had been presented to you.

Dated this _____ day of _____, 19 ____ .

X _____

Note.   The law varies from state to state. No form should be adopted or used by any program without individualized legal advice.

Reprinted from Koeberle 1990.

Form 19

Progress Notes

Date _____

Physician _____

Member's name _____

Weight _____ Date of last program review _____

Medical history changes _____

_____

_____

_____

Exercise prescription _____

_____

_____

_____

_____

_____

Comments _____

_____

_____

_____

_____

Form 20

Incident Report Form

Date of accident _____   Time of accident _____

Member's name _____   Member number _____

Address _____

Home phone _____   Business phone _____

Location of accident _____

Staff attending

_____   _____

_____   _____

Witnesses (nonstaff)

_____   _____

_____   _____

Details of accident _____

_____

_____

_____

Action taken by staff _____

_____

_____

Staff reporting _____   Date _____

Department head's signature _____   Date _____

Form 21

Theft Report Form

Date of incident: _____   Time of incident: _____

Item reported missing: _____

Member's name: _____   Member #: _____

Address: _____

Home phone: _____   Business phone: _____

Location of incident: _____

Description of incident: _____

_____

_____

Witnesses: _____   _____

_____   _____

Reporting by: _____   Date and time: _____

Action taken: _____

_____

_____

_____

Supervisors's signature: _____   Date: _____

Form 22

Special Event Sign-Up Sheet

Event: _____   Location: _____

Date(s): _____   Time(s): _____

Staff responsible: _____

Member's name	Number	Member phone no.	Paid	Comments	Follow call
1.					
2.					
3.					
4.					
5.					
6.					
7.					
8.					
9.					
10.					
11.					
12.					
13.					
14.					
15.					
16.					
17.					
18.					
19.					
20.					
21.					
22.					
23.					
24.					
25.					
26.					
27.					
28.					
29.					
30.					

Form 23

Appointment Sheet

Time	Name/length	Member number	Phone number	CNL	Date	INT	CONF
8:00							
8:15							
8:30							
8:45							
9:00							
9:15							
9:30							
9:45							
10:00							
10:15							
10:30							
10:45							
11:00							
11:15							
11:30							
11:45							
12:00							
12:15							
12:30							
12:45							
1:00							
1:15							
1:30							
1:45							
2:00							
2:15							
2:30							
2:45							
3:00							
3:15							
3:30							
3:45							
4:00							
4:15							
4:30							
4:45							
5:00							
5:15							
5:30							
5:45							
6:00							
6:15							
6:30							
6:45							
7:00							
7:15							
7:30							
7:45							
8:00							
8:15							
8:30							

Day _____

Date ____/____

Therapist _____

Hours _____

Therapist _____

Hours _____

- Use Pencil
- Mark out 15 minutes before and after the appointment
- **Last appointments:**

  Mon-Thur 7:30 pm

  Fri 7:00 pm

  Sat 1:00 pm
- Remind gift certificate and coupon holders to bring them
- Remind clients of cancellation policy and check column that you did remind them

3-hour notice, or a cancellation fee of $10.00 will be charged

Appointments Confirmed

by _____

at _____

on _____

Form 24

Sample Exercise Card

Sex   M ☐   F ☐   Age _____

Resting Heart Rate _____   Resting Blood Pressure _____   Training Pulse _____

History _____

Example:

| wt / sets + reps |

Activity	Prescription								
Resting	H.R. _____ B.P. _____ /		/	/	/	/	/	/	/
Warm-up Exercises									
Seat Heights	1.								
	2.								
	3.								
	4.								
	5.								
	6.								
	7.								
	8.								
	9.								
	10.								
	11.								
	12.								
	13.								
	14.								
	15.								
	16.								
	17.								
	18.								
	19.								

Member name _____

Member number _____

Personal Fitness Motivator's Initials _____

Please see your motivator when finished with your card.

Form 25

Physical Activity Readiness Medical Exam Form
(PARmed-X)

The PARmed-X is a physical activity-specific checklist to be used by a physician with patients who have had positive responses to the Physical Activity Readiness Questionnaire (PAR-Q). In addition, the Conveyance/Referral Form in the PARmed-X can be used to convey clearance for physical activity participation, or to make a referral to a medically-supervised exercise program.

Regular physical activity is fun and healthy, and increasingly more people are starting to become more active every day. Being more active is very safe for most people. The PAR-Q by itself provides adequate screening for the majority of people. However, some individuals may require a medical evaluation and specific advice (exercise prescription) due to one or more positive responses to the PAR-Q.

Following the participant's evaluation by a physician, a physical activity plan should be devised in consultation with a physical activity professional (CSEP-Certified Fitness Appraiser). To assist in this, the following instructions are provided:

Page 1:   • Sections A, B, C, and D should be completed by the participant BEFORE the examination by the physician. The bottom section is to be completed by the examining physician.

Pages 2 & 3: • A checklist of medical conditions requiring special consideration and management.

This section to be completed by the participant

A PERSONAL INFORMATION:

Name _____

Address _____

_____

Telephone _____

Birthdate _____ Gender _____

Medical No. _____

B PAR-Q: *Please indicate the PAR-Q questions to which you answered YES*

❑   Q1. Heart condition
❑   Q2. Chest pain during activity
❑   Q3. Chest pain at rest
❑   Q4. Loss of balance, dizziness
❑   Q5. Bone or joint problem
❑   Q6. Blood pressure or heart drugs
❑   Q7. Other reason:

C RISK FACTORS FOR CARDIOVASCULAR DISEASE:
Check all that apply

❑ Less than 30 minutes of moderate physical activity most days of the week.

❑ Currently smoker (tobacco smoking 1 or more times per week).

❑ High blood pressure reported by physician after repeated measurements.

❑ High cholesterol level reported by physician.

❑ Excessive accumulation of fat around waist.

❑ Family history of heart disease.

Please note: *Many of these risk factors are modifiable. Please discuss with your physician.*

D PHYSICAL ACTIVITY INTENTIONS:

What physical activity do you intend to do?

_____

_____

_____

This section to be completed by the examining physician

Physical Exam:

Ht	Wt	BP i)	/
		BP ii)	/

Conditions limiting physical activity:

❑ Cardiovascular   ❑ Respiratory   ❑ Other

❑ Musculoskeletal   ❑ Abdominal

Tests required:

❑ ECG   ❑ Exercise test   ❑ X-Ray

❑ Blood   ❑ Urinalysis   ❑ Other

Physical Activity Readiness Conveyance/Referral:

Based upon a current review of health status, I recommend:

❑ No physical activity

❑ Progressive physical activity

❑ Only a medically-supervised exercise program until further medical clearance

    ❑ with avoidance of: _____
    ❑ with inclusion of: _____
    ❑ with Physical Therapy: _____

❑ Unrestricted physical activity —start slowly and build up gradually

Further information:
❑ Attached
❑ To be forwarded
❑ Available on request

Following is a checklist of medical conditions for which a degree of precaution and/or special advice should be considered for those who answered "YES" to one or more questions on the PAR-Q, and people over the age of 69. Conditions are grouped by system. Three categories of precautions are provided. Comments under Advice are general, since details and alternatives require clinical judgement in each individual instance.

	Absolute Contraindications	Relative Contraindications	Special Prescriptive Conditions	
	Permanent restriction or temporary restriction until condition is treated, stable, and/or past acute phase.	Highly variable. Value of exercise testing and/or program may exceed risk. Activity may be restricted. Desirable to maximize control of condition. Direct or indirect medical supervision or exercise program may be desirable.	Individualized prescriptive advice generally appropriate: • limitations imposed; and/or • special exercises prescribed. May require medical monitoring and/or initial supervision in exercise program.	**ADVICE**

Cardiovascular	❏ aortic aneurysm (dissecting)
	❏ aortic stenosis (severe)
	❏ congestive heart failure
	❏ crescendo angina
	❏ myocardial infarction (acute)
	❏ myocarditis (active or recent)
	❏ pulmonary or systemic embolism—acute
	❏ thrombophlebitis
	❏ ventricular tachycardia and other dangerous dysrhythmias (e.g., multi-focal ventricular activity)
		❏ aortic stenosis (moderate)
		❏ subaortic stenosis (severe)
		❏ marked cardiac enlargement
		❏ supraventricular dysrhythmias (uncontrolled or high rate)
		❏ ventricular ectopic activity (repetitive or frequent)
		❏ ventricular aneurysm
		❏ hypertension—untreated or uncontrolled severe (systemic or pulmonary)
		❏ hypertrophic cardiomyopathy
		❏ compensated congestive heart failure
			❏ aortic (or pulmonary) stenosis—mild angina pectoris and other manifestations of coronary insufficiency (e.g., post-acute infarct)
			❏ cyanotic heart disease
			❏ shunts (intermittent or fixed)
			❏ conduction disturbances
			  • complete AV block
			  • left BBB
			  • Wolff-Parkinson-White syndrome
			❏ dysrhythmias—controlled
			❏ fixed rate pacemakers
				• clinical exercise test may be warranted in selected cases, for specific determination of functional capacity and limitations and precautions (if any).
				• slow progression of exercise to levels based on test performance and individual tolerance.
				• consider individual need for initial conditioning program under medical supervision (indirect or direct).

			❏ intermittent claudication	progressive exercise to tolerance
			❏ hypertension: systolic 160-180; diastolic 105+	progressive exercise; care with medications (serum electrolytes; post-exercise syncope; etc.)
Infections	❏ acute infectious disease (regardless of etiology)	❏ subacute/chronic/recurrent infectious diseases (e.g., malaria, others)	❏ chronic infections ❏ HIV	variable as to condition
Metabolic		❏ uncontrolled metabolic disorders (diabetes mellitus, thyrotoxicosis, myxedema)	❏ renal, hepatic & other metabolic insufficiency	variable as to status
			❏ obesity ❏ single kidney	dietary moderation, and initial light exercises with slow progression (walking, swimming, cycling)
Pregnancy		❏ complicated pregnancy (e.g., toxemia, hemorrhage, incompetent cervix, etc.)	❏ advanced pregnancy (late 3rd trimester)	refer to the "PARmed-X for PREGNANCY"

References:

Arraix, G.A., Wigle, D.T., Mao, Y. (1992). Risk Assessment of Physical Activity and Physical Fitness in the Canada Health Survey Follow-Up Study. **J. Clin. Epidemiol. 45:4 419-428.**

Mottola, M., Wolfe, L.A. (1994). Active Living and Pregnancy, In: A. Quinney, L. Gauvin, T. Wall (eds), **Toward Active Living: Proceedings of the International Conference on Physical Activity, Fitness and Health.** Champaign, IL: Human Kinetics.

PAR-Q Validation Report, British Columbia Ministry of Health, 1978.

Thomas, S., Reading, J., Shephard, R.J. (1992). Revision of the Physical Activity Readiness Questionnaire (PAR-Q). **Can. J. Spt. Sci.** 17:4 338-345.

	Special Prescriptive Conditions	Advice
Lung	❑ chronic pulmonary disorders	special relaxation and breathing exercises
	❑ obstructive lung disease	breath control during endurance exercise to tolerance; avoid polluted air
	❑ asthma	
	❑ exercise-induced bronchospasm	avoid hyperventilation during exercise; avoid extremely cold conditions; warm up adequately; utilize appropriate medication
Musculoskeletal	❑ low back conditions (pathological, functional)	avoid or minimize exercise that precipitates or exacerbates (e.g., forced extreme flexion, extension, and violent twisting); correct posture, proper back exercises
	❑ arthritis—acute (infective, rheumatoid; gout)	treatment, plus judicious blend of rest, splinting, and gentle movement
	❑ arthritis—subacute	progressive increase of active exercise therapy
	❑ arthritis—chronic (osteoarthritis and above conditions)	maintenance of mobility and strength; non-weightbearing exercises to minimize joint trauma (e.g., cycling, aquatic activity, etc.)
	❑ orthopaedic	highly variable and individualized
	❑ hernia	minimize straining and isometrics; strengthen abdominal muscles
CNS	❑ convulsive disorder not completely controlled by medication	minimize or avoid exercise in hazardous environments and/or exercising alone (e.g., swimming, mountain climbing, etc.)
	❑ recent concussion	thorough examination if history of two concussions; review for discontinuation of contact sport if three concussions, depending on duration of unconsciousness, retrograde amnesia, persistent headaches, and other objective evidence of cerebral damage
Blood	❑ anemia—severe (< 10 Gm/dl)	control preferred; exercise as tolerated
	❑ electrolyte disturbances	
Medications	❑ antianginal ❑ antiarrhythmic ❑ antihypertensive ❑ anticonvulsant ❑ beta-blockers ❑ digitalis preparations ❑ diuretics ❑ ganglionic blockers ❑ others	NOTE: consider underlying condition. Potential for: exertional syncope, electrolyte imbalance, bradycardia, dysrhythmias, impaired coordinations and reaction time, heat intolerance. May alter resting and exercise ECG's and exercise test performance.
Other	❑ post-exercise syncope	moderate program
	❑ heat intolerance	prolong cool-down with light activities; avoid exercise in extreme heat
	❑ temporary minor illness	postpone until recovered
	❑ cancer	if potential metastases, test by cycle ergometry, consider non-weight bearing exercises; exercise at lower end of prescriptive range (40-65% of heart rate reserve), depending on condition and recent treatment (radiation, chemotherapy); monitor hemoglobin and lymphocyte counts; add dynamic lifting exercises to strengthen muscles, using machines rather than weights.

* Refer to special publications for elaboration as required
Reprinted from the Canadian Society for Exercise Physiology, Inc., 1995.

Form 26

Emergency Procedures Sheet

In the event that an emergency should occur and no medical personnel are present, the following guidelines should be followed:

1. A staff person should identify him or herself as a professional rescuer trained in emergency care. This helps to reassure the victim and bystanders. If the victim is conscious, legally we must ask permission to assist the victim. (The law assumes that an unconscious person would give consent.) A senior staff person should stay with the individual at all times. He or she should attempt to reassure the person and protect the individual from personal bodily harm. Senior staff person will assume control of the situation and issue further orders as needed.

2. A second staff member will call 911 and give the following information:

   A. Phone number of location

   B. Title of location (building name, address, specific suite or room number)

   C. Site-specific entrance instructions for ambulance driver

   D. Brief description of the problem. If it is a definite cardiac event, i.e., respiratory arrest - CPR is in progress, an Advanced Life Support unit will be sent. If it is non–life-threatening, i.e., seizures, a Basic Life Support unit will be sent.

   E. After 911 has been called, a staff member will notify building security (list phone #), put elevator on hold (if applicable), and wait in the lobby to meet the ambulance at the main entrance to escort them to the emergency.

3. The individual should be monitored at all times. This will include:

   A. Checking a heart rate, noting the regularity and strength of each heart beat.

   B. Monitoring and recording blood pressure.

   C. Observing skin color and breathing pattern.

   D. Maintaining open airway.

   E. Establishing unresponsiveness and initiating CPR when appropriate.

   F. Before the individual is transported (if unconscious) give the EMT's as much information as possible regarding individual's:

   > Name, age, medical considerations, (folder, if possible) and
   > home phone emergency numbers. The attending physician and
   > the hospital will make the call to the family.

4. Once the individual is transported, the senior staff person in charge should:

   A. Notify the individual's work place so that the employer can decide how to handle the family.

   B. Assume responsibility for personal belongings and valuables. Please remember that it is important to respect the individual's privacy. Be as brief as possible when disclosing the information pertinent to the event.

   C. Fill out an accident report and file one copy in the member's folder, and one copy with the Center Director.

C   The Americans With Disabilities Act (ADA) As It Applies to Health/ Fitness Facilities

On July 26, 1990, the Americans With Disabilities Act (ADA) was signed and enacted into law. The ADA is a landmark civil rights law that was designed to further the goal of full participation in American society by people with disabilities. A critical part of the ADA involves the fact that places of public accommodation must provide access to their facilities and programs to *all* persons, including those with disabilities, unless exclusion or limitation of activity is necessary for safety considerations. Therefore the ADA mandates that most health/fitness facilities must provide equal access to both nondisabled and disabled individuals.

In 1991, the issue of how public places of accommodation (including health/fitness facilities) must afford disabled individuals access to and egress from all areas in a building, including all public accommodations such as drinking fountains, bathrooms, telephones, and so on, was greatly clarified with the enactment and publication of ADA Accessibility Guidelines for Buildings and Facilities (ADA-AGBF). These guidelines provide specific information regarding how health/fitness facilities must be designed and constructed (and, in some instances, existing buildings modified) so that they are readily accessible to individuals with disabilities.

Because by law all health/fitness facilities must conform to applicable local, state, and federal codes of design and access/admissions regarding access for individuals with disabilities, as specified by the ADA-AGBF, facilities must take every reasonable step to ensure that they are in full compliance with applicable laws. One of the first steps that a facility can undertake to conform to the law is to obtain information on the ADA-AGBF. Such information is readily available from both governmental agencies and private concerns. Among the most commonly recommended sources are the following:

Governmental Agencies

- Architectural and Transportation Barriers Compliance Board
  1111-18th St. NW, Ste. 501
  Washington, DC 20036-3894
  800-USA-ABLE (voice/TDD)

Sets guidelines adopted as accessibility standards under Titles II and III of the ADA. Provides information on technical and scoping requirements for accessibility and offers general technical assistance on the removal of architectural, transportation, communication, and attitudinal barriers affecting people with disabilities. Publications: *ADA*

Accessibility Guidelines for Buildings and Facilities; ADA Accessibility Guidelines for Transportation Vehicles; ADA Accessibility Guidelines for Transportation Facilities; manuals on ADA accessibility guidelines for transportation vehicles; ADA Accessibility Guidelines Checklist for buildings and facilities; Uniform Federal Accessibility Standards Accessibility Checklist; design bulletin series explaining various provisions of ADA Accessibility Guidelines for Buildings and Facilities; booklets and guides on barrier-free design, accessible rest rooms, wheelchair lifts and slip-resistant surfaces, transit facility designs, assistive listening devices, visual alarms, airport TDD access, and air carrier policies affecting people with disabilities.

- Centers for Independent Living Program*
  Rehabilitation Services Administration
  U.S. Department of Education
  Mary E. Switzer Building
  330 C St. SW
  Washington, DC 20202

*Many states offer state-level offices of the Centers for Independent Living Program.

Approximately 400 Independent Living Centers, most funded by this program, provide local services and programs to enable individuals with severe disabilities to live and function independently. Centers offer individuals with disabilities a variety of services, including independent living skills training, counseling and advocacy services on income benefits and legal rights, information and referral, peer counseling, education and training, housing assistance, transportation, equipment and adaptive aid loans, personal care attendants, and vocational and employment services. Assistance available to employers includes accessibility surveys; job analyses; advice on job accommodations, job modifications, and assistive devices; recruitment; job training; job placement and support services; and information and referral to specialized technical assistance resources.

Private Organizations

- Barrier Free Environments, Inc.
  P.O. Box 30634
  Highway 70 West-Watergarden
  Raleigh, NC 27622
  919-782-7823 (voice/TDD)

Provides consultation and technical assistance on accessibility design at all stages of construction planning or product development. Conducts on-site accessibility surveys, product evaluations, and work-site modifications and provides cost-effective accommodation and barrier-removal solutions. Offers seminars, workshops, and publications on accessible and universal design and information on design standards for all national and federal legislation mandating building and program accessibility.

- Mainstream, Inc.
  3 Bethesda Metro Center, Ste. 830
  Bethesda, MD 20814
  301-654-2400 (voice/TDD) or 301-654-2401 (voice/TDD)

Provides on-site accessibility surveys and job analyses and offers advice on cost-effective accommodations for people with disabilities. Offers publications on several relevant topics, including accessibility checklists, architectural barriers, and workplace accommodations.

- National Center for Access Unlimited
  155 N. Wacker Dr., Ste. 315
  Chicago, IL 60606
  312-368-0380 ext. 49 (voice) or 312-368-0179 (TDD)

Provides consultation, education, information, training, and technical assistance to business, industry, and nonprofit agencies on meeting ADA requirements for accessible work environments for people with disabilities. Develops accessibility checklists, inspects existing and future work sites, and conducts plan reviews for identifying physical and structural barriers. Offers practical ideas for immediate, low-cost accessibility improvements. Offers consultation on overcoming communication and transportation barriers. Provides training on ADA requirements, accessibility solutions, and attitudinal training.

Once a health/fitness facility has obtained sufficient information on the ADA-AGBF, the next step is to identify how these guidelines apply to the facility. For discussion purposes, at least seven facility-related factors are affected by the requirements of the ADA-AGBF: entrances and exterior areas; floor surfaces; stairs, ramps, and elevators; wall fixtures; toilets, lockers, and showers; emergency warning systems; and assistive learning systems. A number of examples of how the ADA-AGBF can apply to each of these factors follow.

Entrances and Exterior Areas

- A facility must provide free and unobstructed access to and egress from a particular area or location for pedestrians and wheelchair users. This requirement refers to all pathways, which may consist of internal walkways and external sidewalks, curb ramps, pedestrian ramps, lobbies, corridors, elevators, activity areas, rest-room facilities, or any combination of these.
- At least one accessible route must be provided within the boundaries of the facility's property that connects parking and public transportation stops with the facility's entrance.
- If the access entrance for individuals with disabilities is located out of the major path of travel, the access door should be automatic. Automatic doors with independent and separate two-level push plates are recommended.
- At least one door at each accessible entrance to the facility must be designed in accordance with the ADA-AGBF. In addition, at least one door at each accessible space within the facility must comply with this act.
- All doors must have a minimum width of 32 inches for accessibility.
- Lever hardware must be provided on all accessible doors.
- All hardware on doors must be mounted at 36 inches maximum to the centerline from the floor.
- A wheelchair access symbol must be mounted on all accessible doors.
- Door-mounted door stops or panic bolts must not be installed in the toe-strike zone.
- Doors with closures must be set with 8 1/2 pounds or less of pressure for exterior doors and 5 pounds or less for interior doors.
- Fire doors must not exceed 15 pounds of pressure.
- The appropriate signage denoting accessible parking spaces and building entrances must be provided. This requirement includes signage located at the facility's main entrance that provides directions to all accessible entrances for people with disabilities.

- If passenger loading zones are provided, they must have an access pathway that is 60 inches wide and 20 feet long, adjacent and parallel to the vehicle space.
- All parking spaces for people with disabilities must be located as near as possible to entrances that are accessible to these people.
- A minimum of 1 parking space per 25 of the total number of spaces available must be for individuals with disabilities. Each parking space set aside for people with disabilities must be at least 96 inches wide and provide an adjacent 60-inch-wide access pathway.
- The slope of any parking space for people with disabilities must not exceed one-quarter inch per foot of parking space in any direction.
- All parking structures must have ceiling clearances of a least eight feet for parking spaces for people with disabilities.
- Signage indicating which parking spaces are for the exclusive use of people with disabilities must be posted.

Floor Surfaces

- Floors within a facility must be at a common level throughout (no more than one-quarter inch variance) or must be accessible (connected) by pedestrian ramps, passenger elevators, or special access lifts.
- The maximum height for carpet tile or carpet is one-half inch. In addition, all carpet edges must be fastened to the floor.

Stairs, Ramps, and Elevators

- All activity areas (e.g., weight rooms, exercise classrooms, gymnasiums, courts, and swimming pools) and support areas (e.g., pro shop, food and beverage areas, offices, and sports medicine areas) must be accessible to people with disabilities. An accessible pathway at least 36 inches wide must be provided in all activity areas.
- All steps, stairs, and ramps must be stable, firm, and slip resistant. For interior stairs, the top and bottom stairstep (tread) must be marked by a strip of contrasting color. For exterior steps, every step should be marked with a strip of contrasting color.
- Stairs must have continuous-grasp (1 1/4 to 2 inches in diameter) handrails located on both sides of the stairs. These handrails must be 30 to 34 inches in height. If handrails are not continuous, they must extend 12 inches at the top of the stairs and 12 inches plus a tread width (the width of a stairstep) at the bottom of the stairs.
- Stairs must have uniform riser heights and tread widths.
- Access ramps must be designed to accommodate individuals with disabilities.
- Ramps must be provided on external and internal pathways where there is more than a one-half-inch vertical change in floor elevation.
- Ramps must have slip-resistant surfaces that are stable and firm.
- Ramps must have landing areas of at least 60 inches by 60 inches.
- Ramps must not have slopes greater than 1:12, although a slope of 1:16 may be the most appropriate slope for a club environment.

- Ramp handrails must be continuous grasp, 1 1/4 to 2 inches in diameter, and 30 to 34 inches in height and must be provided wherever the ramp has a rise greater than 6 inches.
- Whenever possible, ramps should be installed instead of wheelchair lifts. Ramps are usable by everyone, whereas lifts are not. If alternate means of access are not otherwise available, a wheelchair lift should be put in a facility.
- If installed, a wheelchair lift should be located on major paths of travel.
- If wheelchair lifts are installed, they should have automatic doors and buttons that don't require constant pressure.
- Button heights for any wheelchair lift should be the same as for elevators.
- A wheelchair lift should not go higher than five feet.
- Keys should be required on all unenclosed wheelchair lifts.
- Appropriate signage should be posted for all wheelchair lifts. For example, a sign explaining the location of the key for a lift should be posted in a conspicuous location.
- One passenger elevator must be provided in facilities with more than one floor, and the elevator must serve all floors.
- All elevators in a facility must accommodate wheelchair users.
- Call buttons in the hallway or in elevator lobbies must be mounted at 42 inches above the floor and must be located away from corners.
- All floor buttons inside the elevator must be located away from the corners. These buttons must be mounted horizontally (instead of vertically) on the side panels at the lowest allowable height (35 inches to the lowest button and 48 inches at the highest point is required). All buttons must be raised and at least three-quarters inch in diameter.
- Elevator key locations must be designated by signage.
- The entrance to the elevator must have a minimum width of 36 inches.

Wall Fixtures

- At least 50 percent of all drinking fountains or water coolers provided on each floor of the facility must be in accordance with the ADA-AGBF regarding access for people with disabilities.
- Electrical-cooler water fountains should be installed in the facility as opposed to manual drinking fountains. In the electrical type, a person applies pressure to a button or similar element, whereas in the manual type, a person must turn a handle, which is a more difficult task.
- Telephones must be accessible to people with disabilities. This can be facilitated by mounting the telephones at a height of 48 inches from the center of the coin slot to the finished floor. At least one public phone in the facility must provide a telecommunications device for the deaf (TDD).
- All light and control switches must be located at a maximum height of 36 inches above the finished floor.
- All objects protruding from walls (e.g., cabinets and shelves) must comply with the ADA-AGBF.

Toilets, Lockers, and Showers

- Single-accommodation toilet facilities must have sufficient space in the toilet area (room) for a wheelchair (measuring 30 inches wide by 48 inches long) to enter the room and permit the door to close. A minimum turning radius of five feet in the toilet area must be provided for adequate wheelchair maneuverability.
- Designated toilet facilities must be user-friendly for individuals with disabilities.
- At least one water closet must be 60 inches wide for wheelchair access and another must be at least 36 inches wide with grab bars.
- Accessibility signage must be posted on doors.
- Bathroom doors must swing outward to a minimum of 32 inches of clear opening.
- Lever hardware must be placed on both sides of the door.
- Urinals must be 17 inches high.
- Flush valves must be located on the open side of toilet stalls for people with disabilities.
- Lavatories must have space for maneuverability to permit access by people with disabilities.
- Lavatories must be 34 inches maximum in height, 29 inches maximum height to the bottom of the apron from the finished floor.
- All hot water and drain pipes under lavatories must be insulated.
- The faucet-control mixing valve must be operable with one hand. Lever-operated, push-type, and electronically controlled mechanisms are the recommended, acceptable designs for lavatory valves.
- The force to operate the controls of lavatories must require no more than five pounds of pressure.
- The faucet controls and operating mechanisms of lavatories must not require grasping, pinching, or twisting to operate.
- Towel and soap dispensers must be located on a side wall or clear area, not above or between sinks, and should be placed at a height no greater than 36 inches from the floor.
- Lockers must be made accessible to people with disabilities. A path of access not less than 36 inches wide should be provided to these lockers.
- Appropriate signage indicating which lockers are accessible to people with disabilities should be posted in a conspicuous location in the locker room.
- Showers must be made accessible to people with disabilities. Following are design considerations.
- Showers must be at least 36 inches wide and 36 inches deep and must provide an outside clearance of at least 36 by 48 inches.
- Grab bars must be strategically placed adjacent to a reasonable number of showers.
- At least one shower unit must have a handheld apparatus consisting of a hose 60 inches long mounted 48 inches above the floor, or at least one unit must have two shower heads, one 40 inches above the shower floor and the other set at standard height.
- If the unit includes two shower heads, both shower heads must operate independently and have both vertical and horizontal swivel angle adjustments.

- If the unit includes two shower heads, the lower shower head must have a mixing valve operable with one hand.
- Appropriate signage must be posted.

Emergency Warning Systems

- Emergency warning systems, if provided, must include both audible alarms and visual alarms, in accordance with the ADA-AGBF (1991).
- The center of the alarm-initiating device (box) on manual alarm stations must be located at a height not greater than 48 inches above the level of the floor or other surface.

Assistive Listening Systems

- A facility must provide a permanent assistive listening system in any facility area that will be used for meetings or banquets where more than 50 people are present.

D Climbing-Wall Areas

Rock climbing is a relatively new program activity that an increasing number of health/fitness facilities offer to their members. It is conducted on a climbing wall, an affixed vertical surface that can be scaled by those who choose to participate in this sport. Although most climbing walls are typically indoor structures, some health/fitness facilities have installed them in outdoor areas adjacent to the facilities.

The relative newness of rock climbing and the level of skills necessary to participate in this activity raise several safety issues that should be addressed to ensure that the sport is conducted in a safe, appropriate manner. Although data (i.e., risk statistics) that could help better define safety-related issues pertaining to rock climbing are not readily available due to the newness of the activity, some safety steps have been identified, including requiring participants to engage in preactivity training, using belaying systems, supervising the climbing wall at all times that the wall is in use, placing an absorbent floor covering in the area immediately adjacent to the wall, and identifying and adopting procedures to handle special emergencies.

Health/fitness facilities that either offer or are contemplating offering a rock-climbing program should consider the following list of issues and possible concerns when designing, developing, and operating such a program. (Note: In order to lend organization and structure to the list, the various points are grouped into four broad areas: programming, staffing, safety, and facilities and equipment.)

Programming

- Focus of programming efforts. Recommendation: All activity programming for a climbing-wall area should take into account the unique characteristics of the individuals who will be using the area.
- Types of programming. Recommendation: A regularly scheduled program of both structured and unstructured activities for the climbing-wall area that is appropriate for the needs, interests, and goals of the facility's users should be offered.

Staffing

- Level of on-site supervision. Recommendation: The climbing-wall area should be supervised at all times by staff to ensure that all activities are being conducted according to guidelines established by the facility.
- Qualifications of staff. Recommendation: Staff should be relatively proficient in climbing-wall techniques and have the ability to teach those techniques to users; staff should have basic first-aid and CPR certification.

- Ratio of staff to users. Recommendation: The ratio of users to supervisory staff should not exceed reasonable levels; as a general rule, when relatively untrained users are utilizing the climbing wall, there should be at least one supervisor per six children or 12 adults; when trained climbers are utilizing the climbing wall, a reasonable level of supervision would involve one staff member per 10 children or 20 adults.

Safety

- Safety guidelines and policies. Recommendation: A comprehensive set of safety guidelines and policies for the climbing wall should be developed and posted in a conspicuous place.
- Staff training. Recommendation: All staff assigned supervisory responsibility for the climbing wall should be fully knowledgeable of the rules and regulations for using the wall and should be trained (and periodically retrained) in the skills and techniques involved in using the wall.
- User training. Recommendation: All individuals who wish to use the wall should undergo basic introductory training in climbing and should demonstrate a minimal level of proficiency in at least the following climbing skills: belaying techniques, rope-handling skills, and climbing signals.
- Belaying. Recommendation: While climbing, all users should be belayed except when on the warm-up wall. The ropes that are connected to the climber should be enclosed at the ceiling and controlled by an individual who belays on the floor.
- Risk management. Recommendation: All holds—devices affixed to the wall that are used by the climber's hands and feet to scale the wall—should be checked periodically to ensure that they are securely connected. All holds should be cleaned periodically. All equipment used in the climbing-wall area should be inspected on a regular basis and promptly replaced or repaired if found defective or in a state of disrepair. The floor area in front of the climbing wall should be cleaned on a regular basis.

Facilities and Equipment

- Equipment requirements. Recommendation: The climbing-wall area should be adequately equipped and furnished to meet the material requirements for all activities scheduled to be conducted in the area; for example, nylon ropes, carabiners (lightweight metal clips that climbers use for a variety of functions while climbing), and harnesses should be furnished. Any equipment not provided by the facility should be approved for use by staff.
- Space requirements. Recommendation: The climbing-wall area should be allotted space sufficient for the activities that will be conducted in the area. A space 15 to 20 feet high by 15 to 20 feet wide with 6 to 10 feet of floor space in front of the wall is the suggested minimum area required. As a relative guideline, the climbing wall space should be approximately the size of a racquetball/handball court.

- Warm-up wall. Recommendation: The climbing-wall area should include a warm-up climbing wall in addition to the primary climbing wall to provide users with a means to practice and perform various climbing skills at a low level of intensity prior to using the primary climbing wall. If a climbing-wall area has a warm-up climbing wall, the warm-up wall must have a clearly defined or indicated system that limits the distance a climber's feet may travel from the floor. A maximum distance of four feet is recommended. Typically, a line is painted across the warm-up climbing wall at a height of four feet, the point beyond which no climber may ascend.

- Climbing harnesses. Recommendation: All climbing harnesses used in the climbing-wall area should be designed and manufactured specifically for climbing.

- Carabiners: Recommendation: All carabiners should be capable of sustaining at least a 2,000-kilogram dynamic force.

- Belay bars. Recommendation: All belay devices should be manufacturer tested and friction based. In addition, all belay bars (both top anchor and bottom anchor) should be engineer tested and approved for minimum load-bearing standards. The top-anchor belay bar should be capable of bearing at least 2,500 kilograms of static load force, whereas the bottom-anchor belay bar should be capable of sustaining at least 1,000 kilograms of static load force. All belay bars should also be securely connected. The top-anchor belay bar (which provides a secure anchor above the climber for the climber's rope) is commonly connected using 1-1/2-inch by 1/4-inch steel stock brackets that are attached to structural members behind the climbing wall. The bottom-anchor belay bar (which secures the belay to the floor) is commonly connected to the floor with 1/2-inch by 3-inch expansion bolts if the subfloor is concrete. If the subfloor is wood, the bottom anchor is usually connected through one lug bolted to a structural member beneath the wood.

- Component holds. Recommendation: The design and placement of the holds should be appropriate to the activities planned for the wall. In general, the only design limitation for holds appears to be the manufacturer's imagination. All component holds on the wall should be fastened to the wall per manufacturer's instructions. In general, most holds are bolted to a T-nut behind the wall through a hole in the wall.

- Climbing ropes. Recommendation: All climbing ropes used in a climbing-wall area should be static ropes, certified by the Union Internationale Association of Alpinists (UIAA).

- Surface area of the climbing wall. Recommendation: The surface area of all climbing walls should have a moderately abrasive texture with a high degree of durability. Currently, climbing walls and wall components are constructed from a wide variety of materials (e.g., fiberglass, plastics, birch, steel, concrete, and plywood).

- Floor surface adjacent to the climbing wall. Recommendation: The floor surface adjacent to the climbing wall should be well padded to a distance of at least six inches from the bottom edge of the wall.

- Illumination requirements. Recommendation: An indoor climbing-wall area should have an appropriate source and level of light. Mercury vapor or fluorescent lights are commonly used. The illumination level should be at least 50 foot-candles at the surface of the floor.

E Bibliography

Allen, E. *Fundamentals of building construction: materials and methods.* 2nd ed. New York: Wiley; 1990.

Alston, F.K. *Caring for other people's children: a complete guide to family day care.* New York: Teachers College Press; 1992.

American College of Sport Medicine. *ACSM's guidelines for exercise testing and prescription.* 5th ed. Philadelphia: Lea & Febiger; 1995.

American Lung Association. *Indoor air pollution: an introduction for health professionals.* Shipping list No. 96-0027-P. New York: American Lung Association; 1995.

Americans With Disabilities Act (ADA) Accessibility Guidelines for Buildings and Facilities; Final Guidelines, 56 FED. REG. 35,408 (1993)(to be codified at 36 C.F.R. § 1911)

Asfahl, C.R. *Industrial safety and health management.* Englewood Cliffs, NJ: Prentice Hall; 1990.

Bauer, E.G.; Pinegar, R.D. *The primer for playground safety.* Grinnell, IA: Ashley Scott and Associates; 1987.

Berg, R. Fitness testing can screen out trouble. *Athletic Business* 9(12): 18-22; 1985.

Berg, R. New looks in locker rooms. *Athletic Business* 13(4): 40; 1989.

Bortz, W.M. *Dare to be 100.* New York: Simon and Schuster; 1996.

Boyce, P.R. *Human factors in lighting.* London: Applied Science; 1981.

Brauer, R.L. *Facilities planning.* 2nd ed. New York: American Management Association; 1992.

Brzyck, M. Safety in the weight room. *Athletic Business* 12(1): 30-36; 1988.

Club Corporation of America. *Club Corporation of America standards for design, construction, equipping and remodeling of an athletic club and athletic facility* (unpublished manual). Dallas; 1996. For more information write Steve Tharrett, 3030 LBJ Freeway, Suite 600, Dallas, TX 75234.

Club Corporation of America. *Club Corporation of America standards for operating an athletic club and athletic facility* (unpublished manual). Dallas; 1996. For more information write Steve Tharrett, 030 LBJ Freeway, Suite 600, Dallas, TX 75234.

Consumer Product Safety Commission. *Handbook for public playgrounds.* Vols. 1 and 2. Washington, DC: Consumer Product Safety Commission; 1981.

Dale, J.R. The physiology of floors. *Fitness management* 4(8): 32-33; 1988.

DeChiara, J.; Callendar, J.H. *Time-saver standards for building types.* 3rd ed. New York: McGraw-Hill; 1990.

DeChiara, J.; Koppleman, L.E. *Planning design criteria.* New York: McGraw-Hill; 1978.

Department of Labor, OSHA. *Occupational exposure to bloodborne pathogens.* (29 CFR Part 1910.1030). Washington, DC: Dept. of Labor, OSHA; 1992.

Doggett, L.; George, J. *All kids count: child care and the ADA act.* Washington, DC: GPO, 1993.

Dreyfuss, H. *Designing for people.* New York: Paragraphic Goods; 1967.

Edelson, E. *Clean air.* New York: Chelsea House; 1992.

Fanger, P.O. *Thermal comfort: analysis and applications in environmental engineering.* New York: McGraw-Hill; 1973.

Farren, C.E. *Planning and managing interior projects.* Kingston, MA: R.S. Means; 1988.

Frederickson, D. Space and program development. *Phys. Ther.* 50: 1179-1186; 1970.

Gay, F. *Air pollution.* New York: Franklin Watts; 1991.

Gutman, B. *Recreation can be risky.* New York: Twenty-First Century Books; 1996.

Havrella, R. *Heating, ventilating and air conditioning fundamentals.* 2nd ed. Englewood Cliffs, NJ: Prentice Hall; 1995.

Helms, R.M. *Lighting for energy-efficient luminous environments.* Englewood Cliffs, NJ: Prentice Hall; 1991.

Herbert, D.L. *Legal aspects of sports medicine.* 2nd ed. Canton, OH: Professional Reports Corporation; 1994.

Herbert, D.L.; Herbert, W.G. *Legal aspects of preventative, rehabilitative, and recreational exercise programs.* 3rd ed. Canton, OH: Professional reports Corporation; 1993.

Hiserman, M.A., ed. *Access requirements* (unpublished handbook). Berkeley: Physical Resources Office, University of California; 1990.

Hoke, J.R. *Architectural graphic standards.* 8th ed. New York: Wiley; 1988.

Hollander, C. *How to build a sauna.* New York: Drake; 1978.

Hopf, P.S. *Designer's guide to OSHA.* New York: McGraw-Hill; 1975.

The how-to's of tennis court dimensions and measurements. *Club Industry* 6(12):46; 1990.

Hunsaker, J.; Counsilman, D. Keeping pools and spas safe, sanitary. *Athletic Business* 8(12): 46-47; 1984.

Isernhagen, S.J., ed. *Work injury: management and prevention.* Rockville, MD: Aspen Publishers; 1988.

Izard, R.M., Jr. Treatment setting or service station. *American Archives of Rehabilitation Therapy* 31(2): 6-8; 1983.

Jones, T.L. *The ADA: a review of best practices.* New York: American Management Association; 1993.

Kamm, D. Integrated light and color makes positive contribution to patient rehabilitation. *Contract* 27(2): 116-119; 1985.

Kelly, R.B. *Industrial emergency preparedness.* New York: Van Nostrand Reinhold; 1989.

Kelly, T.M.; Foster, C.; Maier, T.; Glueckstein, J.; Tristani, F.; Keelan, M.H. *How to choose a health club.* Milwaukee: American Heart Association of Wisconsin; 1988.

Kingsbury, D.F.; Vogler, S.K.; Bener, C. *The everyday guide to opening and operating a child care center.* Denver: Vade Mecum Press; 1990.

Koeberle, B. *Legal aspects of personal fitness training.* Canton, OH: Professional Reports Corporation; 1990.

Kroemer, K.H.E.; Kroemer, H.B.; Kroemer-Elbert, K.E. *Ergonomics: how to design for ease and efficiency.* Englewood Cliffs, NJ: Prentice Hall; 1994.

Lahue, K.C. *Interior lighting.* San Ramon, CA: Ortho Books; 1991.

Lang, V.P. *Principles of air conditioning.* 4th ed. Albany, NY: Delmar; 1987.

Lavoie, H.R. Anatomy of a locker room. *Athletic Business* 11(4): 96-102; 1987.

Lechner, N. *Heating, cooling, lighting: design method for architects.* New York: Wiley; 1991.

Lloyd, C. Emergency medical response is a facility responsibility. *Athletic business* 8(5): 34-41; 1984.

MacLeod, D. *The ergonomic edge: improving safety, quality and productivity.* New York: Van Nostrand Reinhold; 1995.

McCormick, E.J. *Human factors in engineering and design.* New York: McGraw-Hill; 1976.

McLendon, C.B.; Blackistone, M. *Signage: graphic communications in the built world.* New York: McGraw-Hill; 1982.

Merritt, F.S., editor-in-chief. *Building design and construction handbook.* 4th ed. New York: McGraw-Hill; 1982.

Micheli, L.F. Pediatric and adolescent sports injuries. *Exerc. Sport Sci. Rev.* 14: 349-351; 1986.

Moses, K. *It's a child's world.* Minot, ND: North American Heritage Press; 1989.

National Spa and Pool Institute. *Minimum standards for public spas.* Washington, DC: National Spa and Pool Institute; 1978.

Neuberger, D. How to avoid common errors in pool design. *Athletic business* 8(10): 86-90; 1984.

Olson, J. Safety standards for athletic and physical education facilities, equipment and practices. *Athletic Business* 5(9): 48-52; 1981.

Olson, R. Safety standards for aquatic facilities. *Athletic Business* 5(3): 49-51; 1981.

Osborne, D.A. *Ergonomics at work: human factors in design and development,* 3rd ed. New York: Wiley; 1995.

Packard, R.T.; Kliment, S.A. *Architectural graphic standards.* Student ed. Abridged from the 7th ed. New York: Wiley; 1989.

Panero, J.; Zelnik, M. *Human dimensions and interior space: a source book of design reference standards.* New York: Watson-Gaptill; 1979.

Paten, D. Keep safety in mind when building a sauna. *Athletic Business* 4(5): 36-38; 1980.

Patton, R.W.; Gratham, W.C.; Gerson, R.F.; Gettman, L.R. *Developing and managing health fitness facilities.* Champaign, IL.: Human Kinetics; 1989.

Peltz, D. Options for child care facilities. *Club Industry* 7(1): 45; 1990.

Penman, K.A. Construction and maintenance of racquetball courts. *Athletic Business* 3(5): 30-32; 1979.

Penman, K.A. How to properly plan locker rooms, showers, storage and laundry areas. *Athletic Business* 4(8): 34-39; 1980.

Penman, K.A. Upgrading your locker, shower, and laundry facilities. *Athletic Business* 7(4): 16-20; 1983.

Peterson, J.; Bryant, C. *The fitness handbook.* 2nd ed. Champaign, IL: Sagamore Publishers, Inc.; 1995.

Pierce, J.R. *Symbols, signals and noise: the process of communication.* New York: Harper and Brothers; 1961.

Pool chemistry primer. *Club Industry* 6(12): 48; 1990.

Price, R.W. Strength equipment maintenance. *Fitness Management* 6(6): 30; 1990.

Putsep, E.P. The consequences of designing for the disabled in general hospitals. *World Hosp. Fed.* **18**: 51-53; 1982.

Puzio, H.; Johnson, J. *Practical heating, ventilation, air conditioning and refrigeration.* Albany, NY: Delmar; 1996.

Ramsey, C.G.; Sleeper, H.R. *Architectural graphic standards.* 8th ed.New York: Wiley; 1988.

Ritzer, J. Designing the optimum aerobics studio. *Club Industry* **6**(10): 49; 1990.

Ritzer, J. Ten steps to follow when building/remodeling locker rooms. *Club Industry* **6**(7): 20; 1990.

Schley, M.K.; ed. *Cad layer guidelines: recommended designations for architecture, engineering, and facility management computer-aided design.* Washington, DC: American Institute for Architects Press; 1990.

Schmid, S. Accident proof fitness centers. *Athletic Business* **12**(7): 52-55; 1988.

Seaward, B.L.; Snelling, A. Essential qualities of a health promotion professional. *Fitness management* **6**(3): 80-84; 1990.

Sorcar, P.C. *Architectural lighting for commercial interiors.* New York: Wiley; 1987.

Tanruther, W.J. Shedding some light on sports lighting. *Athletic Business* **10**(3): 87-90; 1986.

Tregenza, P. *The design of interior circulation: people and buildings.* New York: Van Nostrand Reinhold; 1976.

Turiel, I. *Indoor air quality and human health.* Stanford, CA: Stanford University Press; 1985.

U.C. Berkeley Wellness Letter, editors. *The new wellness encyclopedia.* Boston: Houghton Mifflin; 1995.

Ullman, S.G. Assessment of facility quality and its relationship to facility size in the long-term health care industry. *The Gerontologist* **21**(1): 91-97; 1981.

UMDNJ—Robertwood Johnson Medical School. *Health and safety in small industry. A practical guide for managers.* Chelsea, MI: Lewis; 1989.

U.S. Department of Labor. *Occupational health hazards: their evaluation and control;* Bulletin 198; 1968.

U.S. Equal Employment Opportunity Commission: U.S. Dept. of Justice. *Americans with disabilities act handbook.* GPO Stock #052-015-00074-0. Washington, DC: U.S. Equal Employment Opportunity Commission; 1992.

VanGelder, N.; Marks, S., eds. *Aerobic dance exercise instructor manual.* San Diego: International Dance Exercise Association Foundation; 1987.

Williams, M.R.; Russell, M.L. *ADA handbook: employment and construction issues affecting your business.* Chicago: Real Estate Education; 1993.

Woodward, K.L. *Sign design and layout.* Cincinnati: Signs of the Times; 1983.

F Trade and Professional Associations for Fitness, Health, and Related Recreational Concerns

The organizations listed in this appendix can assist facility managers in creating exercise programming, understanding and achieving qualifications, training staff, continuing staff education, and keeping abreast of current data and trends of the fitness world.

Aerobics and Fitness Association
of America
15250 Ventura Blvd., Ste. 200
Sherman Oaks, CA 91403
818-905-0040

American Association of Cardiovascular
and Pulmonary Rehabilitation
7611 Elmwood Ave., Ste. 201
Middletown, WI 53562
608-831-6989

American Alliance for Health, Physical
Education, Recreation and Dance
1900 Association Dr.
Reston, VA 20191
703-476-3400

American College of Sports Medicine
P.O. Box 1440
Indianapolis, IN 46206-1440
317-637-9200

American Council on Exercise
5820 Oberlin Dr., Ste. 102
San Diego, CA 92121
619-535-8227

American Heart Association
7320 Greenville Ave.
Dallas, TX 75231
214-373-6300

American Massage Therapy Association
820 Davis Street, Ste. 100
Evanston, IL 60201-4444
847-864-0123

Association for Worksite Health Promotion
60 Revere Dr., Ste. 500
Northbrook, IL 60062
847-480-9574

International Council for Health, Physical
Education and Recreation
1900 Association Dr.
Reston, VA 20191
703-476-3471

IDEA (International Association of Fitness
Professionals)
6190 Cornerstone Court East, Ste. 204
San Diego, CA 92121
800-999-IDEA

International Health, Racquet and
Sportclub Association (IHRSA)
263 Summer St.
Boston, MA 02210
617-951-0055

National Athletic Trainers Association
and Certification Board, Inc.
2952 Stemmons Freeway
Dallas, TX 75247
214-637-6282

National Employee Services and
Recreation Association
2211 York Rd., Ste. 207
Oak Brook, IL 60521-2371
708-368-1280

National Institute for Occupational Safety
and Health—Division of Safety Research
1095 Willowdale Rd.
Morgantown, WV 26505
304-285-5894

National Strength and Conditioning Association
916 O St.
Lincoln, NE 68508
402-472-3000

National Swimming Pool Foundation
P.O. Box 495
Merrick, NY 11566
516-623-3447

National Wellness Institute
P.O. Box 827
Stevens Point, WI 54481
715-342-2969

President's Council on Physical
Fitness and Sports
701 Pennsylvania Ave. West, Ste. 250
Washington, DC 20004
202-272-3421

Sporting Goods Manufacturers Association
200 Castlewood Dr.
North Palm Beach, FL 33408
407-842-4100

U.S. Squash Racquets Association
P.O. Box 1216
Bala Cynwyd, PA 19004
610-667-4006

Wellness Councils of America
Community Health Plaza, Ste. 311
1701 Newport Ave.
Omaha, NE 68152-2175
402-572-3590

G About the American College of Sports Medicine

What ACSM Is All About

The American College of Sports Medicine's more than 16,000 members in almost 60 countries are dedicated to improving the quality of life for people around the world.

ACSM's Mission Statement reflects this goal. "The American College of Sports Medicine promotes and integrates scientific research, education, and practical applications of sports medicine and exercise science to maintain and enhance physical performance, fitness, health, and quality of life."

ACSM was established in 1954 in Madison, Wisconsin. Since that time, our members have applied their knowledge, training, and dedication in sports medicine and exercise science to promote healthier lifestyles for people around the globe. In 1984, the National Center was relocated to Indianapolis, Indiana, and our strong heritage, combined with our visionary approach to the future, means ACSM continues to grow and prosper both nationally and internationally.

Working in a wide range of medical specialties, allied health professions, and scientific disciplines, our members are committed to the diagnosis, treatment, and prevention of sports-related injuries and the advancement of the science of exercise.

Our members' diversity and expertise makes ACSM the largest, most respected sports medicine and exercise science organization in the world. From astronauts to athletes, from people with chronic diseases to physical challenges, ACSM continues to look for and find better methods to allow everyone to live longer and more productively. Healthier people make a healthier society.

Membership: Our Greatest Resource

What started with a group of only 11 physicians, physiologists, and educators back in 1954 has evolved into a diversified, professional association, comprising more than 16,000 members in more than 50 different professions today. These many and varied professions are divided into three main categories: basic and applied science, education and allied health, and medicine.

ACSM also is committed to developing students into exceptional professionals. Students are the foundation of the future. The importance of student members is exemplified by their presence on ACSM's Board of Trustees with an elected student Trustee. There is a student newsletter available on ACSM's Home Page to facilitate the needs of the student members.

ACSM offers five types of new memberships:

- Professional
- Professional-in-Training

- Graduate Student
- Undergraduate Student
- Associate

ACSM offers the status of "Fellow" to those who meet the required standards.

Member Benefits: ACSM members in the "Professional," "Professional-in-Training," "Graduate Student," and "Undergraduate Student" categories receive subscriptions to ACSM's monthly scientific journal, *Medicine and Science in Sports and Exercise* (MSSE); ACSM's quarterly newsmagazine, *Sports Medicine Bulletin* (SMB); the *ACSM Membership Directory;* and the annual review of current research topics in exercise science found in *Exercise and Sport Sciences Reviews* (ESSR). "Associate" members receive SMB and the membership directory. All ACSM members enjoy discounts on rental cars, meeting registration fees, certification examinations, and other products and services. In addition, they have the opportunity to purchase the best liability insurance policy available today.

ACSM Interest Groups

These groups provide a forum for focused discussion, activity, debate, and networking among members with similar interests. In addition, interest groups allow members to network on a more formal basis. Each recognized interest group works toward fulfilling the mission of the College.

Regional Chapter Membership

Twelve regional chapters broaden the base of participation and encourage networking at the grassroots level for members, as well as provide valuable professional growth for student members. Local concerns are addressed through annual regional chapter scientific meetings and publications.

Mailing Address: P.O. Box 1440
Indianapolis, IN 46206-1440 USA

Street Address: 401 West Michigan Street
Indianapolis, IN 46202-3233 USA

Telephone: (317) 637-9200   Fax: (317) 634-7817

Internet address: http://www.acsm.org/sportsmed

ACSM Certifications for Health/Fitness Professionals

More than 20 years ago, the American College of Sports Medicine identified a goal of increasing the competency of individuals involved in health and fitness and in cardiovascular rehabilitative exercise programs. With increased public awareness of the benefits of exercise, the College also saw the importance of consumers' being able to recognize professional competence.

With the publication of the ACSM's first edition of *Guidelines for Exercise Testing and Prescription*, the College was able to set the standards and objectives for its Clinical Track certifications. Since 1975, more than 6,000 individuals have been certified in one or more of the Clinical Track's three levels. At the height of the health and fitness awakening in the early 1980s, ACSM introduced its Health and Fitness Track certifications for those working with healthy individuals. In only 15 years, more than 11,000 health/fitness professionals have been certified by ACSM.

In 1996 ACSM established the Certification Resource Center (CRC), which can be reached by calling 1-800-486-5643. In its first year the CRC fielded more than 30,000 calls from individuals interested in ACSM certifications. The CRC is a one-stop resource for ACSM certification information, workshop dates, study packets, as well as for a complete line of certification review, reference, and resource materials.

ACSM Certification is available to any professional in the preventive and rehabilitative exercise field who meets the established prerequisites. Each of the six progressive levels of ACSM Certification requires you to pass a written exam that tests knowledge and a practical exam that measures hands-on skills. Many educational workshops, taught by ACSM-member experts, are offered, but are not required, to earn certification.

Clinical Track Certifications

ACSM Program Director$_{SM}$

ACSM Exercise Specialist$_{SM}$

ACSM Exercise Test Technologist$_{SM}$

These particular levels recognize competence of personnel working in clinical exercise programs for individuals with cardiovascular, pulmonary, and metabolic diseases. Most individuals with ACSM clinical certifications are found in cardiac rehabilitation programs.

Health and Fitness Track Certifications

ACSM Health/Fitness Director_®

ACSM Health/Fitness Instructor_{SM}

ACSM Exercise Leader_{SM}

These three progressive levels of certification are targeted to professionals who work with those apparently healthy individuals who have no history of disease or who have controlled disease. ACSM health/fitness personnel can be found in corporate fitness centers, fitness clubs, wellness programs, and the like.

Certifications of Enhanced Qualification

ACSM has expanded the education and certification opportunities available to those certified at the Exercise Specialist level and the Health/Fitness Instructor level or above with the Certification of Enhanced Qualification (CEQ). The procedure to qualify for the CEQ involves a one-day workshop followed by a one-hour exam. The workshop consists of five or six lectures presented by experts in the topic areas. There is no practicum section. ACSM's first CEQs focused on the "Advanced Personal Trainer" and "Exercise and the Older Adult."

The primary objective of the CEQ workshops is to present selected topics that are relevant to professionals in clinical exercise and applied fitness. These topics focus on a subject and provide the latest research as well as information about applied skills. Exercise professionals are emerging as key players in the continuum of health care, and it is critical that they be prepared to work with all populations. The CEQ is a vehicle that ACSM has created to advance the training to meet these expanded roles in health care. Through the CEQ and other educational opportunities, ACSM is solidifying its position as the preeminent exercise science and sports medicine organization.

After Certification

Once certification has been earned, you will be reviewed every four years to ensure that your competence and the ACSM's high level of standards are maintained. You will be required to document continuing education credits (CECs) or continuing education units (CEUs) and to maintain a current CPR certification. CEQs are good for four years and must be repeated to be maintained. ACSM is developing a new CEQ each year.

For information about workshop and certification dates and sites, recommended study material, and applications for registration, please call ACSM's Certification Resource Center at 1-800-486-5643.

Index

A

ACLS (Advanced Cardiac Life Support) 25, 39
acoustical guidelines 119-120
    exercise classrooms 46, 47, 120
    fitness floors 53, 120
    gymnasiums 56, 58, 119, 120
    pool areas 70, 119, 120
ACSM. *See* American College of Sports Medicine
ACSM's Guidelines for Exercise Testing and Prescription 38, 43, 44, 49, 81
ADA (Americans With Disabilities Act) 7, 10, 185-191
Advanced Cardiac Life Support (ACLS) 25, 39
aerobics coordinator 8
aerobics studios 8, 20, 119. *See also* exercise classrooms
air circulation
    basic guidelines 17
    in specific areas (*see* environment)
alarm systems, emergency 191
American College of Sports Medicine (ACSM)
    certification by 23
    exercise programming recommendations 38, 43, 44, 49, 50, 81
American Heart Association 25, 30
Americans With Disabilities Act (ADA) 7, 10, 185-191
Appointment Sheet (form) 179
aquatics areas. *See* pool and aquatics areas
aquatics directors 8
assistive listening systems 191
assumption of risk 7, 28, 50, 167

B

back care programs 39
badminton courts 57, 126
ball fields 75, 76, 77, 78, 143
baseball fields. *See* ball fields
Basic Life Support 5, 25, 30
basketball courts 56, 57, 122, 124
beauty salon services 26, 105, 106
blood, guidelines for handling incidents involving 31, 33
blood pressure screening 39
BSL (Basic Life Support) 5, 25, 30
building construction. *See* design, of facilities
bulletin boards 20, 84

C

cardiovascular areas. *See also* fitness floors
    equipment 52, 114-115
    noise guidelines 119
    signage 20, 111
Cardiovascular Assessment Data Sheet 173
cardiovascular incidents
    emergency procedures 37 (*see also* emergency procedures)
    equipment for dealing with 40
    risk during exercise testing 37
    screening for risk of 27-28, 37, 38-39, 173
carpeting. *See* floor surfaces
Centers for Disease Control (CDC) 31, 50

certification and licensing. *See also* Basic Life Support; CPR
    documentation of 33
    general standards and guidelines 8, 23, 24, 26
    specific area staff 8, 25, 37, 57, 68
chemicals
    hazard communication program 116
    in laundry room 91
    storage 33-34, 135-136
    for water treatment 34, 72, 73, 106, 135-136
child-care areas and playrooms 9-10, 101-103, 119, 120
children. *See* child-care areas and playrooms; youth services
cholesterol screening 39
climbing-wall areas 193-195
clocks
    nonactivity areas 96
    program activity areas 58, 61, 63, 71, 82
    specialty areas 106
communication systems 17, 31-32. *See also* signage
    hazard communication program 116
confidentiality 41
    Release of Information Form 174
construction standards. *See* design, of facilities
Consumer Products Safety Commission 76
continuing education 26
control desk 89-90, 119
coronary risk, screening for 27-28, 37, 38-39, 173
court sports areas. *See also specific types of courts*
    basic standards and guidelines 59-65
    court dimensions and markings 60, 124-131
    enclosed 61, 62-63
    equipment 61, 63, 64
    indoor 61, 64-65, 132
    lighting 61, 63, 64, 65, 122, 132, 133, 134
    noise guidelines 119, 120
    open 61, 64
    outdoor 61, 65, 133, 134
    safety 60, 76
    signage 20, 111
CPR (cardiopulmonary resuscitation)
    classes in 39
    guidelines for use of 30
    staff certification 5, 8, 24, 25, 39, 193

D

design, of facilities
    child-care areas 102-103
    climbing-wall areas 194-195
    control desk 90
    court sports areas 60-65
    exercise classrooms 45-46
    fitness floors 51-53
    fitness-testing/health promotion/wellness areas 40
    gymnasiums 56-57, 58
    laundry rooms 92-93
    locker rooms 96-97
    outdoor recreational areas 77-80
    playgrounds 76, 77, 79-80
    pool areas 69-73, 142

design, of facilities *(continued)*
  running tracks 82-84
  spa areas 107-108
DIN (Deutsches Institut für Normung) floor standards 123
directors 8, 24
diving pools and platforms 69, 70, 139
documentation, of emergency plan and incidents
  basic standards and guidelines 5, 30, 31, 33
  Emergency Procedures Sheet 184
  Incident Report Form 176
doors, ADA requirements 187. *See also* entrances and exits
drills, emergency 33
drinking fountains 17, 79, 189

E

electrical safety 16, 69, 92, 102
electrocardiograms (ECGs) 39
elevators 189
Emergency Medical Authorization Form 170
emergency plan
  basic standards and guidelines 3, 5, 29-30
  documentation of 33
  drills 33
  signage 32
emergency procedures. *See also* emergency plan
  basic standards and guidelines 3, 5-6, 29-34
  Emergency Medical Authorization Form 170
  Emergency Procedures Sheet 184
  Incident Report Form 176
  signage 20, 31-32
  staffing concerns 5, 24, 25-26, 30-31
Emergency Procedures Sheet 184
emergency warning systems 191
entrances and exits
  ADA requirements 187
  child-care areas 102
  court sports areas 60, 63
  pools 71
  signage 20, 187
environment (temperature, humidity, air circulation)
  child-care areas 102-103
  court sports areas 63, 64
  exercise classrooms 46-47
  fitness floors 53
  fitness testing/health promotion/wellness areas 40
  gymnasiums 58
  nonactivity areas 90, 92-93, 97
  pool areas 72
  running tracks 83
  spa areas 16, 106, 107, 108
equipment
  basic safety guidelines 16-17
  cardiovascular areas 52, 114-115
  child-care areas 102, 103
  climbing-wall areas 194-195
  control desk 90
  court sports areas 61, 63, 64
  exercise classrooms 46
  fitness floors 51, 52-53, 113
  fitness testing/health promotion/wellness areas 40, 41
  gymnasiums 58
  laundry rooms 92, 93
  lifesaving 68, 70, 71, 135
  maintenance schedules 17, 77, 92, 113-115
  massage area 107
  outdoor recreational areas 78
  out of order signage 112
  playgrounds 76, 77, 79, 80, 145
  pool areas 68, 70, 71

protective 56, 60
running tracks 82
signage with 16, 112
executive director 24
Exercise Card (sample form) 180
exercise classrooms 20, 43-47, 120
exercise testing. *See* fitness evaluation/testing
exits. *See* entrances and exits

F

facility, defined 4
filtering and filter rooms, for pools 69, 70, 72, 135-136
first-aid kit 32, 33, 148
first-aid training 24, 26, 193
fitness director 8
fitness evaluation/testing. *See also* screening
  basic standards and guidelines 27-28, 37-41
  forms 171-173
  informed consent for 28, 163-164
fitness floors 49-53. *See also* cardiovascular areas; free-weight
  areas; resistance-training areas
  noise guidelines 53, 120
  signage 20, 51, 111-112
  staffing 8, 49, 50
Fitness Integration Tracking Form 172
floor surfaces
  ADA requirements 188
  child-care areas 103
  climbing-wall areas 195
  court sports areas 62
  DIN standards 123
  exercise classrooms 46
  fitness floors 52
  fitness testing/health promotion/wellness areas 40
  general safety guidelines 14
  gymnasiums 57
  laundry rooms 93
free-weight areas. *See also* fitness floors
  equipment 53
  noise guidelines 119
  signage 20, 112

G

grounds (external areas) 13-14, 87-88. *See also* outdoor recreational areas; parking
guard rooms 135
guests
  Agreement and Waiver With Brief Medical History Form
    169
  health history questionnaire form 155-156
gymnasiums
  basic standards and guidelines 55-58
  noise guidelines 56, 58, 119, 120
  signage 20

H

handball courts 60, 63, 127
Handbook for Public Playgrounds (Consumer Products Safety
  Commission) 76
Hazard Communication Standard 116
hazardous materials. *See* chemicals
health history questionnaires
  basic standards and guidelines 6, 27
  for children in child care 101
  form (guest) 155-156, 169
  form (member) 153-154
health promotion areas 37-41
Heimlich maneuver 30. *See also* Basic Life Support
humidity

basic guidelines 16
in specific areas (*see* environment)

I

illumination. *See* lighting
incident reports
    basic standards and guidelines 30, 31, 33
    form 176
informed consent
    basic standards and guidelines 28
    forms 160-166
instructors/leaders 24

L

laundry rooms 91-93, 119
laws and regulations. *See also* Americans With Disabilities
    Act (ADA)
    on fitness testing/health promotion/wellness staff 37
    general standards and guidelines 4, 10
    on incidents involving blood 31
    on outdoor recreational areas 75, 76
    on parking 88, 187-188
    on pool areas 9, 67
licensing. *See* certification and licensing
lifeguard rooms 135
lifeguards 9, 25, 68, 70
lifesaving certification 8
lifesaving equipment 68, 70, 71, 135
lighting
    ADA requirements for switches 189
    ball fields 77, 78
    basketball courts 122
    child-care areas 103
    climbing-wall areas 195
    court sports areas 61, 63, 64, 65, 122, 132, 133, 134
    exercise classrooms 47
    fitness floors 53
    fitness testing/health promotion/wellness areas 40
    general indoor guidelines 15, 122
    grounds 13, 88, 110
    gymnasiums 58
    nonactivity areas 90, 93, 97
    outdoor recreational and activity areas 77-78, 84, 110, 133,
        134
    playgrounds 79
    pool areas 73
    running tracks 83, 84
    spa areas 107
    switches 63, 189
    tennis courts 122, 132, 133, 134
locker rooms 95-97
    ADA requirements 190-191
    noise guidelines 119, 120
    in pool areas 70, 136
    safety 95-96, 136
    signage 20, 190, 191

M

manager 24
massage services 105, 106, 107, 119
medical clearance (physician's approval)
    basic standards and guidelines 6, 28, 39
    forms 157, 158, 168, 181-183
medical history. *See* health history questionnaires
medical liaison 25
Medical Waste Tracking Act of 1988 31
member, defined 4
message boards 20
multipurpose recreation areas. *See* gymnasiums

N

noise guidelines. *See* acoustical guidelines
nutrition programs 25, 38, 39

O

Occupational Safety and Health Administration (OSHA) 10,
    31, 88, 116
offices, noise guidelines for 119, 120
officials, for competitions 57, 76
organizational chart 117
organizational structure 118
OSHA (Occupational Safety and Health Administration) 10,
    31, 88, 116
outdoor recreational areas 75-80
    court sports areas 61, 65, 133, 134
    lighting 77-78, 84, 110, 133, 134
    running tracks 146
overflow systems, pool 69, 72, 140-141

P

paddle tennis courts
    dimensions and markings 60, 64, 130
    fencing 65
    surface 60-61
parking 26, 88, 187-188
PARmed-X (Physical Activity Readiness Medical Exam Form)
    181-183
PAR-Q and You 6, 27
    form 152
passenger loading zones 188
peer review group 149-150
Physical Activity Readiness Medical Exam Form (PARmed-
    X) 181-183
Physical Activity Readiness Questionnaire (PAR-Q) and You
    6, 27
    form 152
physical therapy areas 25, 119, 120
physicians. *See also* medical clearance
    fitness testing by 39
    as medical liaison 25
Physician's Approval Form 158
Physician's Release for Exercise Form 168
Physician's Statement and Clearance Form 157
platform tennis courts
    dimensions and markings 60, 64, 130
    fencing 65
    surfaces 61
    teaching area 60
playgrounds 79-80
    equipment 76, 77, 79, 80, 145
    safety 76-77
playrooms. *See* child-care areas and playrooms
policies. *See* rules and policies
pool and aquatics areas 67-73
    chemical storage and treatment 34, 72, 73, 135-136
    cleaning 69
    dimensions and markings 69, 137, 138
    diving pools and platforms 69, 70, 139
    equipment 68, 70, 71
    filtering and filter rooms 69, 70, 72, 135-136
    lighting 73
    locker rooms 70, 136
    noise guidelines 70, 119, 120
    overflow systems 69, 72, 140-141
    safety 34, 67, 68-69, 135-136
    signage 9, 20, 68-69, 111, 112
    sources for construction standards 142

pool and aquatics areas *(continued)*
    staffing 8, 9, 25, 68
    water temperature 71, 72, 112
programming
    ball fields 75
    climbing-wall areas 193
    court sports areas 59
    exercise classrooms 43-45
    fitness floors 49-50
    fitness-testing/health promotion/wellness areas 37-39
    gymnasiums 55
    outdoor recreational areas 75
    pool areas 67-68
    running tracks 81
    spa areas 105
Progress Notes form 175
pro shop areas, noise guidelines for 119
public address systems 17

R

racquetball courts
    dimensions and markings 60, 127
    equipment 63
    floor surfaces 62
    noise guidelines 119
    signage 111
ramps, ADA requirements for 188-189
regulations. *See* laws and regulations
Release of Information Form 174
release of liability 28, 159
resistance-training areas. *See also* fitness floors
    design 53
    equipment 52, 113
    noise guidelines 119
    signage 20, 111
rest rooms 78, 79, 102, 190
risk management 34. *See also* screening
rules and policies
    cardiovascular areas 111
    child-care areas 101
    court sports areas 60, 111
    exercise classrooms 44
    fitness floors 111-112
    free-weight areas 112
    gymnasiums 56
    laundry room 91
    outdoor recreational areas 76, 77
    playgrounds 76
    pool areas 111
    racquetball courts 111
    resistance-training areas 111
    running tracks 81, 83
    saunas 111
    signage 19, 20, 76, 77, 83, 111-112
    steam rooms 111
    treadmills 112
    whirlpools 112
running tracks 81-84
    dimensions and markings 82, 83, 84, 146, 147
    440-yard 147
    indoor 83-84, 119
    noise guidelines 119
    outdoor 83, 84, 146

S

safety. *See also* emergency procedures; screening
    ball fields 76, 77
    basic physical plant guidelines 13-17
    child-care areas 101-102

climbing-wall areas 193, 194
control desk 90
court sports areas 60, 76
electrical 16, 69, 92, 102
exercise classrooms 45
fitness floor 51
fitness testing/health promotion/wellness areas 40
grounds 87, 88
gymnasiums 56
laundry room 91
locker rooms 95-96, 136
outdoor recreational areas 76-77
playgrounds 76-77
pool areas 34, 67, 68-69, 135-136
protective equipment 56, 60
running tracks 81-82, 83
signage 4, 8-9, 19, 20, 31-32, 51, 68-69, 76, 83
spa areas 16, 105, 106-107
staffing concerns 5, 24, 25-26, 30-31
salon services 26, 105, 106
saunas
    facilities design 107, 108
    safety 16, 106-107
    signage 8-9, 20, 111
    staffing 106
schedules
    equipment maintenance 17, 77, 92, 113-115
    for program activity areas 43, 55, 59, 68, 81
screening. *See also* fitness evaluation/testing
    basic standards and guidelines 4, 6-7, 27-28
    control desk role in 90
    for coronary risk 27-28, 37, 38-39, 173
    forms 152-158
    for specific activity programs 43, 50
security, for pool areas 68
sharp objects 16
showers 96, 107, 190-191
signage
    ADA requirements 187, 188, 189, 190, 191
    basic guidelines 4, 15, 19-22
    chemical storage 34
    court sports areas 20, 111
    elevators 189
    emergency information on 20, 31-32
    entrances and exits 20, 187
    with equipment 16, 112
    exercise classrooms 20
    fitness floor 20, 51, 111-112
    grounds 13, 14
    gymnasiums 20
    locker rooms 20, 190, 191
    outdoor recreational areas 76
    parking and loading areas 187, 188
    pool and aquatics areas 9, 20, 68-69, 111, 112
    rules and policies 19, 20, 76, 77, 83, 111-112
    safety 4, 8-9, 19, 20, 31-32, 51, 68-69, 76, 83
    samples 111-112
    spa areas 8-9, 20, 111, 112
    about staff 20
    wheelchair lifts 189
smoking cessation programs 38, 39
soccer fields
    design 78
    dimensions and markings 144
    lighting 77
    programming 75
softball fields. *See* ball fields
spa areas 105-108. *See also* saunas; steam rooms; whirlpools
    chemical storage 34

massage services 105, 106, 107, 119
    safety 16, 105, 106-107
    salon services 26, 105, 106
    signage 8-9, 20, 111, 112
    staffing 26, 106
space requirements. *See* design, of facilities
Special Event Sign-Up Sheet (form) 178
squash courts
    dimensions and markings 60, 128
    equipment 63
    floor surfaces 62
    noise guidelines 119
staff. *See also* certification and licensing
    basic guidelines 23-26
    basic qualifications 4, 7-8, 23
    child-care areas 9-10, 102
    climbing-wall areas 193-194
    control desk 90
    court sports areas 60
    directors 8, 24
    emergency procedures and 5, 24, 25-26, 30-31
    exercise classrooms 45
    fitness floors 8, 49, 50
    fitness testing/health promotion/wellness areas 37, 39
    gymnasiums 56
    laundry room 91
    locker rooms 95
    organizational chart 117
    organizational structure 118
    outdoor recreational areas 75-76
    parking attendants 26
    physical therapy 25
    pool areas 8, 9, 25, 68
    running tracks 81
    signage identifying 20
    spa areas 26, 106
    youth services 9-10
stairs, ADA requirements for 188
steam rooms
    facilities design 107, 108
    safety 16, 106-107
    signage 8-9, 20, 111
    staffing 106
storage areas
    for chemicals 33-34, 135-136
    court sports areas 61
    gymnasiums 58
    noise guidelines 119
    outdoor recreational areas 79
    pool areas 71, 135-136
stress management programs 39
support staff 24-25

T

telephones 17, 32, 189
temperature
    effect on performance 121
    general safety guidelines 16
    pool water 71, 72, 112
    of specific areas (*see* environment)
tennis courts. *See also* paddle tennis courts; platform tennis
    courts
    dimensions and markings 60, 129, 130, 131
    equipment 64
    indoor 119, 132
    lighting 122, 132, 133, 134
    noise guidelines 119
    outdoor 65, 133, 134

safety 60
    surfaces 60-61
Theft Report Form 177
toilets 78, 79, 102, 190
tracks. *See* running tracks
treadmill signage 111

U

users, defined 4

V

valet parking 26
volleyball courts
    design/dimensions and markings 78, 125
    gymnasium design for 57
    lighting 77, 78
    outdoor 75, 76, 77, 78
    safety 76

W

waivers 28, 50
    form for guest use 169
walkways
    ADA regulations 187
    outdoor safety guidelines 13-14, 88
    in specific areas 64, 71, 79, 88
wall fixtures, ADA requirements for 189
water fountains 17, 79, 189
water treatment 34, 72, 73, 106, 135-136
weight management programs 25
wellness areas 37-41
wheelchair lifts 189
whirlpools
    facilities design 107
    safety 16, 106-107
    signage 8-9, 20, 112
    staffing 106

Y

youth services 4, 9-10. *See also* child-care areas and playrooms

More great books for health/fitness professionals

ACSM's **Exercise Management for Persons with Chronic Diseases and Disabilities**

AMERICAN COLLEGE OF SPORTS MEDICINE

1997 • Cloth • 280 pp • Item BACS0798 • ISBN 0-87322-798-0
$39.00 ($58.50 Canadian)

Clear, concise guidance for developing exercise programs for individuals with special health considerations. This one-of-a-kind book provides an excellent framework for clinical exercise personnel, health club personnel, personal trainers, and others who work with persons with disabilities, chronic diseases, or multiple conditions.

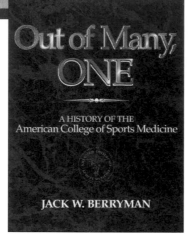

Out of Many, ONE

A HISTORY OF THE
American College of Sports Medicine

JACK W. BERRYMAN

1995 • Cloth • 424 pp • Item BACS0815
ISBN 0–87322–815–4 • $25.00 ($37.50 Canadian)

The first history of the beginnings, development, and impact of the American College of Sports Medicine (ACSM) on the fields of exercise science and sports medicine. More than an examination of the rich history of this premier organization, this book is a record of how individuals from different fields have retained a common focus over decades of growth and change.

New Edition!

ACSM Fitness Book
(Second Edition)
American College of Sports Medicine

1997 • Paper • 152 pp • Item PACS0783 • ISBN 0-88011-783-4
$13.95 ($19.95 Canadian)

This new edition will take the guesswork out of setting up a personal exercise program. The book includes easy-to-follow, color-coded intensity guidelines; dozens of photos showing proper exercise technique; logs for recording progress; and much more. Available Fall, 1997.

To request more information or to place your order, U.S. customers call **TOLL FREE 1-800-747-4457**. Customers outside the U.S. place your order using the appropriate telephone number/address shown in the front of this book.

Human Kinetics
The Information Leader in Physical Activity
http://www.humankinetics.com/

Prices subject to change.

2335